I Sold Myself a Dream

To Bud Riley
with best wishes

[signature]

April 13/28.

I Sold Myself a Dream

Harry Henig

Exposition Press   *Hicksville, New York*

FIRST EDITION

© 1977 by Harry Henig

ISBN 0-682-48928-X

Printed in the United States of America

To those who have traveled a similar road through life—I hope you will find some means of serenity and contentment on the wings of time

Any displeasure caused to anyone by the quoting of names, places, incidents, etc., is purely unintentional

Contents

Preface

I sold myself a dream many years ago, that I would write my autobiography some day.

After many years of wishing and hoping, my dream became a reality.

That autobiography, *Orphan of the Storm,* which describes the joys and sorrows of my life, was published by Pitt Publishing Company in 1974. At the urging of many friends and others who came to know me through this book, I am writing a sequel dealing chiefly with my rewards and disappointments in the business world, as well as my ambitions and aspirations to attain some measure of material success.

Some of the incidents mentioned only in passing in the earlier book will be described in detail, with a broader and deeper explanation and reexamination of those turbulent years as I floundered awkwardly and hopelessly from one endeavor to another, failing in many.

I shall lead you through my selling experiences from the time I was six years of age to the teeming melting pot in the Lower East Side of New York and finally to the unexpected involvement in a retail ladies' wear store in Toronto, in which business I continued until I started my literary venture.

You will become acquainted with the garment industry and the people with whom I have been associated for almost thirty years. I have nothing but praise and gratitude for those who accepted me so warmly into a world about which I knew nothing, and who gave me the confidence that I would succeed.

You will read about individuals I knew in the industry who may also be known to you. We will share many sentimental memories as we take a thirty-three-year journey through the manufacturing and retail business and meet the people caught up in it by choice or through necessity.

To me it was a strange and unrealistic world. I did not speak or understand the language of the garment industry, which is a puzzle to one who doesn't know the difference between silk and cheap lining. Nevertheless, with the help of many sincere people, I learned quickly, and in time became a part of that world.

As I unfold the pages of my mind, memories emerge of bygone years. They give me a feeling of pride and self-satisfaction, even though the deep-rooted insecurity I had lived with since childhood haunted me in my new venture. It is said that success is born when opportunity and ambition meet head-on. This combination, however, happens only on rare occasions. One must have ambition to seek out and create opportunities to achieve success.

One can get out of a business only as much as one puts into it, remembering too that long, endless hours are not necessarily productive if not guided in the proper direction of creativity. Before one can reap benefits from a business, one must first build up an image of prestige and confidence and realize that what may seem insignificant in establishing a profitable business is of utmost importance when combined with genuine sincerity and enthusiasm.

Nothing is so contagious as enthusiasm. It is the real allegory of the tale of Orpheus. It moves stones, it charms brutes. Enthusiasm is the genius of sincerity and truth accomplishes no victories without it.—BULVER

Success in any field of endeavor is largely dependent upon desire to achieve recognition, self-satisfaction, and monetary benefits. One must find the proper methods to reach and fulfill such ambitions through discipline and sincere effort.

I shall share with you a lifetime of diversified experiences in the business world, and outline some of the "dos" and "don'ts" as I have learned them the hard way over the years. I have learned that success should not be reaped at the cost of dignity and self-respect. It is essential to build a solid foundation upon which a strong structure can be erected. If you desire to be a champion in any chosen field, act like one—with courage and conviction.

It is my hope that you may derive some inspiration from reading about my countless experiences in pursuit of my goal of establishing a profitable business combined with self-respect.

Acknowledgments

As readers of *Orphan of the Storm* are aware, I learned to speak English not in formal schooling, but by studying various advertisements and descriptions of the many varieties of merchandise contained in the Eaton's and Simpson's catalogues.

During the long, cold winter nights in Hirsch, Saskatchewan, when sleep wouldn't come to me in the small icy room where a galvanized bathtub was my bed, I would get up in the middle of the night, straighten my spine, restore some circulation to my aching body, and quietly sneak in some books my uncle had accumulated over many years—the books all in Yiddish, of course—and then read by candlelight until about four A.M., when it was time to begin the daily chores.

I realize now that the books I read almost a lifetime ago were, and still are, of great assistance to me. They opened new worlds, new horizons I hadn't known.

I wish to acknowledge in this imperfect way the many writers and thinkers whose books have given me inspiration, faith, desire, and the courage to accept adversity.

I should also record here my gratitude to all of my business associates in one endeavor or another, for their kind acceptance and guidance throughout the years.

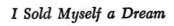

I Sold Myself a Dream

1

Rypiana

Rypiana—one small desolate village in an endless chain of villages scattered on small hilltops and deep valleys, which nestled tightly against the threatening Carpathian Mountains, in a province under the rule of Emperor Franz Joseph of Austria. That's where I was born, in a dark unknown corner of Eastern Europe that has remained a mystery to this day.

I doubt if anyone, except those who lived there, really knew of its existence. Those God-forsaken villages sheltered a unique people who were illiterate and, of course, primitive. "God-forsaken" is perhaps not the proper expression; I remember that the *Chassidim* (saintly men) spoke with God each day; they even argued with Him. I gather that God was there at all times, and saintly men were in constant communication with Him, asking Him for help that never came.

Because there were no schools, no one could read or write. The members of the small Jewish communities, however, miraculously taught each other to read the daily Hebrew prayers and the Psalms. Most of them didn't understand Hebrew but they hung on to the culture of their ancestors tenaciously.

The Jewish communities were small in numbers and existed on miracles. I don't know how they managed to survive. When I sit in the still of the night and reflect on those years, the villages and the people, it seems as if I had lived there a million years ago. In fact, I believe that I am hallucinating, until clear pictures begin to unfold before me.

There was a narrow shallow brook purling down the center of the village. I see myself sitting at the edge. The multicolored reflections created by the hot summer sun make me squint. Thousands of minnows rush around at the bottom excitedly. I lick my chops like a cat. I was almost always hungry then.

I was five years old when I began to daydream, but my dreams

3

were shattered by the First World War. Hundreds of village peasants were killed or maimed on the battlefields. Jews, although despised and considered second-class citizens, contributed more than their share of blood and dead during the war years. Yet they gained nothing. Anti-Semitism, persecution, pogroms were on the rampage again just as soon as the war came to an end. Jews are first-class citizens in time of war, but fall back again in time of peace.

Do all these unjust acts happen because of ignorance? I believe that greed and jealousy are responsible for all acts of violence.

It was the spring of 1915 when the warring armies retreated from our devastated village and the surrounding areas. Most of the squalid huts were demolished, and the peasants worked day and night, clearing the rubble and restoring their dwellings to livable conditions. Our small isolated world finally seemed peaceful, except for the intermittent thunder of distant cannon that shook the ground.

Outside it was spring, in all of its beauty and glory; the trees were in full bloom: white, yellow, purple. Fragrance filled the air. The heavens were crystal clear, the sun was shining, the gardens were smiling, the birds were singing a prayer, and the whole universe was exultant and pulsating vibrantly: Spring—what a beautiful time of year, when everything comes to life again!

I was six years old when I ventured out to canvass the village for some business, armed with a homemade bamboo basket and a box of cigarettes my mother had succeeded in getting from a friend of the family who lived in Lymna, a few miles from our village. My selling career began when I started peddling from house to house, trading cigarettes for whatever I was offered. The threat of starvation kept me going, no matter how tired I was. I walked countless miles each day, from hut to hut, from village to village, my bare feet cut and bruised, my old pants held up with a rope around my waist, but my sidelocks neatly curled.

This last detail is important, because I was the grandson of a Chassidic Rabbi, and whatever else happened, I always kept the faith. My mother made me recite the morning prayers before I took my first step into a strange, cruel world unknown to me until that day. I wore an old cap that was much too large for me but was held up by my ears. This is important too, because it is against the Chassidic religion to go about with a bare head. As is written in the High Holidays prayer book, "Forgive us for our sin we have committed by levity"—going about with a bare head. This is especially true of a Chassidic Rabbi's grandson, who is expected to observe the Laws of the Torah at all times.

I can attribute my small measure of success on my first venture only to my pitiful appearance. It may have been the innocence of my pleading eyes and my pale, hungry-looking face. Whatever the reason, I was doing quite well until fear gripped my heart when I heard dogs barking nearby. The villages were full of dogs running around on the loose and I was terrified of being attacked by them.

I would hide at the edge of a forest and hold my breath, but I was also deathly afraid of forests, where, I believed, demons and spirits roamed in the dark deep silence. I remembered stories told by our learned Chassidim on many occasions about forests and evil spirits. Some even made us believe that they had actually seen, with their own eyes, a spirit wrapped in a white sheet wandering about at the edge of the forest reciting aloud a chapter of the Psalms, and then suddenly vanishing into thin air. What would I do if a spirit suddenly appeared? I would run! Where would I run—into the sharp fangs of a dog? There is no escape from fear that penetrates the mind of a child.

Now that I think back I am convinced that I have never been a child. As a teacher once told me during the time I was in a Kibbutz, "Childhood can be compared to the most beautiful room in the whole world." I have never seen that room; in fact, by the time I was ten years of age I had forgotten how to cry.

Although I was numb with terror, I knew I had to get home somehow to bring back my bamboo basket, which was full of a variety of food and some money. Summoning up my courage, I began the descent to the valley below. When I reached bottom, I made my way alongside the shallow creek, crawling on my hands and knees, dragging my worldly possessions home. That was my first exposure to selling, an endeavor that produced some food for us, plus pride of accomplishment for me.

After this first attempt, I decided to extend my territory to villages I had not canvassed before. As a result of this decision, I ran into serious trouble.

I came upon a gang of young peasants who were tending cows and goats in a community pasture. They saw me approaching and were about to confront me. This is terrible, I thought. They will probably make fun of me, which they usually do, and then beat me up for good measure! I swiftly sneaked into the thick brush growing alongside the river and sat quietly praying that they wouldn't find me. After searching for a while, they went back to their flock.

I sat there, watching the river purl on its way to distant lands, listening to the trees rustling, the cows lowing, and I heard the peasant boys singing Ukrainian songs while roasting potatoes over a bonfire. The sun was slowly sinking beyond the horizon of the high Carpathian Mountains as I made my way home. It was a frightening experience but somehow rewarding. I remember that evening with nostalgia: we all sat in our hut and recited the Benedictions, thanking God for our survival.

Life was ugly but we didn't know it. Joys were rare unless there was a wedding in the village; otherwise there was no emotion. Life and death were accepted with indifference!

I remember spring in my little village, the time when the old earth heaved slowly over, and all things became beautiful and promising. Blackbirds and robins were picking worms on the lawn; others were perched on tree branches singing, chirping, busily building nests.

I can't just sit and dream away precious time! I climbed down to the little creek. On the right, brush and old grass covered a slope leading to the creek. Across it, green grass polished in silver was disturbed by warm breezes, and the weeping willow tree seemed to weep even though it was bathed in sunshine. To my left, hills and mountains rose. Granite rocks towered above them, their brilliance shadowed for a while by a scattering of clouds, then reappearing brighter than ever in the blinding sunshine. The wind rushed hotly by and the mountains around me fell away to either side, reaching for pieces of cloud and sky.

It was time to make my rounds. Spring and summer wouldn't last forever. I took my bamboo case and peddled while the world around me was so breathtakingly warm and serene.

Long ago the Talmud said, "The Voice of the people is the Voice of God." I was a part of that eternal people who lived in the midst of ignorance and hate, intolerance and persecution. They were honest, unworldly people. They were a unique people; they didn't desire or know how to be corrupt. This is the kind of world I was living in during my childhood years, which was beyond my understanding.

My selling career came to an end with the first cold winter

day, when I could no longer go out barefoot, and of course I had
hardly even *heard* of shoes! The time had come to climb up on
top of the clay oven and stay put until summer. This hibernation
period was long and painful. Endless days turned into months of
hopeless apathy.

Despite such pains, I often recall my childhood years with
nostalgia, reminiscing about the villages and mountains, the green
valleys, the ripples on the shallow creek winding its way through
the center of our village on its way to join other rivers in unfamiliar,
faraway places. I think of the village bathhouse that I was given the
privilege of tending for a few days while Reb Shamshon, our
bathhouse attendant, was ill. I can visualize the flaming fire and
the choking smoke forcing its way out through holes in the log
walls and the straw roof.

Friday afternoon was the beginning of the Holy Sabbath, the
time to shed all the worries and frustrations of the week, take a
deep sigh of relief, and say "Oh, God, it's time to forget the past
week." On the Sabbath one must meditate a little and not think
of the weekday activities, but devote time to relaxation and singing *Zemirot*, songs and praises to God. One can also sleep a little
after lunch when the Zemirot are completed, but who wants to
sleep away the loveliest day of the week, the Holy Sabbath? It is
a day of rest, but one should also pray and refresh the spirit with
a little learning. We may not know where next week's food will
come from, but we try to forget it, for today is Sabbath.

> *Thou beautiful Sabbath, thou sanctified day,*
> *That chasest our cares and our sorrows away,*
> *O come with good fortune, with joy and with peace*
> *To the homes of thy pious, their bliss to increase!*
>
> *In honor of thee are the tables decked white;*
> *From the clear candelabra shines many a light;*
> *All men in the finest of garments are dressed,*
> *As far as his purse each hath got him the best.*
>
> *For as soon as the Sabbath-hat is put on the head,*
> *New feelings are born and old feelings are dead;*
> *Yea, suddenly vanish black care and grim sorrow,*
> *None troubles concerning the things of tomorrow.*

New heavenly powers are given to each;
Of everyday matters now hushed is all speech;
At rest are all hands that have toiled with much pain;
Now peace and tranquility everywhere reign.

—SPINOZA

Crushed under the burden of exile and poverty for so long, one must take respite each Sabbath, and as the sun sank beyond the horizon, haunting melodies began to float in the air from the improvised synagogue, echoing from the mountains. Those melodies were not songs, but chants full of melancholy—"Bim, Bim, Bom, Biri, Biri, Bom." It was a sort of lamentation, melancholy, and meditation all in one.

We would linger over the passing of the Sabbath, trying to make it last, because we feared the coming week, the harsh world, the daily struggles. The bitter life would soon return, a life of poverty and despair, as soon as the Sabbath was over.

What kind of Sabbaths were they? They came so very slowly but passed, oh, so quickly, leaving us and the world around us unchanged, and the battle for survival would begin all over again. Only the Talmud could keep one happy during the week, and make one forget the ever-present hunger. Meanwhile, the wives during the entire week, carried the burden of searching for food for the hungry children.

Otherwise things never changed, unless something out of the ordinary happened that would excite us all. An unexpected group of hoodlums could suddenly decide any day at any time to go on a rampage, break windows, doors, smash the old bits of furniture, or even demolish the clay oven, terrorize the Jewish community for as long as they had fun doing it, and then retreat to wherever they came from. In those incomprehensible times peasants even argued about whether Jewish people had souls.

Such acts of violence, horrible as they were, did not deter us from practicing our Chassidic religion. Windows and doors were somehow repaired over a long period of time, and the clay ovens were rebuilt with sweat and blood, so that our way of life came back to its normal melancholy tempo. In fact, the violence actually strengthened our faith and devotion to God.

We didn't know the word *adversity* or the meaning of it, for we had never experienced anything different from the daily struggle.

In the opinion of the Chassidim we were a privileged group chosen by God to be punished in this world, rather than to be judged and suffer in the world to come, for that is eternal, and who would be so foolish as to forfeit such an opportunity by living a better life in this world? Even if the opportunity had presented itself it would have been rejected.

Our Chassidim should have studied more closely in the *Pirkey Avot* (Sayings of Our Fathers), the most widely known of all the sixty-three tractates of the *Mishnah*, (a collection of traditional laws), written over a period of more than five hundred years. They would have found, in the teaching of Hillel, that salvation is not conceived by the Rabbis as confined to Israelites only. Righteous people of all nations have a portion in the world to come. This was recognized as the universal belief of Judaism.

Judaism or humanism is an endless thread. It represents religious democracy according to our forefathers, and the Torah is the heritage of Israel. Simon the Just was one of the last survivors of the Great Assembly. He used to say that the world is based on three things: Torah, Divine Service, and the practice of charity.

To us, Chassidicism represented the foundation of truth and justice; it embraced everything that was noble. Chassidicism was morals, ethics, principles, and reason. We believed that without them the world would fall apart. Perhaps we were right. As we know today, it should be considered a miracle that the world hasn't destroyed itself already.

Prayer was, for us, the soul's reaction to terror. We hoped that, through prayer, we could withstand tragedy and find courage, for without hope or courage life had no meaning or purpose. Thus, although we were considered unworldly by some agnostics, we thrived on our philosophy and our culture.

As unworldly as we were, we got to know the meaning of the word *alrightnik*. We knew a peasant who had returned home from America. He couldn't speak English but he could say one word —*all right*. That made him the envy of the village. The Jewish community referred to this individual as the "Alrightnik"—the man in the navy suit, with a large watch attached to a heavy glistening chain pulled through a buttonhole in the vest he was wearing, the large watch tucked away into the pocket.

He was respected by all peasants. After all, he had just re-turned from America. He was a special type of peasant who had seen the world outside the confines of the village. He had spent years in the coal mines of Pennsylvania. He would wear his navy suit and watch to church on Sundays, so that all would look up to him with envy and respect. His peasant friends, who wore hand-made white linen shirts and pants, stuck to him like glue and thanked him for letting them touch the navy suit or the huge watch and chain.

I also remember some of the anti-Semitic peasants complaining that the few Jews who lived in the village were contaminating the air. I remember a discussion between two peasants who happened to meet in a marketplace in a distant town:

"How many Jews do you have in your village?" asked Nikolay.

"Oh, about fifty. How about your village? How many Jews do you have?"

"About two hundred," Yurko replied with satisfaction.

"Why do you need so many Jews?" asked Nikolay.

"Oh, they come in handy sometimes in case of a pogrom," replied his friend.

When I was seven years old I thought that I would want to be like Reb Moishe ("Reb" is an expression of respect in Hebrew), the most respected Chassid of the village—to wear a long beard and sidelocks, a long black robe, and a sash about my waist. A few days later I thought I would like to live a carefree life—to be a peasant like my friend Panko, who helped his father fix the straw roof and chop wood, and who wandered about aimlessly in the fields, carving flutes from reeds as the shepherds did. I once made such a flute with the help of my friend. I brought it home and showed my mother that I could really play Chassidic melodies on it, even a Rabbi's *nigun* (a melody without words).

When we were in dire and desperate need for food, I was exposed to selling again. I always felt that I would excel in business if given the opportunity. After I had done a hard day's work in a peasant's field, or peddling, my mother would say to me, "I'll be proud of you yet, some day, God willing." Then she would confide to her sister, "The only thing that worries me is that Hershel doesn't behave as is befitting a grandson of a Rabbi. God shouldn't punish me for what I'm going to say but I have a feeling that the chain of Rabbinical generations is coming to an end." She watched me and seemed to observe my restless behavior and my apparent indifference to the Chassidic culture and way of life. She called me "the little rebel."

I was very confused at this point and spent sleepless nights thinking about my future. Would it have affected the world or the deep endless universe, the sun, the moon or the stars—would it have been against the rules of nature or unjust to others if I were to have a father? Then I could have the feeling of being wanted and loved, and have a sense of security. The greatest need in one's life is to be needed, and loved.

I understood why my father had been compelled to leave the village. Apparently he was not one of the so-called "Holy Chassidim"; he was more progressive-minded, and for that reason he set out to seek a new life in a new world. This would, it was hoped, result in a better life for all of us.

I was six months old when my father left our village and ventured to a new world called New York. Two of his brothers were already there. He left my mother, my sister Sarah, my older brother Sam, and myself behind, promising to bring us over just as soon as he got himself established in the new land.

I cannot recall how we survived those five years, except by stealing fruit and vegetables from peasant property in the summer time. I also remember my mother speaking to my sister, who was the oldest, about five dollars that had apparently come in the mail from our father.

I remember the terribly cold winter nights, when I was about three years old, and Reb Shamshon, our community bathhouse attendant, knocking on the door at four each morning. "Open the door," he shouted. Although we couldn't see through our tiny ice-covered window, we knew it was Reb Shamshon. My mother would let him in. I could look out from under a heap of rags and see that he was covered with snow from head to toe. Icicles hung from his eyelashes, nostrils, and his long thick beard.

My brother Sam was two years older than I. He was always first to crawl out from under a pile of covers. I had noticed on many occasions that he was sort of shaky when he stood up; because he was a sickly child, this was to be expected. My mother would touch his forehead and remark, "Your forehead is hot, but your hands are ice cold. Don't worry, Reb Shamshon will warm you up. You'll feel better just as soon as you begin to read the morning prayers and the Chumish section of the week." (*Chumish* is a part of the Five Books of Moses.) She then proceeded to pull me out of bed.

I remember the hut being so cold that, to have my hands

washed, the thick ice that formed on the wooden bucket had to be broken in order to reach some water. A lit candle was placed on a small table, or we would light a kerosene lamp, hang it on a hook in the wooden ceiling, huddle together, breathe at each other to feel warmer and begin—

"*Mah Tovu Ohalecha Yaakov . . .*" (How goodly are thy tents, O Jacob . . .) while Reb Shamshon was pointing his thick dirty thumb to each word. It was apparent that he was satisfied with my progress. He would look at me sometimes and remark, "You'll be a great Chassidic Rabbi some day, if only your mother could afford to send you to a *Yeshiva* [a Rabbinical seminary] when you get older." To this day, I have a feeling that, had the First World War not broken out in 1914, I might have become a Rabbi either in Poland or in the United States, because that was my mother's greatest wish.

When our morning lesson was over Reb Shamshon sometimes remained seated, trying to engage us in Talmudic discussion. One morning I saw him double up in pain and turn pale. "The pains in my stomach are unbearable sometimes," he murmured. "I am a sick man." After a few minutes he continued: "You are going to be a Rabbi some day. With a brain like yours what else can one be?" While my mother was standing behind me, her fingers intertwined, she would shut her eyes and say in the tone of a prayer, "From your mouth into God's ears."

Reb Shamshon then proceeded to pat the cover of the Chumish gently, lovingly, and say, "There is a lot of wisdom in these pages." I have to admit that I didn't know what he was talking about at the time.

He then turned his attention to my brother Sam and said, "Your older boy also has a brilliant mind, but may God give him strength, he is a sick child. Only an invisible super power or a miracle can make him well."

I knew that my brother was ill because of the attention he was getting from all of us. He stayed indoors most of the time, even on hot summer days, when the grass was green and soothingly cool, when the birds were flyng around from tree to tree, jumping from branch to branch, when the shallow creek was glistening under the Carpathian sunshine, when carrots, peas, apples, and pears were begging to be stolen from the orchards and fields, to be hidden in a pile of straw and eaten only when intense hunger demanded.

I listened to Reb Shamshon's remarks and my heart cried inside me, even though I didn't fully understand the complexities of our lives.

On such occasions my mother stood behind us and cried silently. I could see large tears rolling down her beautiful, angelic face, but pretended that I wasn't aware of them. How can one remain unmoved by tears when one sees his mother cry?

I sat gazing down at the Chumish but my mouth was sand-dry.

One day preceding Yom Kippur (the Day of Atonement), Russian soldiers rode into our village. By the time we managed to escape into a nearby forest, several elders of the Jewish community had been slaughtered. It was the beginning of the First World War. I was five years old and wondered why people were slaughtering each other, but I remembered what Reb Moishe, the oldest of our community, once said:

"Each man is born with a bit of goodness in him, and a soul to feel compassion, but evil always overpowers the good, for evil is relentless in its pursuit to destroy, while 'good' stands by innocently waiting for an opportunity. Good must be developed, nurtured, guarded; ugliness of evil is persistent brutality that chokes the sparks of good and reduces them to ashes. Good is forever battling the wicked and the evil. Unfortunately evil is so widespread and appears in so many different forms that 'good' is not able to get the upper hand."

It was in 1914 when we were compelled to leave our village and wander in forests for days and nights until we reached Skorodna, a village very close to the Hungarian border, where my uncle Isaac lived. He had a nice home with many rooms where we believed we would be safe from the warring armies. But within a few days bullets began to whistle through the air, cannons shook the ground. The Austrian armies were in full retreat, while Russian troops were advancing. The entire region was occupied by them within a few days.

One night in particular stands out in my memory. It began on a severe, cold Carpathian winter's night, when Mongolian troops, who were known to be "cannibals," were approaching the village of Skorodna. We escaped into a nearby forest and hid in prearranged ditches filled with leaves and straw, while the entire village was turned into an inferno and a bloodbath. My brother became very ill that night as we sat in the forest, clinging to an animal or to each other in order not to freeze to death, while snow fell slowly and methodically all night.

When morning finally came we made our way back to the house. We found that the Mongolians had left the devastated village, and my uncle's house was declared a first-aid station. Doctors and high-ranking officers took possession of the entire house, except for one room that was reserved for all of us and two cows, which my uncle was allowed to keep. Everything else was confiscated by the military.

I remember one gruesome, unforgettable night, as we tried to sleep on the bare floor right behind the cows and the manure; the room was in complete darkness because it was against regulations even to light a candle. That night my brother was deathly ill, burning up with fever; he was delirious. My sister and I sat with mother while she cradled my brother's head in her arms. After many hours of hopeless despair that seemed like an eternity, we dozed off. Suddenly we heard mother pleading "Children, please help me find Sam!" We crawled around on our hands and knees in the dirty, dark room; the manure stench was unbearable, but we kept pawing away between—and under—the cows. We found him lying in a pile of dung covered from head to toe. He was dead!

I think that night was the most tragic experience of my childhood. It was the first time that I had seen my mother weep bitterly while cradling my dead brother's head in her arms, murmuring a prayer: "God, my God, how can You do this to us? Are we to suffer the punishment of the cruel world? Why hast Thou forsaken us?"

To get him to a Jewish cemetery, which was miles away, for burial was an unbelievably impossible task, but my mother and uncle managed to bring him to eternal rest, while machine gun fire and cannon bullets were exploding everywhere, reverberating against the mountainous forests into the muddy road below.

Some nights when we were very cold and numb, and the stench of the manure was unbearable in the dark cold room, we crawled out in search of a drink of water, but to do so had to walk over the wounded and the dead soldiers who were lying on the floor packed like sardines in a can. We were so accustomed to seeing such inhuman slaughter and suffering that it didn't even bother us any more. It was a matter of daily existence and survival; nothing else mattered.

The following morning when the dark clouds enveloped nearby forests and heavy snow was falling, we watched soldiers digging long deep ditches only a few yards at the rear of the house and dump most of the bodies into one grave. Very few wounded survived when morning came; those who did survive were loaded onto wagons and taken away.

The day was dark and very cold. An endless stream of troops and supplies were heading for the battlefront, but very few were returning. The full concentration was in front and behind us and we were right in the middle, caught in the crossfire. Bullets were flying from every direction, some going through the walls and rolling across the floor.

A few days later, I got very sick. At the same time we received orders from the officers to vacate the house, in anticipation of a major confrontation of the armies in that part of the village. All I remembered of that day was that I was wrapped in a blanket and carried on my mother's back, while the bullets were whistling all around us and dropping like pebbles into the mud. I was taken to another house at the far end of the village and fell into a deep coma. Two weeks are missing from my memory—I only remember that when I woke up, the first thing I said was: "Mama, I am hungry."

Spring came again, but by sheer bad luck I had to attend *Cheder* (elementary private school). The community had succeeded in hiring a young man from a distant town who claimed to possess all the knowledge necessary to teach youngsters such as myself. Where my mother got two dollars as her share of payment still remains a mystery to me.

I sat at a long table with other students but couldn't concentrate on the section of hte Chumish for that particular week. I was disconcerted. It was probably due to the unorthodox methods our new teacher was using. He insisted that we learn to translate Chumish to Polish. Why not to Yiddish as we were accustomed, I asked.

"You can speak Yiddish, can't you?" he said.

"Yes."

"Now you'll learn to speak Polish. It's a language you must learn anyway."

What a crazy idea, I thought. Polish—of all things. That man must be nuts!

I looked out the small window and observed. The sun was shining brilliantly, and cool shadows were climbing up the walls. They winked at me, calling me: "Come on out, fellow. You want to play, don't you? It's beautiful out here. One sprint to the left and you are on the little bridge under which a small shallow creek is bubbling noisily over thousands of tiny pebbles and minnows. One more sprint and you are across the bridge where green grass is growing, where tiny yellow flowers are smiling, where birds are flying, where a fly is dancing, where cows are grazing, and the green meadow is begging you to come out and throw yourself on the soft fragrant ground."

"But how am I to get out of here?"

"Don't be silly. Pretend you're sick."

I suddenly doubled up in excruciating pain and began to cry, "I am sick. Please let me go home!"

My teacher looked me over carefully to make sure I wasn't bluffing; the act apparently appeared to be genuine. "Go home," he said.

A few minutes later I bathed in sunshine, and rolled in the cool green grass, speculating at the same time why we were so poor. Why didn't we have a school? Why did the illiterate peasants persecute us? Why? Why? Why? I couldn't find an answer to a single question that tormented my mind. I was just a casualty of the times, an era of illiteracy, hate, and ignorance. I, like many others, happened to have been born into a dark corner of Eastern Europe that was never mentioned in history books. Perhaps we were a lost "tribe" hidden in a deep valley, looking up to ominous mountains hovering above.

The day passed quickly. I realized it was getting dark and hastily sprinted home. Not that my brother-in-law missed me; in fact, he would have been happy if I had gotten lost, but I didn't want to worry my mother. I was in the habit of daydreaming, wondering if there was more to the world than our village and the town Sambor I had recently visited with my mother.

I had heard grown-ups talk about cities, oceans, and ocean liners that sailed across the sea to distant lands. Someday, I thought, they'll reach the edge of the world and fall off. There must be an edge; one either has to turn back or fall into an endless, dark, eternal space. I looked up at the clear blue sky and saw a pale moon smiling at me. I wondered if the same moon shone in America. If it did, I thought, then my father may be looking at it right now.

Some years later, when I crossed the ocean on the way to Hirsch, my curiosity about oceans and ships was satisfied. I had seen the ocean, silently, majestically resting on the wings of time, united to the endless horizon. In my earlier book, *Orphan of the Storm*, I describe my first winter in Canada.

> *By now I had become used to seeing large cities and many people, but here we were disembarking in Halifax. I trembled with fear of the unknown. My bamboo case in my hand, we were led to a large hall by a representative of the Jewish Immigration Aid Society. We were then sorted out according to our destination. A group going to Montreal, Toronto, and Winnipeg were put on the same train. By the time the train pulled into Winnipeg, I was the only one left. My destination was Hirsch, Saskatchewan, a Jewish colony of pioneers and recently arrived farmers who were settled there with the aid of the Jewish Colonization Association. One of my uncles was a pioneer of some thirty years; the other a recent arrival, who had lived near Lemberg prior to his departure for Canada.*
>
> *I had a badge with the word Hirsch on my lapel, so that the train officials would know where to take me—just like a piece of baggage that does not speak nor understand, neither did I.*
>
> *After about three weeks of traveling I was finally on the train heading toward Hirsch, my final destination, an innocent lamb on the way to the slaughter house. I sat on the train not knowing where I was going nor did I have any inkling as to what I could expect when I did get to wherever I was going. I was in a strange looking world with strange customs. All I could see was flat open prairie as far as the horizon, a farm here and there miles apart, a couple of pitiful bushes shaking in the November wind. No rivers, no hills; the endless prairie had the appearance of desolation. I thought of my mother, my sister, my village that suddenly had become so dear to me. I sat on*

the wooden bench as the train puffed along the open prairie. Loneliness gripped my heart and I began to cry, hot salty tears rolling down my face.

I wondered if my mother missed me as much as I missed her. I thought I missed everything in the village—the God-fearing Chassidim, all of the things I had hated before departing for this strange land. It looked lifeless, desolate. Years of misery penetrated my soul to the extent of enjoying it, while hating it all at the same time. I missed the misery I had left behind and freed myself from hunger and despair.

I felt I must write a Yiddish poem to my mother, perhaps it would calm my emotions. I dedicated it to my mother. The poem kept repeating itself in my mind over and over. I couldn't think of anything else. I wondered if they missed me at home? Perhaps they did. People are inclined to take things for granted until a sudden change takes place, I thought.

The following, an approximate English translation, retains my yearning and sorrow, even though the rhyme and meaning have been lost.

> *The bygone years begin to surface*
> *I remember them with a feeling of nostalgia.*
> *An enemy bullet in my heart wouldn't pain me as much as*
> *it pains me, my dear mother, that I have left you alone.*
> *It is possible that we may see each other again some day*
> *and maybe this was the last time*
> *But whatever may happen*
> *I'll always remember you and pray for your health.*

I can hardly think back on those days and not cry a little. She was my mother—and how about my sister, my relatives, my friends? The beautiful green summer meadows, the shallow creek with millions of pebbles and tiny glistening minnows in the summer sun. I suddenly began to miss all these things; they seemed so important to me then.

My anticipation became unbearable when the train conductor said something to me that I didn't understand, while removing the badge from my lapel. I strained my eyes into the dark night but couldn't see a light or a single sign of life anywhere. It must be Hirsch, I thought. The train came to a stop, but where was the town; where were the people? I questioned.

As I stepped off the train on to the dark, wooden platform, a few people with flashlights in their hands appeared out of the darkness. They were my cousins. It was a great moment of joy to see all of them again, but a feeling of disappointment flashed through my mind. What a town! It was so dark, hardly any people around.

My trip had come to an end. Perhaps my wanderings would too. God only would know. Hirsch consisted of a huge grain elevator alongside the train tracks, a muddy road, two general stores, a pool room, a small shack used for a post office and miles and miles of open prairie dotted with farm homes and barns at two to three mile intervals.

My cousin drove me to the farm in a very impressive 1927 Ford car. In actual fact this was my very first car ride. A hug and a kiss by my dear aunt was an encouraging welcome to me. It made me feel better, even though my heart was pining of loneliness.

I experienced loneliness most of my young life, but somehow each case of loneliness is different. Some times it is despair that is mistakenly interpreted as loneliness, but sometimes it was not despair, it was homesickness.

My uncle Morris was about sixty years of age, his face and forehead deep furrowed. He told stories of the suffering he had endured during the pioneering years. Homestead life was harsh all over the west in the 1880s and 1890s, but for the Jewish families of Hirsch it was even harder. They had no synagogue or other religious outlet. Only on Sabbath were their lives brightened a bit when they gathered around the Sabbath table each Friday eve and a few fermented raisins provided wine for the Kiddush. God was thanked for the self-baked bread and the potato pudding that graced the course on a snow-white table cloth.

The winters were long and bitter. Thirty degree-below-zero temperatures were considered mild. The normal winter temperature hovered between forty degrees to fifty degrees below, with non-stop, heavy snowfalls. Once a storm stranded a peddler for three days until it was clear enough for him to leave.

The year 1927 was one to be remembered for many years to come by Saskatchewan farmers. It was a year of plenty; the wheat and flax crops were heavy, though the prices were very low and the granaries were full. I walked around in a trance for days. I couldn't fathom the wide-open horizon and the sunny days. So this is Canada, I thought, it is an unbelievable world.

One could see as far as the horizon. The first year I arrived, one could see machines come out of the haze and the dust, like giants harvesting crops.

Then ended the prosperous years; soon hot winds turned the top soil into a desert of dust. Dust clouds so heavy that they covered the burning sun choked everything that must breathe to survive. If you have seen one part of Saskatchewan, you have seen it all; if you have seen one town, you have seen them all. The only freak of nature is Qu'Appelle, in a hilly terrain. Fat, tall hills sat proudly, overlooking the town, the valley, and the river below. If you haven't seen Saskatchewan summers and winters from the inside by living there, you don't have an imagination strong enough to understand it. It can be tame but scorching hot in the summer, and cruel and deadly in the winter.

There were no stores within a thirty-mile radius; the closest general store was in Frobisher. There were no trains operating through the west during the pioneer days. My uncle used to enjoy telling about the thirty years of pioneering on the barren prairies, until he was able to grow some wheat.

According to him, this was paradise now. There were nice cultivated fields, some modern machinery, horses, cows, chickens. The first supper was a rare satisfying experience for me. My aunt placed a huge dish full of meat on the table and said, "Hershel, take as much as you want." I took chunks of meat and thought how wonderful. I had never tasted anything like it before. "Come, take more," she urged, but I was embarrassed, although I could have eaten the lot.

That was an evening of contentment and tranquility. Perhaps the time had really come for me to start a new life. Time would tell. Obviously I was in the land of plenty. My uncle Peretz and family stayed on in his brother's house for a while, while a three-room house was being built for them about two miles away. The Jewish Immigration Aid Society were financing all Jewish farmers who had a desire to stay on the farm and become self-sufficient. My uncle's son Howard began training me how and when to do farm chores.

Within two weeks I had my hands full—physically unable to handle all the responsibilities, feed ten horses, milk three cows, feed the chickens and water the horses by drawing buckets of water from a deep well and pouring it into a trough. Ten horses and three cows consumed a lot of water! The rope tied to the bucket handle was covered with ice in below-zero weather, which made it difficult to hoist buckets of water. By the time I was finished I was completely exhausted, but that was only the beginning.

I proceeded to milk three cows, clean out the manure accumulated in the barn; clean the chicken coop, bring two or three pails of water into the kitchen. At forty degrees below zero, perspiration was soaking through my overalls and sweater by the time all the chores were finished.

I was exhausted to the point of collapse. All work was done between 4:00 a.m. and 7:00 a.m. By then my uncle and aunt would shuffle out to the kitchen, and serve me some breakfast. I was so tired I could hardly bring the food up to my mouth with my trembling hands. Some time later I found out that there was a one-room school about three miles away, but I couldn't get permission to attend because there was always work to be done around the farm. Despite all the hard work I had to perform each day, a repetition of the day before, I began to imagine that my uncle was my father. I looked up to him lovingly, respectfully and devotedly. He took on a father image in my mind which turned into disaster later. I looked up to him and obeyed his slightest or most difficult wish. Nothing was too hard for me to do for him, as long as it was his wish.

I would carry pail after pail of water, heat it on the stove, and prepare a bath for him. The harder I worked the more satisfaction I derived from doing it. For all the hard labor, I got food and board free, but nothing else. But it was rewarding. I had the satisfying feeling of belonging; that to me was more important than money.

The long cold winter had created sleepless, torturous nights for me. The metal tub I slept in was short, the room was freezing at all times. The one tiny window facing northeast was forever frozen solid, I could feel the icy wind blowing inside the room. I was used to suffering; I grew up on it, but this was unbearable. During such nights I would light a candle, sneak in a couple of books, and read all night through. Finally my first winter was over, and gophers ran in and out of holes in the pastures.

My brother-in-law was a sick, neurotic, paranoid man. He was the food provider, and would often take time out to give me a beating and throw me out of the house. He wanted me to leave so there would be one less mouth to feed. But where should I go, I pleaded. "Go into the ground," he would say in Yiddish. I was ten years old, too young to fend for myself, but he couldn't care less.

Relatives came to my rescue by advising me to join a small Kibbutz in Stzylki Topolnica. I managed to find my way to that town and got a part-time job with Mr. and Mrs. Siegal, who owned a log yard and had a year-old baby. I was assigned to take care of the log yard and attend to the baby in my spare time. They allowed me to attend evening classes at the Kibbutz three times a week, for which I was extremely grateful.

Within a few days, I learned how to measure logs, so that I could easily arrive at a cubic feet total in order to be able to buy and sell, but I couldn't manage the baby. Whenever I was really tired, I would squeeze its leg to make it cry. The mother would then take it for a while.

I was fatherless and had no home. My brother-in-law didn't want to have me in the house, especially after my father passed away in New York in 1921. I had only one hope—to go across the ocean, as told in my autobiography, *Orphan of the Storm.*

2

The Lower East Side

Many years came and went before I got the opportunity to try my selling talent again. I arrived in New York, via Canada, in November 1929, just prior to the Depression, which was to spread like a plague throughout North America. It was a time when bank presidents and wealthy financiers would suddenly become poor. Suicide would be considered quite normal, and many would make this choice, rather than bear the humility of standing in relief lines. After being accustomed to a life of luxury, how could one face complete defeat?

In spite of all this, I was fortunate to get a job with a paper and twine wholesaler, helping to prepare items for delivery. The orders were brought in daily by ten or more salesmen who constantly called on their accounts at the retail level. Despite their efforts, business continued to decline, so that their services were no longer required.

One day my employer suggested that I should call on some accounts that were located on the Lower East Side of New York.

"But I can't speak or write English," I said.

"Don't worry," he reassured me. "Just write them the best way you know how. You'll also have to fill them and have the orders ready for delivery."

Although I was elated at this opportunity, I was very apprehensive at the same time. The first few days were not as satisfying as I had anticipated. I was unfamiliar with the goods and the customers, and also worried when I thought of the streets where I had to work. I had witnessed many frightening acts of violence on many occasions and remembered an unforgettable experience I had had one Sunday morning.

I was on my way back from visiting the Statue of Liberty. Descending the stairs at Delancey Street and the Bowery, I noticed that the city was still in deep slumber, except for homeless, lazy hoodlums, Bowery bums, drunks and drifters, sleeping on the sidewalks or inside large culverts scattered about underneath the overhead trains. As I reached street level, I was accosted by two dirty, unshaven winos. One of them held a long knife to my stomach while the second one turned my pockets inside out in search of money. He found $1.35, which was supposed to have lasted me for a whole week—until payday, which was on Friday.

I was in a state of shock and remained in my room for the rest of the day. It wasn't easy to ignore the hordes of cockroaches that invaded my room. They were everywhere—on the floor, on the ceiling, on the walls, on my bed. It was sickening. I opened the window for a breath of fresh air and listened to Chassidic students studying aloud, in singing voices, in the Yeshiva across the street. I was filled with mixed emotions when I thought of the Chassidim I had left in my village. What a waste of lives consumed by piety and superstition!

The first few days on the streets of the Lower East Side were an experience I shall never forget. I was mesmerized by the unbelievable activities of the merchants—the pushcart peddlers, with fish stands parked in puddles of water from the melting ice. The pushcarts were loaded with all sorts of fish exposed to the sun and millions of insects. The stifling heat and the stench were unbearable.

"Watermelons," one vendor shouted in a hoarse, panicky voice, trying to make himself heard over the screaming sirens of an ambulance, and then the ear-piercing blares of fire trucks agitating humanity to near hysteria.

Orchard Street was the boiling pot of New York, where pennies were made and lost each day. Open-door taverns were doing a roaring business. Vapor and smoke drifted out of open doors like the steam and smoke from the bathhouse in our little village.

I remember one peddler in particular who was pushing a cart loaded with knishes. He was screaming, "Heyse knishes—delicious". Each time he screamed, two thick veins would appear on each side of his neck as if they were about to burst.

His competitor, not to be outsold, bellowed in a thunderous voice into the heavy, smelly air, "Get a two-pound pickle for only a nickel."

I have never seen a mass of humanity fighting that hard for survival. This was the jungle I was to face in my job as a salesman!

I was told that, because of the Depression, one had no choice but to join the ranks and hope for the best.

One particular day stands out in my memory. I was browsing around on Norfolk Street. A fat, husky, short man with a huge stomach appeared, wearing a royal blue suit with wide white stripes. The jacket was very short, double-breasted, and far too tight, with the buttons about to pop off. He was carrying what looked like a doctor's case, and perspiration was trickling down his face from under his wide-brimmed hat, like small streams of water from melting snow. I saw horses hitched to wagons loaded with wooden crates of live chickens, dogs chasing around the wagons and pushcarts. What a mass of sweaty humanity!

A woman with a black shawl draped over her head began to scream, "Benny, Benny, you look like a doctor. Are you really a doctor?" The short stout man stopped and screamed back, "Yes, I am a doctor."

"Now I can afford to get sick. Benny is a doctor. Isn't that nice?"

While they tried to get closer to each other so that they wouldn't have to shout, a group of Lubavicher Chassidim appeared on the street, and people began to run toward them to get a closer look. Some of the horses got nervous and also began to run, the wagons hitting against stands and pushcarts, smashing everything to smithereens. Crates broke open and chickens were running everywhere, with dogs chasing them in all directions.

In the confusion, a fight erupted between a group of Jewish and Italian neighborhood boys.

"Your mother looks like a *krepel* and your father looks like a pizza," screamed a Jewish boy.

"Oh, yeah? Your mother looks like an old knish," retaliated the Italian boy. "Wait until I get my hands on you at school tomorrow."

Things were happening so quickly that I couldn't decide if I should run or stay and watch the spectacle. Then I saw a woman fall down, apparently knocked over by a dog.

Benny, the doctor in the royal blue suit, came running over. The woman had fainted, and when the doctor had revived her and examined her, he said that she had sustained a concussion. She was now resting in the shade of a store front, under an old canopy.

I heard her say to Benny, the doctor, "You know, I can't afford to pay you because my husband has been unemployed for over a year."

"Don't you worry your sick *kepale*," he said.

"You mean my credit is good?" she asked.

Benny waved his hand, saying, "I wish I had a hundred patients like you, but the trouble is I have two hundred."

She was taken by ambulance to the hospital, and Benny arranged for a neurologist to see her. She apparently had suffered a concussion. His parting remark to the group that had started the fight was: "You guys should only fall into a sewer hole so you won't create such havoc on our otherwise peaceful streets."

It seemed to me that the entire Lower East Side was fighting a losing battle by strongly resisting integration into the American way of life. Everyone spoke Yiddish, and no one understood a word of English.

A few weeks later I was told that Benny, the doctor, had moved to another area and had taken a partner. We can't do everything alone, he defended himself, we must have help at one time or another; we have an investment to protect in each other.

The Depression was tightening its noose on the unemployed and hungry, and English-speaking Jews also took to the alleys of the tenements. I remember a man who used to come by the alley where I lived and play the violin and other instruments, hoping that someone would open a window and drop a few pennies.

This brings me to a story told to me by a neighbor as we sat on the Williamsburg bridge late one night, waiting for a breeze to penetrate the heavy, stifling air that came from the murky river and the rat-infested tenement buildings.

A man, in desperation, approached some of his relatives one day and asked them to advise him as to how he could earn a few pennies. His cousin, Mr. Shtupnik, came up with a brilliant idea.

"Let's buy him some small items such as needles, combs, thimbles, and thread in a variety of colors so that he can walk the alleys as others do, and perhaps he will be able to earn a few nickels."

"But I can't speak English," the man protested.

"Don't worry, we'll tape the name on each item so that you will only have to shout out loud the items you have for sale."

Our big provider appeared in the alleys of a Jewish neighborhood one day and proceeded to call out loud the names of his precious inventory. While he was straining to look up to the top of a building, a window opened and a lady appeared.

"Mister," she called him in Yiddish, "please come a bit closer. I am so sorry to see you walk these smelly alleys hungry and thirsty in such unbearable heat. Come up and I will make you a sandwich and give you an ice-cold glass of seltzer water to quench your thirst."

The man ran up the stairs quickly and was greeted by a middle-aged lady who was apparently very compassionate and eager to make her guest comfortable. After a while, they both agreed to do some loving. Upon leaving, he said, "Would you please tell me the English word for what we have just done?"

"The word is sex," she replied.

The following day the man walked the alleys calling out his inventory: "Needles, thimbles, thread, shoelaces, and sex too!"

It seems that necessity knows no boundaries to morals. One becomes indifferent to the methods one has to use to make a living. It was the Great Depression, when even men of prestige were selling apples out of baskets on street corners. Unemployed men walked the streets carrying signs: "I am desperate." "I need a job." "Please help me, my children are starving."

The soup kitchens set up by the local government were overcrowded, and the lines of humanity were endless. Dignity and self-respect were destroyed while waiting for a bowl of soup.

It is sad to think that it took a war, a Hitler, and millions of innocent victims to put the world together again so that people could survive those ugly Depression days, thus creating a better life for humanity.

Today we see a repetition of the so-called recession. It doesn't sound as severe and hopeless as "depression." After all, we are a "sophisticated" people. We have nicer words and phrases for poverty in general, which do not carry as much indignity or deep despair in our affluent society, but the situation is nevertheless just as destructive. Its ugly origin, moreover, is in the hands of those who were fed and clothed for years by the nations of the world, but no country has the "guts" to initiate a program whereby all nations collectively could put a stop to the blackmail and thievery.

In order to survive as a salesman, I sat up nights planning a proper approach to succeed in obtaining the desired results. First of all, I decided that positive thinking was essential to create self-confidence. Second, I was not to ask questions, such as "Do you want—?" or "Do you need—?" I knew I would get negative answers. Instead, I took charge the minute I stepped inside a store. I checked out the items of inventory I had to sell, then wrote the order. Once the order was written, my customer couldn't help but accept the copy and smilingly surrender, even though his expression of disapproval was quite obvious. After a few weeks, I won the confidence of my customers. I even began adding new items to the orders, items they had never handled, but I got to know what types of goods were required in that particular area.

The country was in deep depression, but my accounts were doing well. One day, I called on one of my customers, whose first name was Eliezer, and found the store door locked. I ran up one flight of stairs above the store, where the family occupied a dark, cold, damp apartment, and knocked on the door. It was opened by the man's wife, Reizel. Upon seeing me she began to cry.

"Am I glad to see you! My husband is very ill," she lamented. "Maybe you can help me."

"What happened? Where is he?" I asked.

"There." She pointed her finger to a dark room. "He is in bed, very sick."

"Did you not call a doctor?" I asked.

"Yes, I did, but our Jewish doctor is away on vacation in the 'Catsill Montans.' An English-speaking doctor came and left some medicine and instructions how to give it to him."

"So why don't you give it to him?" I asked.

"Because it says on the paper that it should be taken through the rectum, but we don't have one. Here—read it," she said, handing me a piece of paper. I, too, didn't understand the word.

"Whatever it is, let's try and get it. Perhaps some of the neighbors have it, or your Jewish drugstore."

"The Jewish drugstore is also closed for vacation," she cried.

Reizel and I ran from door to door, inquiring if by chance anyone had a "rectum," but no one knew what it was. Furthermore, no one had heard of the word.

In desperation, I called the doctor and asked him, in my broken English, if he would be good enough to tell us where we could get a "rectum." After listening to me for a minute, he burst out laughing and I bet he still is!

"I'll be over in twenty minutes," he chuckled.

He walked into the bedroom, Reizel and I right behind him. He turned to us and said, "Come here and I'll show you what a 'rectum' is." He told Eliezer to crouch into position, forehead resting on the pillow.

"Here," he said, "is the rectum," while he proceeded to insert a suppository. "Mr. Eliezer has infected hemorrhoids. These will clear up the infection." Reizel let out a scream and covered her eyes with her apron.

"*Riboinoi Shel Olam!* [God of the universe!] What is he doing to my poor husband? Such a thing I have never seen!"

I stood as if I were paralyzed, my ears burning with embarrassment. I had become so involved with these two nice people that I had to be at their home at a precise time each day to perform the undignified task of inserting suppositories. Reizel would have no part of it. A lifetime has gone by since then, but I still remember the melodrama and laugh inwardly with a feeling of nostalgia.

I had gained the respect and confidence of all my customers, even though I was only nineteen years of age. My genuine sincerity and honesty seemed to have penetrated their hearts, and they accepted me as a friend and not just another salesman who is always looked upon with a feeling of distrust and suspicion. I had to listen to their problems and tribulations on each visit. If I had told them that I had seen a cow jump over the Empire State Building, or a chicken laying brass eggs, they would have believed me.

I was gaining more experience with each passing day, which was a prelude to my business career. What made my relationship with my customers so warm and intimate was probably my concern for their general well-being, and apparently my sincerity was obvious. They never construed my concern as meaning that I was after larger orders, and, as a result, I got more than my share of business. I was young, ambitious, and enjoyed my work immensely—I thrived on it.

The Jewish storekeepers were decent European immigrants without any worldly knowledge or ideals. They were just hardworking people desperately trying to create a better life for their families in a new democratic land. They enjoyed their freedom in this wonderful America—no persecution, no pogroms such as they had had to contend with in Europe. When they could take some time off from their work, they could even roam around Central Park and bring with them a shoe box full of rye bread corned beef sandwiches, sit on the lovely green grass in the shade of a tree, watch the ducks and swans swimming in the pond—they appreciated their freedom. They had escaped oppression and discovered a new land, which gave them a purpose in life for the first time, and they thanked God for their liberation.

I now pay tribute to those wonderful people who held on to their Jewish identity and traditions, passed on to them by their ancestors, in the midst of a hostile world and anti-Semitic persecution. As cruel as we then thought the world had been, it wasn't nearly as indifferent to suffering, murder, and slaughter as it is today. Human life lost its value during the years of the Nazi holocaust and went progressively downhill until it reached bottom. Numbers of victims no longer matter; whether they be six hundred or six million, the feeling of indifference on the part of world society is the same. There is no feeling of guilt or remorse. Human lives have succumbed to an inflation of quantity but a *deflation* of values.

Perhaps this is because of the sophisticated methods that are used to make death supposedly less painful. Less guilt seems to be attached to murder and terror, so that the worst crimes have become an accepted pattern in world society. Modern technology has penetrated into the minds of leaders and warped their way of thinking, and, like a contagious disease, has poisoned the minds of all people.

Human lives have lost their value as a result of warmongers and agitators. I believe that if all nations were to mind their own business there would be less hostility and threats of war in the world. One can see this by drawing on past experiences and observations of the Second World War, which took years of planning and preparation by the German people. Hitler had been chosen to do the dirty work as prearranged over many years. I can't help but quote Kahlil Gibran in *The Prophet*: "As the leaf turns yellow with the silent knowledge of the whole tree so the wrongdoers cannot do wrong, the murderers cannot murder innocent people without the hidden will of you all."

Politics is an institution for the participants and a tragedy to humanity. If nations were left alone to settle their differences in their own free way without outside pressures, many wars would never come to pass, and millions of innocent victims would be spared slow death by starvation, or other more sophisticated methods. Nations are constantly being instigated to war by outside influences. Politics and diplomacy forced upon such countries are cruel and misleading. The diplomats thrive on seeking supremacy through the suffering of other nations, simply to prove that they are desperately trying to bring peace to the world, and therefore earn their fat salaries and prestige.

I can only compare them to one who sees two friends locked in a barehanded fight. He steps in between them and admonishes them, "What are you two fighting for? Break it up! But—here is a gun for you and one for you. These guns are not to be used for fighting by either one of you; they are strictly for protection."

This is how "have" nations supply the "have-nots" with all sorts of war materials—not for war, but for "protection." Should they refrain from doing so, there would be no wars, simply because the nations would have nothing to fight with. They would then be compelled to settle their differences in a peaceful manner without the influence of others, and thus retain their dignity, rather than flex their "war muscles."

But as unemployment begins to rise and the economy begins to drop, war—wherever it may develop—is the only solution to regain prosperity, at the cost of millions of innocent lives. "Wars are fought with the hidden will of all."

I think that if only one percent of the world's population would practice meditation even for five minutes each day, famine, hate, crime, murder, and wars would become nonexistent within a few years. I have learned over the years the great value of meditation. It calms your rebellious mind; your hostilities and cynicism gradually disappear as if by magic. If only a very few people were to begin the practice, it would spread like the healing of a contagious disease. It's not as easy to do good as it is to do evil, but I am confident that meditation would, over a period of years, make this mad, mixed-up world a better place in which to live.

Some people, directly or indirectly, do some horrible things to their fellow men. When questioned about an evil deed the usual reply is "I didn't mean any harm by it." We know of course that this is only an excuse or a coverup. This reminds me of a joke I read some years ago.

A man had been arrested for stealing a horse. The judge asked him, "How do you plead? Guilty or not guilty?"

"Your honor Judge," replied the man, "I am not guilty of anything that I know of!"

"You are charged with an offense of stealing a horse!"

"Me, stealing a horse? Never! I was walking down the road and noticed a rope lying in the dust. I picked it up to take it home. How was I to know that there was a horse tied to the other end? You call this stealing?"

"Ten days in prison," said the judge, banging his gavel. "Next case."

Evil is a state of an eroded mind. Men are blinded by jealousy and greed. "It [jealousy] is the green-eyed monster which doth mock the meat it feeds on" (Shakespeare). "As rust corrupts iron, so envy corrupts man" (Antisthenes).

Time passed quickly, bringing unexpected and traumatic changes in my life. One morning I received a registered letter from the Immigration Department, giving me notice that, because I was not a landed immigrant of the United States, I had to leave the country within ninety days and return to Canada. The notice was final, and no application for an extension would be considered. I was compelled to give up my job and wandered around aimlessly for many days not knowing what to do. I still had ninety days, however, and had to do something.

Fortunately, and unexpectedly, I was offered the opportunity of a job in the fur business. Most of the fur and garment industry in New York was, and still is, concentrated in one area from Twenty-third Street to Forty-second Street and from Broadway to Eighth Avenue. Entire high-rise buildings were occupied by the industry.

I got to know a Greek furrier who occupied a small part of a basement on Twenty-seventh Street and Seventh Avenue. He made Persian lamb plates, as they called them in the fur trade. A plate is made from Persian skin paws that are trimmed away when making Persian lamb coats. The paws are either sold or given to anyone who is willing to clean up all of the trimmings that accumulate when cutters prepare skins for expensive fur coats. That Greek was one of the paw collectors who trimmed paws and machine-stitched them together to create large plates, some as large as a tablecloth. He would then cut these plates and make coats, which were called Persian paw coats. He was badly in need of paws and was prepared to pay a reasonable price to someone who would supply them; he suggested that because I was not busy I should go out and gather up some paws.

"Where do I start and how?" I asked.

He pointed to a twenty-three story building and said, "This building is exclusively occupied by furriers. Go up to the top floor and work your way down."

"How do I go about collecting the paws and bringing them to your basement?"

He gave me a white coat of the type furriers wear and a handcart on two wheels, half a dozen bags, and a rope.

"This is all you need, and most of the furriers will be only too glad to have you clean away the mess. If you meet up with a furrier who insists on getting paid, here is ten dollars, but if you are asked to pay for some paws, make sure you take the paws only; don't take anything else."

I felt very self-conscious as I noisily pushed the cart up Seventh Avenue.

I entered the building he had pointed out to me and, after going to the different furriers, began bringing out load after load of fur paws, dumping them into his basement.

He paid me eight cents per pound.

Things went well for a few days until I unfortunately walked into a trap. One day, an Immigration official was doing a spot check of the employees on one of the floors while I was in the process of packing bags of Persian paws. He noticed me and called me over, asking to see my papers. All I had was a Polish passport. As a result of this unexpected incident, I was compelled to sign a form stating that I would leave the United States within ninety-six hours or face deportation to the Old Country.

I was now in a very desperate position. I had to leave the U.S. or be picked up and transported back to Poland. After the first panic wore off a bit, I began to think more rationally, and decided to seek help from the Immigration Aid Society on Lafayette Street.

The Immigration Society couldn't be of any help to me, because the time limit of my temporary passport had expired. I had to take my chances and board a train to Canada, aiming for Portal, North Dakota. Sitting on a slippery wooden bench I listened to the noise of the wheels. I got caught up in the rhythm that seemed to keep repeating one word with each turn: "Trouble, trouble, trouble." The word was driving me insane. I covered my ears to block out that agonizing word and fell asleep.

When I awoke, the train was coming to a halt and the conductor announced that we were about to pull into Portal. After about forty-five years, I can still see the Canadian flag fluttering in the summer breeze, just across a narrow dirt road. But it was forbidden territory to me. A Customs official took me off the train politely and informed me that I would be detained until further notice.

At that point in time, I was very anxious to remain in the United States rather than go back to a hopeless life on the farm, but I thought: If you own something that's very dear to you and you can't hold on to it, let it go. It will come back in time, if it doesn't, it was never yours in the first place.

I had hopes of returning to the U.S. some day. However, things did not materialize as I had planned.

3

A Cruel Winter

Today is the first day of the rest of my life.
—JOHN DENVER

The shame and bitterness can never be erased from the mind of a "relief" recipient. The most shameful moment of my life came when I was compelled to stand in a relief line for the first time in my life. I felt as if I were about to commit a crime. I was signing away my manhood, my pride, my self-respect—never again to feel dignity or have the courage to sit at my own table, should I ever own one, and feel that I was worthy of it.

The relief line left its scars on me, as it does on anyone who lives through it. Wounds of humiliation are the worst kind—they never heal. Unemployment was a form of slavery, degradation, and criminality, all in one. Even though I know that this experience doesn't make pleasant reading, I feel that to omit it would be committing conspiracy. I think it is important to describe events as they happened, and the feeling of hopelessness associated with the times.

The year was 1932. I was married and living in Winnipeg. My wife and I had adjusted to the horrible, humiliating, and ugly word *relief*. I shudder to this day when I think of that word and its implications. It is a hopeless, demoralizing word, as is the existence of the recipient. "Relief"—just the sound of it made me squirm; it sounded so degrading and hopeless. Everyone I talked to was on relief; everyone was apathetic and dejected and finally resigned. We, too, were ready to surrender, as we had no choice; we told ourselves, as the saying goes, "If you can't fight them—join them."

We had no idea how to go about applying for relief, but we soon found out. The government had built long bunker shacks

35

in a field outside the city. These shacks were buried in snow most of the winter. It is an unforgettable experience having to line up for hours, in forty-below-zero weather, waiting to sign up, while your face freezes in the blustery wind, and you think that the line will never move as you rub snow on your freezing face to restore circulation. Looking back, I often think of those days and how different things are today, living in our sophisticated society, forever in a hurry getting nowhere. We sit in comfortable warm cars, but swear when we fail to make a green light or miss a turn in a revolving door.

Today we have fancy names for relief—unemployment insurance, mother's allowance, welfare. Checks are mailed to us, and there is no need to stand in line for hours and freeze to death. These benefits are no longer luxuries; now everything is a "necessity."

My wife and I got some soap, on consignment of course, and peddled from house to house. Once we got inside the hallway, she made her sales pitch downstairs, while I ran upstairs where another family lived. We were both completely exhausted at the end of each day.

Over the years, I have had time to think how one can overcome such hardships—climbing stairs while peddling a product from house to house—and I now know the solution. If I were rich, I would demolish all two-story houses and build new ones with ground floors only, so that one wouldn't have to climb stairs while peddling.

The cruel winters in Manitoba are terribly cold, and our peddling business came to an abrupt end. In such winters the snow never seemed to stop falling and a temperature of twenty below zero is considered mild, until a northwest wind begins to howl, accompanied by walls of drifting snow of blizzard proportions, so that just breathing outdoors or walking becomes impossible. These weather conditions continue through the long winters until one thinks that summer will never come, but it eventually does arrive. Yet even summer in the prairie provinces is far from enjoyable because of the mosquito season, when millions invade the province, and people wish for winter to return so they can be rid of them.

January in the prairie provinces is considered the Valley of Winter; it is a time of year when the earth lies dead, buried under heavy snow and ice, cold shadows of a deep sleep and a sun that is as cold as an iceberg. It is a time of fire—flames hidden in forty to fifty degrees below zero that are as cold as the hopeless winter. The earth lies cold and dead, cracked by the below-zero temperatures wherever it's exposed: the gophers, the frogs, the robins, seemingly stilled forever. The leaves that glowed like hot coals on huge branches of poplar trees during autumn are now bare. They look as if they had raised their dried-up frozen arms in surrender to the cruel, merciless winter.

January is a month when no one believes that spring will ever come again. The scattered poplar trees are silent, except in blizzards, when they sway and crackle from the force of the northern winds, and when it's really cold for a long period of time, the trees explode and their juices pop in the intense cold. At the day's end, the sun's rays reach out from the northwest horizon, reflecting redly on the barren, open, snow-covered prairie. You can almost envision it spinning its cold web across endless reaches, its Northern Lights in a bizarre mixture of colors hundreds of miles away reaching into the darkness. The livestock will die if winter is especially long and harsh, and all living creatures will fall victim to the seemingly eternal freeze.

But spring will follow after winter; it always does, riding on a warm south wind on a sunny day. Lilacs and roses will fill the backyards; their fragrance will fill the evening air with a heavenly scent, promising a dream of another summer to come. Trees, orchards, grass—they are reborn in the spring, year after year.

Spring is the beginning of things, as childhood is the beginning of adulthood, but men cannot be reborn and grow new blossoms in the spring. Still, I love spring. Spring brings renewed hope to men and nature. Blackbirds and robins are everywhere—in the pastures, in the trees, even on windowsills, singing, chirping. All is hope and promise.

A few months had passed without any noticeable change except in the weather. It was May again and the snow was slowly melting under the bright, warm sun. There was hope in the air, but people wandered the streets aimlessly.

The day had finally come when I received my inheritance. Eight hundred dollars! It was a lot of money and required careful planning as to what type of business we should go into. We decided to purchase a grocery store, which we considered a safe investment —a business, we thought hopefully, from which we could make a living.

Unfortunately, however, the Depression was taking its toll in this as in all other endeavors. We thought that the south end of Winnipeg, where unemployment was not as high, would give us a better chance. I was impressed with one particular store, in the shape of a small freight car without wheels, which sat in the middle of a long block of nice homes. Upon inspecting the store, we found it to be very quiet because there was no walking traffic, but the telephone didn't stop ringing, and we learned that orders were apparently being called in to be delivered because of the severe cold. We were quite impressed watching the people in the store write out orders and deliver them.

"You see," the storekeeper remarked, "this is the way we do business each day, except Sunday, of course. It's an ideal business for a couple like you."

Needless to say, we bought the store, and later found out that while a prospective buyer was in the store, a sister would get a signal to keep on calling in orders. After we had left, all of the orders were returned to the store. Weeks and months passed and we sat there, hoping for someone to call in an order as we had expected, but the telephone was silent. The cold miserable winter was upon us. A tiny wood stove in the rear of the store was the only way we could get our hands warm. We felt hopelessly dejected.

I am not at all proud of the way we disposed of the store a few months later. We sold it in the same tricky way we had been made to buy it. We thanked God the day we walked out of there and handed the key over to the new "proud owner."

We had no alternative but to move back with my brother-in-law and begin planning our next step for survival.

4

Saved from the Snow

I have been obsessed with a wanderlust since childhood. Curiosity for discovery and adventure forever nagged at my mind. This was as good a time as any to explore the possibilities and satisfy my desire to travel. I believed that it was far better to bring goods to customers rather than wait for customers to come to me.

I therefore decided to buy a car so that I could do some traveling in and around Winnipeg, but where could I get the money?

My wife came up with a solution and approached our kind lady at the corner grocery store for a loan. This lady gave her a loan of $25 and I started to look for a low-priced used car.

I got to know a Hungarian Jewish boy who had recently arrived in Canada and who claimed to be a first-class mechanic. He had a few old cars in a wooden shack he called a "garage." His name was Jean.

"What a name for a tall, robust man like you!" I said.

"It's a Hungarian name which is quite common in my country," he replied.

He showed me a beautiful, shiny black, second-hand Essex car, with a shiny canvas top covered with glossy tar.

"This car is in first-class condition," he said. "I overhauled the engine and it runs like an expensive watch."

I knew very little about cars but took Jean's word that, in fact, the car was worth $150, but because it was my first car he would let me have it for $75, including driving lessons, until I got my driver's license. I couldn't wish for a better deal, and handed him the down payment of $25, the balance to be paid within six months.

On a nice sunny day in June, I pulled up in front of my brother-in-law's house as proud as a peacock. The whole family was standing outside, awaiting my arrival.

"Look, everybody, this is my car! Isn't she a beauty?"

"Oh, look how shiny she is!" they all agreed, and they also agreed that I had made an exceptionally good buy.

I thought to myself that if I were to tell some of my friends that I was the proud owner of this car, I'm sure they wouldn't believe me. They would think I was in a state of hallucination, or a liar.

"What are you going to peddle in the car—shoelaces?" my brother-in-law asked.

I ignored his sarcastic remark because I felt great joy in my heart. I thought of an appropriate quotation by Emerson: "Hitch your wagon to a star." That's just what I'll try to do, I thought, and perhaps I can make another beginning.

My wife and I drove up to our friend, who at one time had supplied us with soap. We loaded the rear of the car with a variety of goods, on consignment, of course. Each time I placed another few boxes of chocolate bars inside the car, I looked at the tires and saw that the car was gradually getting closer to the ground.

Within a couple of hours, I was driving down Main Street, overwhelmed with excitement and anticipation. Then, suddenly, my car began to tremble and belch. Steam was coming out of the radiator, with thick, smelly smoke like a black cloud shooting out of the exhaust pipe. With one more belch and a deep sigh, the car came to a halt. I was beside myself with despair and ran back to complain to Jean. I was completely out of breath by the time I reached the garage.

"Jean, Jean . . ." I tried to tell him that the car had broken down but couldn't explain because I was panting. He towed the car back to his garage, looked it over and said, "Don't worry. I'll do the repairs while you wait."

He tinkered around the motor for a while, but without results. I could see his face getting paler. His teeth clenched tightly and without a word he burst out crying. He kicked a wheel so hard that he hurt his foot; he hit the hood a vicious blow with his fist and squirmed in pain. Then he sat down on the cement floor, leaned his back against the car and burst out crying, while cursing in Hungarian, resting his head between his two enormous, grease-covered hands. I was petrified by his behavior. I thought he had gone berserk.

"God of the universe," I said to myself, "the man has gone mad!"

Have you ever seen a tall, powerful, grown man, a "mechanic," break down and cry, simply because he couldn't find the problem in a car he tried to repair? I watched him silently, scared to utter a word, waiting to see what the outcome would be.

Within half an hour his crying subsided; he got up and without a word calmly resumed work on the motor. By evening the car was in running order again. As a result my trip was delayed until the following morning.

I drove into Morrison, Manitoba. I don't recall whether it was fifty or sixty miles out of Winnipeg. I remember driving on a bumpy dirt road at a top speed of twenty miles per hour. I had some success in Morrison, and decided to try Emerson.

Traveling salesmen were a common sight in those years. Some even resorted to selling directly to farmers. I struggled along the highways and byways until one night, on my way back to Winnipeg, I had a flat tire. While I was trying to put on the spare, I was hit on the head and passed out. When I recovered from the blow, I realized that my pockets had been ripped out and the $35 I had was gone. All I had left was an oversized headache and a large lump on the back of my head.

Yet I was determined to go on. I thought of a quotation by Kahlil Gibran:

> *Your daily life is your Temple and your religion. Whenever you enter it, take with you your all. Take the plow, the forge and the mallet and the lute, the things you have fashioned in necessity or for delight. For in reverie you cannot rise above your achievements nor fall lower than your failure.*

Determined to find a road to success, or at least to self-respect, I decided to take on a partner. Perhaps two of us could explore towns off the beaten track.

My newly acquired partner was a newcomer to Canada, and he could speak very little English, but when one deals with Chinese in small prairie towns—and their cafes have enough grease on the ceilings to make French fries for a year—it really makes very little difference whether one can speak English, as long as one can persuade the customer to buy one's goods.

My partner still had a deep identification with the past, as when he cursed in Yiddish, or gave a blessing in Hebrew. Both languages are endless reservoirs of unique quotations. One gets a real thrill in vocally expressing a *"Geshmaken* curse." (There are many definitions of the word. It can mean delicious, pleasurable, appetizing, depending on the subject it is used on.) Hebrew and Yiddish expressions are as impressive today as they were in ancient times. Yiddish humor in particular depends on its drama and the inflection of voice, a pause, a raised eyebrow, or a wave of a hand.

My partner liked the Canadian way of life, but he couldn't forget the sheets of dough his mother used to roll out to make noodles *"Lekavod Shabos"* (in honor of the Sabbath). He was proud of the fact that he was a Hungarian *"Yeshiva Bachur"* (a chosen one who had participated for some years in Talmudic studies). His name was Shmuel. It's not a common name. Unlike any other name, it invites respect and is an expression of dignity. Shmuel was of small build, very short, almost fragile, as befits a Yeshivah Bachur. But I must admit he was really smart, which made me very uneasy at times. In fact, it made me raging mad too, when he called me *"Cheder Yung"* (a young man who had only an elementary education), who had been taught some Talmud by an old-fashioned *Melamed* (teacher).

Circumstances had forced him to leave his native Hungary and his Yeshiva and seek a new life in Canada. His Yiddish cursing was superior to mine, even though I had thought I was a champion curser prior to meeting him. I soon realized that I didn't possess half the vocabulary of Yiddish curses he had. Shmuel, however, was my partner, and I began to learn new curses, new blessings, and other *shtick* unfamiliar to me.

As mentioned in previous pages, winter in Manitoba makes one feel as if the world were about to come to an end; roads are blocked with deep snow, winds howling, the blizzards blinding. No one dares to venture out of the house, much less to leave town in such weather.

One day we decided to drive to Beausejour, about thirty miles east of Winnepeg. The sky was clear, the streets were passable when we left the city, but, about fifteen miles out, we met a severe snowstorm head-on, on a deserted, snow-covered road. We struggled for a while, hoping to reach our destination, but got stuck in deep drifts. High mountains of snow accumulated by snowplows were hovering above us, forming a deep, seemingly endless tunnel. We were hopelessly locked in a death trap, unable to move.

"Shmuel! What are we going to do?" I asked.

"Holy men and invisible spirits have powers we don't possess or understand," he said. "Their direct conversations with God are real; help will come."

"What holy men? Where are they going to come from out of the snow?"

"I consider myself a holy man," he said calmly.

"You are insane!" I screamed. "In the meantime let's not leave everything to God and holy men; let's shovel some snow from under the car and perhaps we can get rolling." But it was hopeless. Dark clouds were moving in, accompanied by winds of storm proportions, and heavy snow was falling. We will probably freeze to death by morning and no one will know where we have disappeared until late spring when the snow will have melted, I thought.

I was a young man at the time, reaching out for life and meaning, but how was I to reach the point of it all if I were doomed to die there?

As a result of our different beliefs we carried on arguments while sitting inside the car waiting for a miracle to happen. We even argued about the logic of believing in the "Baal Shem Tov," Israel Ben Eliezer, a name given to a saintly man in the eighteenth century. He was endowed with mystical powers attained through the manipulation of God's name. He claimed that unity with God is achieved by emotion, and, according to Shmuel, we were in a very good position to achieve that unity and to be rescued in some miraculous way. I confess that I too had been indoctrinated with such philosophy. I did not, however, believe as strongly in invisible powers as he did; I was inclined to be superstitious rather than believe in miracles.

While the road and the fields were slowly being buried in the swirling snow, Shmuel said, "You see, snow comes from heaven and brings peace to our souls, according to the 'Kabalah,' which is incomprehensible and steeped in the deep mysticism of the Middle Ages. Snow is white and it is therefore a sign of mercy, which is the Chassidic belief of hope, purity, and reward."

I thought he was going insane because the things he was muttering didn't make sense. On the other hand, I thought, perhaps he is right. Here we are, two faithfuls, being punished by nature. Isn't it always the case? The world always punishes virtue and truth. Subsequently we will perish here and no one will ever know the thoughts milling in my mind while we are waiting for a slow death.

In spite of his strong belief in miracles he kept on nagging me to push the car.

"But what good will it do?" I screamed almost incoherently. "Look at the giant mountains of snow towering above us, and down here we are struggling hopelessly like two sick worms. With the approach of night perhaps the sky will clear. How do I know? I don't; I'm only hoping."

Shmuel huddled into a corner of the car and began to tell stories about miracles that had come to pass in bygone generations. He was delirious at this point; his stories weren't making any sense as he spoke in whispered monotony.

He was mumbling a story about a girl who had been possessed by an evil spirit while outdoors on a cold winter night. Her voice changed to that of a man. When she was brought to a Rabbi he suggested that prayers and portions of the Torah be read backward in order to force the spirit out of her.

Another story Shmuel told me was about a corpse that had haunted and tormented his former partner. In this case, a cane that belonged to a Holy Rabbi had to be used to free the man of the corpse.

Only a "Yeshiva Bachur" could be so naive as to believe in stories of the Middle Ages, I thought.

He concluded by saying, "If I were to die here, I would be inclined to think that I too could keep my wife invisible company." While I listened to his monologue, hopelessness was painfully creeping into my heart.

Hours passed and the frightful darkness closed in. We sat in the car huddled under the blanket that we used to cover our merchandise. I was awake and aware that my partner was asleep. I tried to keep him awake too, but he was delirious and indifferent.

Suddenly, as if by a miracle, large, bright headlights pierced the falling snow and the dark of night. I squinted and rubbed my eyes. I was seeing something unbelievably large approaching us. At first I thought it was a mirage, but the bright lights were coming closer.

I shook my partner violently and screamed as loud as I could: "Open your eyes! We are about to be rescued! Look at the huge snowplow coming toward us!"

He slowly opened his eyes and said, "Don't you believe in God? In demons, in spirits, and in miracles? I do!"

Perhaps it *was* a miracle. Had I fallen asleep that snowplow would have probably scooped us up on its huge protruding blade and buried us alive under tons of snow. I quickly turned on the lights of our jalopy, and our lives were saved. The two men operating the plow towed us back to Winnipeg.

I was in a state of shock when I got home and was confined to bed for several days. Thoughts of various experiences were going through my mind in disarray until I collided with a story that was told to me by a friend some years ago.

A successful businessman, Mr. Goldring, decided one day to take in a partner to look after the office and local accounts so that he would be free to travel in order to expand to potentially new territories. But where does one get a dependable, trustworthy partner? Discussing the idea with his wife, she suggested Morris Luftring: "He would be the ideal man. He is our friend. We have known him for years. He is honest, hard-working, but has no *mazel* [luck]. He can't make a living. Take him in," she pleaded with her husband.

"I'll speak to him tomorrow," said Mr. Goldring.

The following day the two friends discussed the proposition and mutually agreed that it would be a most attractive and profitable arrangement for both of them. They shook hands and the partnership was sealed.

Mr. Goldring began to travel to distant cities searching for new business, while Mr. Luftring capably looked after local sales and production. Out-of-town trips were becoming progressively more frequent and of longer duration, so that Mr. Goldring's wife began to feel lonely. Mr. Luftring was a good friend and felt sorry for his partner's wife. "The least I can do for you is to keep you company once in a while while your husband is away," he said.

As time passed the children got used to his frequent visits, although they were a bit disturbed each time Mr. Luftring paid them a visit. They were ordered to play in the family room and not to come out until told.

One day Mr. Goldring came home sooner than expected and found his children sitting dejectedly in the playroom.

"Where is your mother?"

"Upstairs with Mr. Luftring," they replied in unison.

His wife and partner heard him coming up the stairs, but there was no escape. Mr. Luftring jumped out of bed in the nude, and hid in a clothes closet; his wife remained in bed, pretending she was sound asleep.

As her husband entered the bedroom he removed his jacket quietly, so as not to disturb her. While he was reaching for the clothes closet door his wife let out a scream and jumped out of bed: Max! You know that I always hang up your clothes, let me do it!"

But it was too late. By the time she reached him Max was staring at his nude partner.

After a few minutes of silence, Mr. Goldring admonished his partner for his unworthy action. "Shame on you, *Paskudniak*," he said. (In Yiddish the word expresses distaste, low morals, contemptibility, and vulgarity.) "I took you out of the gutter, gave you a nice office and a share in my business, where you didn't invest a dime. I made a businessman out of you. Now you have the audacity to come and roam around in the nude in my house and frighten my children, while I am out breaking my neck in search of extra business. Don't you dare do that again. My children are terrified. Should I find you in the nude in my house again our partnership will be terminated."

I remained in bed for a few days, sick, dejected, and thankful at the same time. We actually had been saved by a miracle!

Our attic was damp, and cold water was dripping from the ceiling and down the slanted walls, turning to ice when it reached the floor. But on Friday night I felt a divine presence when my wife lit the Sabbath candles. It's a feeling one cannot explain; it's symbolic. It doesn't make one richer or ease the hunger pains, but it lifts your morale and spirit. It's a time when a family finds a bond and a feeling of interdependence, when all feel but one emotion—*love*. It's the glue that binds; it's an anchor for a wayward ship tossed about in the stormy sea of life.

That particular Friday night stands out in my memory because of the incredible miracle that had saved me from certain death.

Jean, our mechanic, sheltered our car in his garage during the remainder of the winter, although the canvas top had many tar-covered patches and the sickly-looking tires were almost threadbare. Nevertheless we were about to take a calculated risk and prepare for a long trip to what we thought might be worthwhile destination—Winnipegosis. It took a lot of courage to undertake such a trip, but I have always said that courage is a sort of endurance of the soul and the pursuit of reward. The trip sounded irrational simply because of the location of Winnipegosis and its isolation from the outside world. One could get there, but only by an Indian trail, so to speak, over rough, rocky terrain, strewn with muddy ditches and forests. Why did my partner choose that unreachable end of the line? A friend of his had a general store there, and assured him by mail that he was in need of goods.

When we reached the end of the beaten trail, we found ourselves on what was called the Indian Trail. An old black sign on a tree pointing in a northerly direction had the name "Winnipegosis" on it.

While I was driving, crawling slowly over large rocks and deep ditches, my partner was busily marking down various landmarks along the way, so that we would know how to get back to civilization. After several hours, we unexpectedly found ourselves facing the town of Winnipegosis. There it was, just as we emerged out of thick brush. We were facing a few houses, two or three sad-looking stores, and a yellow, muddy lake that fronted the entire town. The lake appeared to be calm, unlike other lakes that form waves and whitecaps especially on windy days. This lake just sat there like an oversized pond, heavy and muddy, silently still, except for the wind riding on the surface, creating tiny ripples. We were told that this lake was the lifeline of the town and the only link with the outside world. This town, in fact, existed on exports of fish. It was sad-looking, almost dejected, facing the lake with brazen nerve and determination, braced to absorb any and all cruel elements of nature.

The summers in that part of Manitoba last only three months at the most, but the winters are terribly cold and endless. The population of the town and surrounding area of scattered huts hidden in the depth of the brush, apparently drew their living from fishing. They are a hard, tough people. They have to be in order to survive. Looking at the lake, I got the impression that the end of the world was where sky and water united in eternal embrace. Yet fishing boats were coming and leaving the harbor, churning the muddy waters. They apparently aimed at some destination.

My partner's friend was very apologetic, and his wife very benevolent, as they tried to explain to us that business had been very poor and that they didn't need, and couldn't afford to use any of the goods we had to offer. But because we had traveled such a long distance, he would take a few boxes of chocolate bars.

I was fuming mad and naturally very disappointed. The trip was apparently a complete failure that spelled disaster to us.

On our way back, as we were chugging along on the trail in deep silence, I remembered a quotation I had read years before: "Fear knocked on the door, faith opened it, and there was no one there. Fear without faith can destroy one's life." While quotations were milling around in my mind, I noticed a dark brown shack in the thick brush some distance away. After considerable manipulation over water-filled ditches we reached the dilapidated structure.

When I stepped inside I was confronted by a vicious-looking dog. He looked at me, growled, and I froze in my tracks. My childhood experiences had given me a fear of dogs.

"Don't worry, he won't attack you," I heard a heavy voice come from behind an old black counter.

I turned around and saw an Indian leaning on his elbows. He turned to the dog and said, "Wolf, go to your room." The dog obediently turned around and disappeared behind a dirty old curtain.

I slowly, patiently, drew the man into conversation and was told that he was supervising a trading post for the hunters and lumberjacks in the nearby forests. Slowly, methodically, I began to show him some of the goods we carried in our car and proceeded to display the entire inventory on the floor and counter.

"If I were to take it all, how much would it cost?" he asked.

His unexpected question unnerved me, and excitement began to creep up my spine. He must be joking; it's too good to be true, I thought.

We made a list of our entire inventory and began to add up the figures, but because of the excitement we came up with a different total each time. We compromised for a total figure of $78.90. I held my breath waiting for his reaction. He slowly reached behind the counter, brought out an old yellow tobacco can, pulled out a roll of bills, and counted out $79.

"Keep the change," he said.

I had to restrain myself from giving him a big brotherly hug.

Some hours later in the day we were back in civilization. I don't correctly recall the town now, whether it was Dauphin or Roblin, Manitoba. It was one of the towns, a division between two worlds, the known and the unknown.

Our homecoming from that successful trip was quite unlike our return from other trips that had ended in financial failure. This trip netted us a profit of $20 each. My partner, the Yeshiva Bachur, remarked, "You see a miracle crossed our path on this trip. Do you now believe in the impossible? Just when we are on the verge of questioning the One above as to what we can attribute our survival, a miracle happens."

This brings to mind a sermon I once heard an Orthodox Rabbi deliver to his congregants, in which he offered an example of religious thinking. A religious woman fasted for three days and nights, praying that God should reveal to her in some way the secret of what keeps people alive. On the fourth day a divine message penetrated her mind, but she passed out before she could convey her findings. After she was revived and fed she revealed to her friends that she had found the secret she had been searching for. "And what is the secret?" she was asked. "Food," she replied.

We began preparations for another long business trip. This time we were to try our luck in Yorkton, Saskatchewan. I believe it's about five hundred miles northwest of Winnipeg. We were fortunate to have accumulated a variety of goods, plus four fifty-pound crates of chocolate drops. They weren't in the best of condition because of some worms and discoloration, but we worked many days brushing, cleaning, and applying olive oil to each one to restore them to their original color. We removed the rear seat of the car and loaded the back of the car to capacity.

It was a very hot day in July and the humidity was stifling as we set out on our long trip. We were troubled, however, by the frequent stops we had to make in order to keep filling up the radiator. The water was apparently boiling out, because it constantly hissed and steamed. It appeared as though we were heading for trouble, but we kept on going.

I sat in the car worrying and gasping for a breath of air, when a thought suddenly flashed through my mind. I wondered how our chocolates were doing in the heat? They might have melted. "Stop," I said to my partner. "Let's check out our goods." How can I forget the sight when we opened a few boxes of chocolates and removed the wrappers? They were melted so badly that the wrappers had the appearance of freshly soiled baby diapers.

We quickly drove down to the edge of a nearby river and began to pour water all over the car in order to cool it off a bit. We then got a large chunk of ice at a nearby railway station, wrapped it in rags, and placed it on the floor inside the car.

That night a miracle happened that saved us from a complete disaster. As the sun was slowly sinking behind a fiery red horizon, a cold northwest wind was gathering momentum while we sat under the branches of a huge tree cleaning and rewrapping our precious chocolates. The chocolate drops were dumped out of the crates and slowly cooled in the cold breeze.

Yorkton was a small town, consisting of two short business blocks and very poor-looking homes some distance away to the rear. Farther out were farms scattered over a wide area one to two miles apart. There was one hotel built of lumber that hadn't seen a paintbrush in perhaps a decade, and a thick rope hanging out of an upstairs window, which was to be used in case of fire.

The two of us checked in to a room at $1.50 per night (double occupancy). Sanitary facilities were at the rear of the hotel, and so was the drinking water in a deep well in the backyard. There were two Chinese cafes where we hoped to do some business the following morning.

That night remains unforgettable to this very day. As the hot, parching prairie sun was sinking to the edge of the horizon, heavy black clouds began to move in, covering the fading light of day. Within minutes we were enveloped by complete darkness. Dull outbursts of thunder shook the building. It seemed as if the entire town were about to be destroyed. My partner and I looked out the one small window, while mice were excitedly scurrying around for cover; one ran up my pants leg in search of a hiding spot.

As the storm was slowly closing in on the town, high winds of tornado force were whipping up the dust on the dirt roads and the fields, creating a heavy, multicolored cloud that rose swiftly and was absorbed into the wild, threatening atmosphere.

The main street was completely deserted. The gas lamps on the street poles were flickering as if gasping for breath and life, and yet the air was still and lifeless: nature's upheaval was in the making. Stars were appearing and swiftly disappearing while long black clouds were moving fast in all directions. It seemed as if worlds were being born and destroyed in the depths of the endless universe.

There are billions of stars, I thought. Each one represents a world of its own. Perhaps they had been created by billions of souls who joined the celestial expanse over billions of years.

It was a frightening sight. As the clouds moved in, the thunder was getting louder and deeper. Chaos spread quickly as people ran for cover in all directions. Sharp, bright flashes of lightning stabbed sky and earth amid hopeless gloom. Hail and rain came down in torrents. I braced myself against a wall of the dark room and thought of a poem by Longfellow:

> *Be still sad, sad heart, and cease repining,*
> *Behind the clouds is the sun still shining;*
> *Thy fate is the common fate of all,*
> *Into each life some rain must fall.*

The following morning the sun rose red-hot, as if to apologize for the devastation the storm had left behind. The town was a shambles; houses were flattened; poles and wires were strewn everywhere. If and when we get out of this catastrophe, I thought, we will go to a Synagogue and *Bentsh Goymel* (thank God for our survival).

In the meantime, while we sat around waiting for the flood to subside, we got acquainted with two other salesmen we met in the Chinese restaurant. We began to play cards. At first it was for fun, but the game gradually became more heated, because one of them had lost a dollar and we were the winners. The game finally broke up in an unfriendly manner.

This reminds me of a story told by one of the great storytellers, none other than Myron Cohen. If you have heard it before, bear with me; otherwise "laugh a little."

Four friends were in the habit of playing poker three or four times a week. One night they were gambling for big money; the bets were high and the tempers short. Suddenly, one of the fellows had a heart attack and died. They finished the game standing up out of respect to the dead friend. They were now faced with a problem. Who was going to tell his wife of the unfortunate incident? After some deliberation, one of them voluntered to handle this unpleasant task. "How do you plan to break this horrible news to the widow?" "Leave it to me," the informer replied. He walked up to the widow's house and knocked on the door. Sheindel opened it, and asked in astonishment, "Jacob! What are you doing here at this late hour?"

"I came by to tell you that your husband lost $5,000 this evening."

"He should only drop dead, that bum!"

"He did!" the informer replied.

We dug ourselves out of Yorkton mud and headed north. After about fifteen miles we found a prosperous, thriving Dukhobor colony. Dukhobors are members of a Christian sect of the eighteenth century. Their culture and traditions are unique, but they are very hospitable people.

We stopped in front of a general store that looked neat and prosperous; the sign above the door was white and painted in black "Ferguson's General Store." The man was tall, strong-featured, and wore a long red beard. He was almost handsome, spoke fluent English, and his behavior was that of a gentleman.

"Are you boys Jewish?" he asked.

"Yes, we are, why do you ask?"

"I am Jewish, too," he said.

"How do you come to be located in this colony?"

"Oh, it's a long story."

He then slowly unfolded a story as to why his name was Ferguson. "It certainly doesn't sound Jewish," he said apologetically. "Many years ago my grandfather emigrated to Canada. When he arrived with his two friends in Halifax, the immigration officer asked him, 'What's your name?' Since he didn't understand a word of English he excitedly turned to his friends and said, in Yiddish, *'Ich hob fargessen mein pashport'* (I forgot my passport).

"The officer, hearing the word *fargessen*, said "Okay, Mr. Ferguson, here is your landing card!' The name has stuck with us from that day on."

That day was quite rewarding. Mr. Ferguson bought our entire inventory, which consisted of a variety of items, ranging from medicine for ingrown toenails to long woolen underwear and birth control instructions. About the only thing we weren't selling was snake oil.

When we finally returned to Winnipeg, we had a net profit of $1.50 each. This low net was mainly due to the expense of repairing the car, which had refused to start after plunging into a ditch when the lights failed while we were driving on a muddy country road. Our partnership thus came to an abrupt end.

Shmuel began to look for a position as a Hebrew teacher, while I sat on a bench in a park for days planning my next venture.

I suddenly realized that Jean, our mechanic, had repaired our car; perhaps we could dispose of it. I suggested to my partner that we see Jean and ask if he knew anyone who would be interested in buying it. "Are you kidding?" he asked. "With 90,000 miles on the odometer who would even look at it?"

I had once heard a story about a man who had a car for sale, and the odometer registered 80,000 miles. He consulted a friend to advise him what to do in order to sell his car. "Turn the mileage back to 15,000 miles, polish up the car, and no one will ever know the difference." He took his friend's advice and left. About a month later the two friends happened to meet again, and the one who had sought advice was driving the same car.

"How come you didn't sell the car as you said you would?"

"I changed my mind. Why should I sell a car with only 15,000 miles on it?"

I asked Jean to do the same for us. He agreed, and within a few days our car was sold.

I didn't grow up in a world where I had to give daily or weekly demonstrations of being a well-adjusted individual. Life was difficult at best; frustrations and defeats were never-ending. With each defeat, however, I became more determined to try again.

Beware of self-pity, I always thought. Pity is erosion of the mind. It comes in the form of compassion, which sometimes weakens the will.

I looked up a wholesale grocer who had hundreds of canned goods, some slightly damaged, which were being sold at a fraction of the original price. I knew how to select the ones that were in fair condition: You press the top of the can with your thumb; if the dent springs back, the food is suitable for consumption, but if it doesn't you know it's bad.

I roamed around the huge wholesale store, picked and chose a sufficient quantity of various fruits and vegetables and had them delivered to our attic. Then I walked from store to store soliciting orders for sauerkraut, peaches, pears, only to find the following day that I had no means of delivery. I purchased a small, flat-bottomed cart, loaded the goods, and proceeded to deliver my orders. But winter had set in again, and I had to abandon my business.

You'll probably wonder how I had managed to be involved in so many different ventures in such a comparatively short time. Simply because they were all of short duration, but highly diversified. I had learned a lot about business, which I found to be dishonest, most of the time, and certainly not to my liking or practice.

In a way it was a tremendously exciting time. We found strength we didn't know we had. We learned to endure more and more. Suffering can be compared to exercise in a way: the body and mind get adjusted to it over a period of time. Suffering, too, can be endured for longer periods of time; one gradually finds extra strength within that makes it less painful.

We were apparently made of solid stuff and had the will to work hard. Faith was also of great significance; it's easier to face unrealistic reality when one has faith.

One who has stood in a relief line knows that we weren't treated as humans, not even as animals. We were shameless, faceless, silhouettes.

I remember one miserably cold day in January. I stood in line for hours to get my measly $2.50 token for the week. When I finally got to the wicket, I was handed a paper to fill out in preparation for being sent to a relief camp. My protestations and pleading fell on deaf ears, until I went to see a doctor and informed him that my wife was due to give birth any day. When I brought the doctor's report to the relief office, the "jerk" looked me over in disgust and said, "You should be horsewhipped. Don't you realize that there is a worldwide depression? How dare you make babies in times of depression?"

I stood there with my head down without uttering a word. I turned and walked away in indescribable humiliation.

A few days later I received a letter of reprieve, due to the fact that I was about to become a father, and a note enclosed saying that an error had been made in my case, but it didn't even contain an apology.

I was absorbed into the relief lines, again, this time without any feeling of guilt or humility. In fact, I was indifferent. I had analyzed how and why a gradual feeling of indifference develops. It comes in stages. First, one feels panic, frightened of the anticipated consequences; then one begins to hope that whatever it is will not come to pass and, if it does come, it will, one hopes, be short-lived. When hope wears off, unrealistic courage takes over and creates a bold approach to any given situation. When everything finally fails, one becomes indifferent; you surrender to a situation or circumstance without a feeling of guilt, remorse, fear, or frustration. There is no other way. This is how I felt when I rejoined the relief lines. I remembered some lines by Robert Burns:

> *Life was but a day at most,*
> *Oh life, thou art a galling load,*
> *Along a rough and weary road.*

Convinced that I was fighting a losing battle, I became apathetic. I wasn't troubled by ambitions or aspirations any longer; at that point all feelings had failed me. I was, however, facing one problem: my wife was due to give birth any day to our first baby. I was deeply concerned as to how to handle it when the day came!

I went to see my wife one day in the hospital and found her walking the corridors. I tried to call her doctor but didn't get an answer. It's impossible to believe now that in the thirties doctors were doing house calls twenty-four hours a day at two dollars a call, but were unreachable when emergency demanded, and had no answering service to convey an urgent message.

I decided then and there to take my wife to another hospital. Within two hours of admission, our daughter Sheila was born.

Let's go back now to the world of business, its complexities, frustrations, and rewards. We were exuberantly happy, but unfortunately we had to face hard, cruel reality. Man is the only species in this world that doesn't live exclusively for the sake of being happy. There is always that unpredictable tomorrow that shadows one's daily joys. As someone has said,

> *Joy is like a gentle summer breeze; sadness is like a heavy*
> *storm that numbs our feelings, downbeaten by a blast, and*
> *remains shivering on the brink of despair that spreads like a*
> *ripple in the water from a thrown stone.*

Urgency penetrated my mind. I had to find some way of earning a living. By sheer coincidence, I met an acquaintance who confided in me that he was giving up his present job of delivering bread and he was about to open a soft drink plant.

"Max, how about a job?" I asked.

"Like doing what?"

"Well—like driving a truck and promoting sales for your new product."

"Oh, I have already got someone to do that," he said, dismissing me impatiently. But I had a feeling that sooner or later I'd get the job. People are misled by their own ignorance of what it takes to put a new product on the market, and of the complex ideas one has to use to make the product known, so that it eventually becomes in demand.

After a few weeks, I came to see him one day and he agreed to let me prove what I could do.

A few months later we bought our first house on Magnus Avenue for $1,900, with a down payment of $200. It looked like a Japanese hut from the outside, and the stucco walls and the low roof looked as though they were going to crumble any minute, but to us it was a palace. We had three nice rooms and a good solid basement, where I had stored all of the books my uncle had given me, only to lose them in the first rainfall, when the basement flooded.

That's when Sheila began to take piano lessons from a young, promising pianist, Gordon Kushner, who is now musical director of the Beth Tzedec Synagogue in Toronto. Life was more or less bearable as I was struggling to live up to the promise I had given to my employer: "Give me a chance and I swear I'll make you rich."

I don't think I have ever been more accurate in my predictions!

I had thoroughly analyzed my position and had formulated a definite approach and method of putting the product on the market. I loaded a few cases on a truck and began to canvass grocery and variety stores.

"Mr. Yankevitch, would you please allow me to leave two bottles of cola in your store? I am not asking you to pay for them; just let me leave them here for a couple of days."

"Leave them if you want! But I am not responsible."

"Of course not." (I might mention that the two bottles amounted to fifteen cents, contents included.)

That was back in the thirties, when I was hoping for bigger and better things in the future. I was promised five cents' commission for each case of drinks I sold.

On winter days when the falling snow united with the murky sky and numbed my senses, I carried on with determination, reaching for the unpredictable future.

5

Defeat and Determination

About this time I should explain why I had been summoned to New York by a group of lawyers to deal with a dispute over my father's estate. One lawyer had been assigned by the Polish consulate. A cousin of mine also happened to get involved in the whole mess.

I worked by day, and traveled in subways by night, gathering information and witnesses in preparation for the case, which was to be heard in the Supreme Court of New York at some future date. I also spent a lot of time in the Hall of Records, accumulating photostatic copies of mortgages, insurance, ownership registration, and other documents. Every document had been drawn on and signed by my father and my uncle. We had accumulated proof beyond any doubt that my father was a full-fledged registered partner in the entire operation. Preparations took two years, by the time the case finally reached the Supreme Court.

These two highly qualified lawyers were especially interested in the case after reading an announcement in a New York newspaper. They had agreed to take it on a percentage basis, because of my lack of funds for a retainer. I had done all the preliminaries of gathering all the information necessary under the direction and guidance of my lawyers.

One man who was considered most valuable to our case could not be found. All I knew about him was his first name. How is one to find someone in New York who is known only by his first name? It's like looking for a needle in a haystack.

I was walking down a street one Sunday morning, when I heard someone call out the name I had been looking for. Upon investigation I found a few men working in a stable attending to horses, and found the man I was searching for. He told me that he had been very close to my father and had worked for him until he suddenly got ill and passed away.

"I'll be only too happy to come to court and testify," he said, with satisfaction. I walked away with a feeling of triumph and gratitude. Talk about miracles, I thought. One just happened, even though I was under the impression that miracles happened only in the Chassidic communities in our Old Country villages. I was amazed at the timing. Was it coincidence, or a miracle? How are we to know? It is what we believe it is.

I had also lost my job at the paper and twine wholesaler as a result of the investigation by the Immigration Department, which forbade me to hold a job while in the country on a visitor's visa.

Nevertheless, I walked into Ratner's Restaurant on Delancey Street one day and succeeded in getting a job on the night shift, from six P.M. to six A.M. I carried dishes, cleaned tables, served water, scrubbed floors. I was told by the manager that I would not receive any pay but would have to rely strictly on the tips that the waiters might or might not give me at the end of each week. I was making $12 a week in tips and had the days free to do all the investigations in preparation for the upcoming trial.

One late Friday afternoon stands out vividly in my mind. It was a hot summer day. I was walking to my cousin's house for supper. Inadvertently I walked by a short block where my uncle lived. He happened to be sitting on the porch when I was passing. He saw me coming and began to scream, "Here he is! Get him!" I kept on walking, not realizing that the screaming was a message informing someone that I was in the vicinity. Within a minute three young hoodlums jumped me, swinging baseball bats. I managed to knock two of them to the street and then I ran inside a corner milk store and hid behind the counter. The storekeeper got terribly excited and called the police. They put all four of us into a police car and took us to the station. After they had it all sorted out they let me go. Bruised and bleeding, I showed up for supper two hours later than expected. This attack, I imagine, was planned to scare me off the upcoming trial. However, this only strengthened my determination that I had a fair chance of winning.

Time dragged on and I kept riding the subways seeking people who had worked for my father. It was too costly to pay two dollars to a sheriff, so I looked after things during daylight hours, serving witnesses with summonses to appear in court.

The day of the trial had been set and the political maneuvering began. I can't recall whether my lawyers were Democrats or Republicans, which can mean a great deal because of the influence a group has over someone who has been appointed to a position by a certain political party. We were aware of what was taking place, and decided to counteract with a politician of our own.

I was on the witness stand for hours for the first two days of the trial. I produced letters my father had written to us prior to his sudden illness, and all sorts of evidence was produced that established beyond any doubt that my father was a registered partner, according to the Hall of Records, the mortgage company, the telephone company, and so forth, and of course all the witnesses who had worked for him.

Those were exasperating days as the case continued for more than a week. The judge kept sustaining all objections raised by the lawyer for the defense. It was crystal-clear that we were in trouble, and my lawyers even made an effort to bring my mother over for a few weeks. That, too, was denied.

The day finally came when my uncle was called to testify. He made a very dramatic entrance wearing a shabby old suit and supported by a white cane. He was pretending to be blind! He was led to the witness stand, sat down and stared into space. If he was blind how did he see me across the street, so that he could scream to the three hoodlums, "There he is! Get him!" It was a comedy disguised by drama.

Our politician, Mr. Peters, was instructed by my lawyers to put pressure on his party, which in turn would put pressure on the judge, but it all seemed in vain, even though the pressure was mounting.

I had been invited to party meetings on many occasions when my case was the main topic of the evening. Discussions and opinions were exchanged, motions were passed, resolutions were typed and signed by the members to be delivered to the judge who was hearing my case.

The maneuvering had gone on for months, until one Friday afternoon while I sat in my lawyer's waiting room, hoping to hear from Mr. Peters, who had promised to call us immediately after a meeting with the judge was over. According to him this was the day a miracle was about to happen, and happen it did.

At about three P.M. he called from the judge's chambers, instructing my lawyers to prepare a final brief and stipulate in detail the total amount claimed for the three heirs. Within an hour everything was ready. All that was needed was the judge's signature, which we were to obtain within half an hour or so.

Mr. Peters called again and instructed me to bring the documents down to the Supreme Court, wait for him in the lobby, and he would take the documents directly to the judge's chambers and have him sign them while he waited.

I was overwhelmed by the incredible sudden turn of events: A miracle was about to happen, just as soon as I took the brief down to the court lobby.

It was about three-thirty when I got on the subway to meet Mr. Peters and get the final signature. I rushed into the court lobby expecting my proud politician to be there, waiting for me—but he wasn't. I paced the lobby back and forth watching the minutes tick away on the big clock on the marble wall, and realized that at four P.M. sharp the guards would make everyone leave and lock the gates for the weekend. I was desperate and decided to go upstairs. Perhaps I had misunderstood the instructions and Mr. Peters might be waiting for me there. I then commited the unforgivable sin of my life.

As I walked into the secretary's office, she was preparing to leave, and asked me politely if she could help me. I, like an idiot, impatiently handed the documents to her. She took them and remarked, "I'll see that Mr. Peters gets them."

I took the elevator down and found my politician pacing the lobby waiting for me. "Where in the hell have you been?" he asked me angrily. I told him the whole story and began to cry quietly, for I knew there and then that I had committed a deed that had probably wrecked the desperate hopes I had lived with for so long, and shattered them beyond repair.

Mr. Peters turned pale and said, "You just threw thousands of dollars down the drain. For your information I was supposed to have seen the judge after hours," he added.

How was I supposed to know? I can't even begin to describe the hopeless despair and the sinking sensation. I knew that I had just buried my future. I also knew that all of my hopes and my dreams had ended at that moment.

It's pure speculation to this day whether things would have happened as anticipated, had I not been so impatient—but who is to know? Fate, or perhaps it was coincidence, sealed my destiny that day.

There is no need to belabor that episode of my life: the decision was reserved by the judge, as requested by the attorney for the defense.

Three months later my lawyers got a court notice. According to the records the case had been settled "out of court". Knowing my circumstances, it was done without the risk of an appeal. I was awarded $800, which I did not receive until 1932.

Thus ended a nightmare that haunted me for years, and the piece of rainbow that had held out some promise vanished forever. As the Dutch proverb says, *"A handful of patience is worth more than a bushel of brains."* How true it was in my case! I believe that impatience can be destructive, just as clear thinking and rationality can be constructive.

No one will ever know the tormented days and sleepless nights I endured for years. I was so close to victory, so close to seeing justice triumph, and yet all the sparks of hope that had illuminated my dark depression had turned to ashes. My hopes were shattered in the shadows of a ruined dream, never to be recaptured again.

Now back to my efforts in the soft drink business. I had thought about New York, the trial, the injustice, and the unfair judicial system I had lived through, but one cannot dwell too much or too long on bad experiences one faces at one time or another. One must strive and challenge the present, especially while one is young and the world is wide open to be conquered, if one has ambition and determination. I found it much easier to overcome disappointments while I was young, and in a shorter period of time, but it became more difficult as I grew older.

By nightfall I had distributed close to a hundred bottles of drinks and waited with anticipation to find out the results.

On my return visits, two days later, I was happy to find that all of the drinks had been sold. I then increased my sales to four bottles in each store. By the time the hot weather came, the storekeepers were calling the plant for delivery. I could visualize that my promise was indeed becoming a reality; big business was in the making and perhaps the beginning of some security resulting from my hard work and relentless efforts.

Storekeepers had become less resistant because the drink was in demand. That's when I began to feel that my peddling days were about to come to an end, and began selling. I remembered a quotation I had read when I was involved with my lawyers, to the effect that selling can be compared to a rule that lawyers practice: "Don't ask questions of a witness unless you know what answers you are going to get." When you ask, "How many cases of drinks will you have today?" the answer will be one, or two— if you are lucky—but on my own I left five or up to twenty cases, depending on the weather and the volume of business the store was doing.

My loyalty to my job and the promise I had given in anticipation of a vague hope that I might or might not succeed as originally planned tortured my mind. If I were not successful it could only become another persistent memory that would torture me and turn into frustration, even though there was not that much to lose, but the feeling of anticipated failure diminishes one's confidence. One wants to become accustomed to pulling the weight of responsibility, which is tied to loyalty and promise.

I once heard a father giving a few words of advice to his son, who was about to venture into business: "Remember two very important words in conducting a profitable business."

"What are the two words?" his son asked.

"Integrity and wisdom. Integrity means that you must live up to your promises at all times, even if it means going bankrupt. Wisdom means that you should never promise something you may not be in a position to fulfill."

While I carried thousands of soft drink cases, perspiration running down my back into my shoes, German storeowners showed resentment toward me, and toward Jews in general. I had heard them mention an unfamiliar name on many occasions. I didn't have the vaguest idea what the name "Hitler" represented.

I was informed sometime later by a friendly German that Hitler was in the process of organizing a new dictatorial regime and wanted to become the Führer (dictator) of Germany. Anti-Semitic attitudes were becoming infectious, like rabies, or some other poisonous and contagious disease. All this, of course, ultimately resulted in war, concentration camps, gas chambers, and other inhuman practices to exterminate innocent people.

I remember when a Jewish store on Selkirk Avenue had its windows smashed during the night. The police report was very brief after a so-called investigation: "Suspect or suspects unknown."

I also remember a movie theater on Notre Dame Avenue; its name escapes me at the moment. It was packed with Germans nightly and on Sundays. They were showing Nazi films to enhance the glory of the Aryan race. Of course we didn't think much of the propaganda. The police will take care of it, we consoled ourselves. Unfortunately, the police were busy watching the Communist organization, which was, in their opinion, a threat to democracy.

I remember "Bund" members marching on Osborne Street, a short distance from River Park or Assiniboine—I am not sure which—where a rally was to be held that day. I was familiar with that area; it had been my route for some months. A large sign with the Hitler insignia and a slogan painted in German, *"Für Das Vaterland,"* was carried by two youths. While delivering soft drinks I overheard some gruesome predictions in that area. A sizable number of the young Germans were Canadian-born; nevertheless they too were influenced by the glamour and the inspiring, agitating music. They even tried to show their superiority on school grounds against British-born students.

All of this was happening right here in our wonderful democratic country. That was a prelude to the atrocities and complete holocaust throughout Europe on those who refused to surrender to Hitler's philosophy.

Other bunds, seeking not to be too conspicuous, were called "The Canadian German Youth," which was apparently also quite acceptable to the police, even though fights and arrests usually resulted at such meetings. The Mounted Police, to my knowledge, never raided German Bund headquarters, where poisonous propaganda was being prepared.

About two years later we began to realize what the speeches, the singing, the marching, the strange-looking flags with unusual emblems (later identified as "swastikas") the brown shirts with arm bands were all about. The world stood by and passively watched the growth of a deadly cancer that subsequently tried to annihilate an entire race. Hitler's armies set out to conquer the world. Transportation systems were organized and assigned to deliver en masse all who were to be destroyed.

Nations—"the whole world"—should hang their heads in shame and guilt. Even though that part of black history belongs to the past, it will never be erased from the present; it will be remembered for centuries to come.

Have you ever stopped to think for one moment of the strange behavior of the bombing raids? The magnitude of the bombing? The thousands upon thousands of bombs that were dropped on German cities, military installations, and railway yards to disrupt communications and supplies? But have you ever heard of one single incident where bombs, or a bomb, were dropped on the train tracks leading to the places of extermination? Have you ever asked yourself, or others who were in charge of the war machine, why that was the case? I can only quote Kahlil Gibran again, from his celebrated book *The Prophet*: "So the wicked and the weak cannot fall lower than lowest which is in you also."

I am aware that thousands of books have been written, hundreds of movies have been produced, dramatizing those dark, agonizing years of bestiality. But the world tried to vindicate itself, tried to clear its guilty conscience by granting a home, called Palestine, to the remnants who miraculously survived against all odds. Some even survived who were floating around aimlessly on the oceans in broken-down tubs called "ships," like the *Exodus*, but were refused temporary asylum by all nations. A trickle of them somehow managed to reach Cyprus, where they were held in detention camps like criminals.

When some of the starving souls finally reached Palestine, they were not allowed to land in their own old historic country, but were shot down like animals by the British rulers. Some were fortunate enough to slip in unnoticed in the dark of night. "The mighty shall fall, and the meek shall some day inherit the earth." This is my prediction; it's so written in the Bible. We are witnessing that right now; the trend has already begun downward. Perhaps the hunting season on Jews will come to an end soon.

Did religion, nationality, or origin have something to do with it? We know it did, but do we know *why*?

Don't we believe that all men were created equal and in the image of God, and ultimately pass on in the same humble way? If we don't believe in creation or even in Darwin's theory of evolution, then we are nothing more than talking animals, but unfortunately highly sophisticated. We possess the power and the knowledge to destroy weaker minorities, or even each other.

Remember that history repeats itself, and we can see signs of that now. When it happens, I don't think that any one particular race or religion will be a victim or a scapegoat of another holocaust. An atom bomb does not believe in discriminatory practice, and is not interested in who, or what, you are. The unanimous promises and the recognition of the need for peace—the acceptance of peace by the world—have gradually eroded and fallen by the wayside over the years.

New history is now in the making. If we let it spread as we have in the past, it will destroy us all; let us not sweep it under the rug and pretend it's not here. One guilty conscience in one of the blackest centuries in history is enough.

Why can't we accept facts intelligently? China is for Chinese people, Japan is for Japanese, America is for Americans, Canada is for Canadians, and so forth. This does not mean that people of other countries and nationalities are not allowed to live in countries other than their own. Why is Israel not for Israelis? It's been their country from the time of Abraham.

Each one of us has a native country. We can either live there, or choose to live elsewhere, depending on circumstances. It should be a matter of choice, as it is with other nations.

I look into a not-too-distant future, and my humble, unsophisticated mind tells me that Israel is the only sliver of democracy that will remain in the Middle East, struggling to sustain its identity with democratic dignity and ideals.

The most surprising aspect in this complex struggle is deceit. I feel that Israel has been pressured to a degree by political factions, which claim to be democratic, to perform actions that are against Israeli principles, and then is later censured by these same factions. Not only does Israel get very little assistance from the so-called do-gooders, but it is impeded by them because they need a scapegoat at all times. Israel, moreover, is forced into situations in which one cannot tell the difference between friend and enemy.

There is an ancient saying I have remembered since childhood: "Dear God, protect me from my friends, and I shall protect myself from my enemies, for I know who they are." My opinion, for what it's worth, is that the troubled world is being tormented by overzealous politicians, and Israel is being used as a scapegoat.

If a study of geography could but lead the people of one country to understand the conditions of life in other countries, and bring about an intelligent sympathy among the people of the world, it would render its greatest possible service to mankind. Ruthless criminality can't always be blamed on oppressors or persecutors. Such acts of violence are planned, instigated, and finally provoked by political forces, whether for monetary reasons, political recognition, or gains in prestige. Whatever the reasons, they are inhumane and unjust, but who is interested in justice, now or ever?

How long can the world go on denying the Jews their birthright, namely, Israel? It's a historical dream that rose from desolate deserts into a paradise. The Israelis are being denied their rights, which stretch all the way back to the time of Abraham. I remember learning as a child, in a section of the Chumish (a part of the Five Books of Moses), that God said to Jacob, "The land you are lying on, I shall give to you and to your children," meaning the Israelites. "And I shall be with you to watch over you wherever you shall go, and will return you to this land. I shall not neglect you nor forsake you until I have done what I had promised to you and to your forefathers."

This is a land of promise that unites a human being to a country, to a love of a historic home. Israel is entitled to its country, and to its freedom as a nation, and should not have to beg for it. People without a country are like a country without a people; it is dead; it is desolate and barren. Israel is a vision, a beautiful dream fulfilled. Israel is vibrant, alive, where justice, reason, and ethics are permanent and unbiased.

We are hopefully witnessing a new beginning for the Jewish people. A *Shofar* (ram's horn) is sounding. Although as yet it is faint, we hope it will become louder with the passing of time.

It is a historical fact that a gulf exists between the Jewish and the non-Jewish world. This gulf has existed for thousands of years, and yet no one has come up with a legitimate answer or reason as to why those of minority religions—Jews in particular—become not only privileged but are expected and ordered to sing the same national anthem of the country in which they reside and chant the prayers for their secular leaders in time of war. They are expected to defend the country and fight for some sort of victory. We never fought for the victory of morality and the principles on which brotherly love is based; we fought for victory—victory for what? To be classified as racists by countries who have just recently gained their own independence? Is Americanism or Canadianism racism? Most people will answer no. Then why should Zionism be called racism?

I am appalled that nations who recognized Israel as a state

when it was first established, should sink to a level of voting with countries that either know nothing of the tremendous issues at stake or have consistently opposed Israel for their own selfish reasons.

This is one of the many "victories" for which millions of lives have been sacrificed to create a better understanding among nations. Had Hitler concentrated more on the war effort and given less attention to annihilating the Jews, chances are that he would have won the war. Think about that!

Perhaps this is the reason why the inheritance of Abraham, Isaac, and Jacob has thrilled the Israelites for they have inherited a promised land that has been unjustly taken away from them many times during history when they were driven into exile.

Time teases me with the feeling that tomorrow will be more significant than today. I take it for granted that there will be a tomorrow when life will be easier for all righteous people, and the oppressors will become the oppressed.

Hundreds of questions come to mind when one begins to delve a bit into the subject. One cannot help but express some feelings and criticize the world a little. All I can say is, Forgive them, O God, for they know not what they are doing!

I am about to quote a poem from a collection of poetry by the late Annie Rutzky, which was originally written in French. Born in 1920 in Antwerp, Belgium, she was one of that country's finest pianists. During the German occupation she was prevented from playing publicly, and turned her talents more and more to composing and writing poetry. Her Scherzo for piano was composed in 1942, one year before her death in Auschwitz. This poem is entitled "Suffering":

> *It takes a time of suffering to make her aware of living.*
> *Because then she feels herself greater than all her own kind.*
> *She rejoices in this atmosphere of bitterness and sorrow,*
> *A softness possesses her spirit, which is not an ordinary thing.*
> *She is capable of transforming an intolerable noise into a sweet harmony;*
> *It is unpleasant to malign everyone in spite of all she suffers and of all she will yet endure.*

She almost will find it dreadful—yet painfully sweet.
She must be able to triumph over the great injustice
*   reigning over our world.*
She must look kindly upon her own people, a kindness
*   mixed with both charity and strict virtue,*
If only to conquer hate and to try to live infinitely.
It is so easy to forgive.

6

Secrets of Selling

The country was in deep depression, and the storekeepers refused to part with a penny. I didn't blame them, for we all existed on pennies. When they were one empty bottle short to a case they refused to pay. I carried a bottle opener in my pocket for just such occasions—to open a bottle and pour the contents down the drain, while gathering up the empties, thus making another case of empties. Poor *schmoks*, had they been willing to advance five or ten cents they wouldn't have lost its contents. But necessity knows no limits or sympathy when one has the opportunity of making another five cents' commission. Although I felt guilty and sorry for doing it, I fought for survival, not for saintliness.

I have learned a lot during my selling career, and the human way of thinking. It can vary, depending on circumstances and approach.

Isn't it a fact that when you ask a customer, "May I help you?" you are answered, "No thanks, I am just looking." You are then disarmed and in no position to follow up. You'll be resented if you do.

Questions are "don'ts" in business, unless they are put in the form of a positive statement, gradually developed into a chatty conversation. Increased sales mean an extra degree of self-satisfaction and profits. When you are happy you can perform more efficiently. Enthusiasm is contagious; it can promote and create, while apathy gives one an inferiority complex. If you don't think much of yourself or your ability, how do you expect others to feel about you?

A happy, outgoing personality draws attention and confidence, provided one knows how to use it, while a troubled person is ignored. You must also remember that a person's thinking is affected by his personality, which is unique, just as his fingerprints are.

You must therefore adjust your approach and conversation

accordingly, but *don't* ask questions! Tell your customers, suggest to them, with confidence and sincerity, in a positive manner.

One must also remember to leave all personal problems behind. The minute you step into a business a complete transformation of your personality must take place. A pleasant smile breathes confidence—that's what good business is all about.

The main point in selling is not to appear as if you are rushing the customer. Even though you are dying to make the sale, you are the only one to know. We are so intoxicated with self-indulgence that we fail to notice other people's problems. We are out to annihilate each other openly; greed is deeply engraved in each one of us; nothing deters us from selfish practice, simply because we are beyond caring. Be nonchalant but with dignity. Honesty combined with honor will make you a really good salesperson. Obvious pressure creates suspicion.

If your customer obviously likes a garment and tells you stories about why she can't buy it now, you have to become politely persistent. You may not make the sale, but you'll at least know the reason for her hesitation, rather than waste time. Chances are she'll return when she is ready to make a purchase.

Happiness is also comprised of different things for different people. To some it's attainment of an ambition; to others it's a feeling of contentment. It is instrumental, however, in accumulating friends and achieving serenity, as in the practice of meditation.

As I have said before, I think that meditation, among other things, creates good human qualities and gives one a feeling of tranquility. It can also free one from a feeling of depression and anxiety.

You begin to enjoy the things you are doing, rather than feeling that you are compelled to perform certain tasks because of circumstances. Consider it a privilege and you'll find pleasure in your work. When you reach that point of tranquil thinking you begin to respect and love yourself; consequently you begin to breathe confidence and become more efficient in your profession. You can rise to unbelievable heights of serenity you never thought possible, look and feel younger, enjoy your life and your work, rather than looking pathetic and projecting an impression of being a martyr. Walking tall will contribute and create happiness within you.

You should always strive to feel as if you are on top of a high mountain looking down at the world of weakness and fear lying below. You'll get a feeling of strength and importance that will help you to endure the frustrations and disappointments of life. Some sunny day in the future you'll look back and your heart will be filled with gratitude. You'll begin to see your dreams being fulfilled and standing there shimmering in the air, because you have never lost faith.

Any constructive dream can be realized if you honestly believe in it and constantly do the things you must—fertilizing, watering, weeding. It's hard work to develop self-discipline, but you can do it if you try hard enough to be a success in your chosen endeavor.

No one has ever had a nervous breakdown from hard work. I worked for years day and night, worrying at the same time about tomorrow (which made life difficult). But, as the years passed, I gained a feeling of gratitude, because I have never lost faith or felt sorry for myself.

Remember, youth is hope and anticipation; old age is hopelessness and despair. So take your time getting old while you are young. A child is someone who passes through your life, and then disappears into an adult. So are you—young—passing into old age.

Patronization is a habit carved into the subconscious over a long period of time. One automatically associates a certain retailer or supplier with his tentative needs. I know this from years of observation of customers who traveled fifty to eighty miles, when I finally owned a store in Toronto. They bypassed hundreds of stores similar to mine and came to make their purchase in my store. Why did they go to all the trouble and a time-consuming trip? Simply because they felt that no other store could give them the courteous service, the prestige, and the good value for their money. Such confidence can be created only by sincerity and integrity, consistent honesty, not eroded by daily complexities or an overinflated ego when business is good.

Within one year from the day I started promoting, four trucks were in operation. I felt that I was directly responsible for the success as a result of my relentless drive to live up to my promise.

The work was indescribably hard. Some days I thought that I wouldn't live through another, but, as time passed, I became conditioned, even though I often thought that it was beyond human endurance, but I thanked my lucky stars that I had a job. I endured unbearable heat in the summer—snow and freezing temperatures in the winter.

I shall always remember how my wife silently cried and prayed seeing me drive a monstrous, heavily loaded truck down the street. I can't help but refer to a quotation that expresses so much: "A quitter never wins, and a winner never quits."

I stuck to that inhuman torture simply because I wanted to be a winner. I was at least assured of earning $8 to $10 weekly in the winter, and $15 to $25 in the hot summer months. Because of the stupidity of all the employees our employer was getting wealthier by the day, but my hopes for better times never wavered.

One morning in December I was slowly driving down Main Street in forty-five-below-zero weather and noticed a man waiting for a streetcar that I knew wouldn't come by for at least half an hour. I stopped and asked him to get in and drove him to the center of town. As he stepped out of the truck he thanked me, gratefully slammed the door, and shattered the window. Because I couldn't afford the $3 it cost to replace it, I drove around all winter without a window, sitting in snow waist-deep on stormy days. I cursed the man quietly each day, because if it hadn't been for him I would at least have been sheltered from the swirling snow and wind, but then—he didn't mean to do it; he simply tried to express his gratitude.

One day a stabbing pain in my right side became unbearable. I parked the truck in front of a doctor's office and went in to seek relief. He told me that I had pleurisy and ordered me to stay home for a week. I was fed up and hopelessly tired but didn't obey his orders. I hope I get pneumonia, I thought with satisfaction, as I was walking back toward the truck.

One day, in July, 1944, after eight and a half years, I walked into the office and announced in a shaky voice (I have never been good at quitting or firing), "I quit as of today." My employer was caught by surprise.

"You are joking," he said.

"No, I am not. I have had enough of you and everything you represent."

The accumulation of hate and resentment had broken my will to continue working.

"But why?" he asked in surprise.

What a question, I thought. My mind was made up regardless of the consequences I might have to face. I just couldn't carry another case.

I despised that man. He was brutal and merciless. I remember when my daughter Louise was born. It was forty below zero that day. I finished my route about four P.M. and asked him to allow me to go to the hospital to see my wife and baby. He seemed to think about my request for a moment, and to my surprise he handed me a check for $25 as a gift for the baby.

The following morning when I arrived at the plant (it was six A.M.) he casually asked me if I had the check he had given me. I said, "Yes, I have it; here it is." He took it from me and, with a gleam in his eyes, tore it into pieces and walked away. I asked him why he had done that and he replied, "You had the nerve to leave the plant yesterday at four P.M. You don't deserve the check." I felt terribly humiliated and decided to quit the job as soon as possible.

7

The Renewal
of the Moon

The chapter containing some detailed accounts of my life and experiences was not meant to boast about my capabilities, nor was I seeking a sympathetic ear. I merely wanted to familiarize you in some small way with what it was like to live in that era, so that you can make some comparison with existing values and conditions, and count your blessings.

I had suddenly found idle time just to roam around and sit in a nearby park off the main street facing the Red River. The park was hypnotically beautiful at that time of year, with flowers drenched in sunshine ablaze in the hot summer sun. The grass was as thick as a heavy carpet and smiling at the world. The leaves on the trees were whispering a prayer to the universe. What serenity! To me, especially it was hypnotic, because I hadn't had the time in countless years to observe or appreciate nature and its beauty. As I sat there, tranquility penetrated my aching bones. I was at peace with myself and the world, agreeing with Kossuth, who wrote, "I am a man of peace, God knows how I love peace; but I hope I shall never be such a coward as to mistake oppression for peace."

We lived only a short distance away, so my wife came over and joined me. The two of us sat there for a while listening to the murmur of the river, the singing of the birds, and the hushed rustle of the leaves, created by a soothing breeze. Had it not been for the pesky mosquitoes we could have sat there until nightfall. But the mosquitoes were biting as if they hadn't eaten in months.

I haven't accomplished much materially, I thought, but I am proud of one thing: I breed confidence in whatever I do and this alone is quite rewarding, even though I can't pay a bill with it. I am, nevertheless, proud of it. Facts speak for themselves when they are arranged and analyzed. To be liked and trusted is a satisfying achievement. It creates a certain inward happiness. Society claims that everyone should try to be happy. If you are depressed you'll develop a feeling of guilt for feeling that way. It takes a mature mind to control such emotions. Unfortunately some people never mature. They just grow taller. It depends on one's capability for stretching the mind and the imagination.

The summer of 1944 was passing slowly. War factories were in full production, creating materials for destruction, but the Western Provinces have always been in sleepy oblivion as compared with the Eastern Provinces. Western people seem to possess inborn tranquility; they are never in any particular hurry and yet they get to wherever they are going just the same. One can always feel the serenity of a satisfied people, moving about to the slow rhythm of the West.

Although the factories were humming day and night, the pulse was beating slowly with calculated monotony. Many unemployed were still seeking work and I was one of them. If I were a son of a wealthy man, or were rich myself, I would probably get a job in no time, but how does one go about getting rich?

Oh, I thought, to hell with the system. I had battled inequality for years and gained nothing. Had I been in a position to get a formal education I might even have had a chance to work in some sort of public or government office. I remember hearing someone remark one day that "public office is the last refuge of the incompetent." But why worry about it, I asked myself. We have a fairly nice home covered by a mortgage halfway up the roof. Whatever is beyond that is ours, which is very little.

The Second World War was still raging. I had lost my family some years before. I was the lone survivor. I can visualize the hump on the otherwise flat ground where the entire community is buried. It's probably level by now, and green grass is growing, smilingly covering the bloodstained spot of butchery.

People in general are prone to be neutral in any given situation, even to declarations of war. Individually we grumble, but obey. We follow regulations of our leaders not by choice but by pattern. All of the opposing or agreeable comments by the media do not seem to make a dent in our behavior, even though we applaud wholeheartedly or oppose as strongly.

My wife went home but I sat in the park, and was surprised to meet my ex-partner, Shmuel. I hadn't seen him in more than eight years, during which time he slowly got assimilated into Canadian life to some extent. We compared notes as to how we were doing and found that we had one definite thing in common—overdue bills we couldn't pay.

According to Shmuel's belief it is written somewhere in the Talmud that Chassidim consider this world as a vestibule or a stopover on the way to the eternal world. When the day of retribution comes, one has to face his creator and give an account of all his deeds before he is permitted to enter the "Golden Palace" of infinity. The following is the story told me by Shmuel.

A Jew—a *Misnaged* (a sinner—one who doesn't believe in Chassidic culture and Chassidic Rabbis)—passed on and came to the gates of Heaven. He arrogantly demanded to be allowed to enter, saying, "I am Aryeh Ben Yehuda" (*Ben* means son). "Not until you give us a full account of your life on earth" came the reply.

"I could lie!"

"I know" came a voice out of the void. "You were an evil man, a liar, and committed many evil deeds in your life under misleading pretenses. You robbed widows and orphans of the money they had earned by sweat and blood, and pretended to be a philanthropist. You became a rich man while your victims were starving, and you covered your sinful deeds by publicity for which you had paid in order to be known as a compassionate man and a humanitarian. You covered yourself with glory in order to win the trust of innocent people."

"I admit that I have cheated, I have lied, I have obtained money by evil and devious methods, but am I not entitled, as every Jew is, to enter the gates of Heaven? It even states in the *Pirkey Avot* that 'every Jew has a share in the world to come.'"

"You are excluded and you shall burn in Gehenim [Hell] forever. You have inflicted too much pain on too many during your life time. Now is the time for *Din Vechesbon* [judgment and accounting] so that the books will be balanced."

It's an unbelievable story, as usual coming from Shmuel. I paid very little attention to him, but he made me think.

I began to analyze it. Perhaps there is a moral to what he was saying. How many individuals do you and I know who thrive on evil, on misleading pretense, and project piety and honesty? They almost succeed in making us believe that they are saints. They win our trust and confidence, only to turn them to their own gain, regardless of the grief and tragedy they cause to others in the process.

His story reminded me of a man who had killed his parents. He was tried and convicted. Just before passing sentence, the judge asked him, "Do you have anything to say for yourself?"

"Your honor, all I can do now is ask that you have mercy when pronouncing my sentence."

"Why?" asked the judge.

"Well, you see, I am an orphan!"

I feel that it is important at this time to quote the Talmud regarding sin and forgiveness, also the penalty that is subsequently paid by the sinner one way or another.

I remember learning in Cheder that an evil man doesn't necessarily suffer the penalties of his deeds, individually. In many cases children, brothers, or sisters pay the price for the evil deeds committed by one within a family circle. When life is good to you despite all devious methods you have used to get rich, don't beam with satisfaction, because someone, somewhere, someday, will pay for it dearly. In other words, don't think that you have gotten away with it. A debt must be paid regardless of who pays it.

I remember a story told by Rabbi David Monson during a sermon many years ago. The story pertained to greed and evil, when enough is not much, and much is never enough.

I believe that most of us are familiar with the particular time in history when Jews in Russia who lived under the rule of the Czar were deprived of the right to live in certain areas, towns, or cities. It was also against the Russian law for a Jew to own a piece of land. The oppression was unbearable but they somehow lived on, as Jews always do. One day the Czar proclaimed that all Jews of a certain area would be allowed eight hours during which they would be permitted to own the land they could encircle within that specified time. Most of the Jews were quite content to walk slowly and stop when the time had expired; the greedy on the other hand set out to encircle as much territory as possible; they didn't walk, they *ran* to the point of exhaustion and dropped dead of heart attacks in the process. I must refer to the *Pirkey Avot* again, where it's cleverly written, "*Eizehu ashier?* [Who is rich?] He who is satisfied with his lot, and is not about to kill himself or others for fame and fortune."

"Fame is usually short-lived, and in his ambition to attain great fame a man often loses his good name, vaulting ambition which overleaps itself."

—SHAKESPEARE

"However, you can derive so much joy in giving help to someone, you feel like thanking him."

—HENRY DEMONTHERLOND

There are many things that money can't buy—health, happiness, contentment of the soul and spiritual serenity, just to mention a few.

I am at this time reminded of a story told to me by a friend of mine.

A very rich man had a beautiful daughter and wished to find an intelligent, educated young man for her. Because he possessed great wealth he was certain that he would achieve this, if he were to approach a matchmaker with the proposition. He was an illiterate individual, and was known as a cheater and a devious character, but he thought that money would cover everything.

The matchmaker brought him a fine, educated young man, reared in a good home, presented him to the rich man, and introduced him to his daughter. A few days later a lavish engagement party was prepared, as befits a rich man.

After the party the young man lingered in the neighborhood before returning home. He consequently began hearing all sorts of stories about his future father-in-law, Mr. Tarber. He was told that the man was a crook, a cheater, a conniver, but was very rich.

The young man had a change of heart, and said so to Mr. Tarber. "You see," he said, "my parents are God-fearing, ordinary people. They would be very unhappy if I were to marry your daughter. I am sorry, but I must insist that the engagement contract be canceled."

"Wait a minute," said Mr. Tarber. "Don't pay attention to what people are saying, come with me and I'll show you something so that you wouldn't be so naive."

He escorted him to his beautiful den and said, "Do you see this billiard table? It is covered with the most expensive felt money can buy. Here is a piece of white chalk and you print on it what I tell you, okay, ready—'Crook,' 'Thief,' 'Cheater.'"

He then took three thousand-dollar bills and covered each word. "You see," he said gleefully, "money covers everything."

The young man looked at the money for a few seconds, then bent over and with one blow of his breath blew away all the thousand-dollar bills. He turned to Mr. Tarber and said, "You see, money can easily be blown away, but the words I printed on the green felt remained."

He turned and walked out.

The moral of the story is that money is important, but not to the point of being able to erase a bad name. Monetary achievements are not to be construed as success. A feeling of reward and contentment can be achieved only by being a kind and compassionate human being; only then can one claim success and experience a feeling of serenity that soothes the soul.

As the sun was slowly sinking behind the horizon, Shmuel got up and with a deep sigh said, "Good luck We shall meet again, I hope!" That was more than thirty years ago. I have never seen him since. I think of him many times; maybe he wasn't too much out of line in his beliefs and his unique philosophy on life!

As I was walking slowly home, my wife met me halfway. It was apparent that she had been crying. She slowly took my hand and began to tell me about a long distance telephone call, a call that changed our lives. Nothing has been the same from that day on.

My wife informed me that her sister, who owned a ladies' wear store in London, Ontario, had called to tell of the sudden passing of her husband. Would we consider moving to London? Perhaps I could help her in the operation of the store.

"How do you propose we do that?" I asked. "Our elder daughter, Sheila, has many friends here and is doing very well in piano. She even stages plays in our old garage for her friends. She is a natural musician. How can we dislodge her from all of this and move to London? Louise is only six months old. How can we consider such a drastic change?"

"This may well be our last opportunity to perhaps become a bit more independent and somehow manage to find some solid ground and a future for our children," she replied.

I resisted the idea at first, but my wife subsequently talked me into selling our house, and we got busy making preparations to leave Winnipeg.

On a hot humid Sunday in August, 1944, we were standing in front of the house waiting for a taxi to take us to the CNR station.

I heard a train thunder by and cross the road where the steering rod of my truck had once broken and I had veered into a deep ditch in fifty-below-zero weather. There I was, standing on the threshold of leaving Winnipeg and about to face the unpredictable future in a strange city. I felt a chill penetrate my body.

Later, looking out the train window at night, all I could see were fences and poles swishing by my eyes. The full moon, set in a deep-blue, crystal-clear sky, reminded me of my village Chassidim, who prayed all month for a clear sky so that they could welcome it with song and prayer. On a beautiful clear night like this we would stand outside our little house of worship and pray loudly in unison. This was called *Mechadeish Halvanah* (the renewal of the moon), according to the commentaries by Rabbi Hertz.

In ancient times the proclamation of the moon was the supreme function of the *Sanhedrin* (Supreme Council), who sat in Jerusalem ruling on certain ethical and political matters. In Judaism all beginnings are holy, and the beginning of the month would be a serious reflection for a better life in the future.

I, too, hoped that our new beginning would be blessed with success. We had reached bottom now; the only way left was up. Something must have beckoned in my mind to urge me on to a goal. Maybe my luck would change, but I could not depend on good luck alone. Good luck is simply a readiness for opportunity if and when it comes. Perhaps I was prepared, although I wouldn't express my feelings openly. I didn't possess the confidence I once had. It had deteriorated slowly with numerous failures over the years.

As I looked out the train window again, it seemed as if the moon were moving, smiling at me, daring me. In deep thought and fascination with the night I kept thinking that no matter how dark the night, daylight would follow.

Each of us has our own hopes and frustrations, fantasies and aspirations that we do not wish to share with others. All we do is silently hope for a better tomorrow.

The day we arrived in London, we were sorry we had left Winnipeg. There were a handful of Jewish families, most of them in retail ladies' wear. We lived with my sister-in-law. Business was poor, probably because of the sudden tragedy. A feeling of guilt and dejection penetrated my senses. I also noticed that my wife appeared to be very unhappy.

I knew nothing about ladies' wear. Necessity, however, really is the mother of invention. I possessed a lot of experience in promotions and prepared a storewide sale. We were successful in raising enough money to pay most of the accounts.

I was interested in a soft drink plant, because that was the business I knew best. I commuted to Belleville, Ontario, for several weeks with the idea of entering into partnership with, or buying outright, a plant that was on the brink of bankruptcy. The deal did not materialize, however, and I unexpectedly entered into a partnership in a ladies' wear store in Toronto. It was my last hope of endeavor at the time. I plunged, moreover, into an unfamiliar business in a strange city. I felt that it was wrong in character as well as in principle, but I had no alternative.

8

A New Dawn

In 1945, our daughter Sheila presented us with an anniversary card that we treasured for many years:

It takes a special day like this
To just look back and reminisce,
And think of all the things you've shared
Since that first day you knew you cared. . . .
Of course things change, for that is life,
And love between a man and wife
Cannot remain "Romantic Bliss
Forever flavored with a kiss,"
But always there's that "Bond of Love"
There's just no explanation of,
And with the storms and trials it grows
As flowers do beneath the snows.

Sometimes it's hidden from the sight
Just as the sun gets lost in night,
But always there's the bond of love,
There's just no explanation of. . . .
And every year that you are together,
Regardless of the "Kind of Weather,"
The bond of love grows that much stronger
Because you've shared it one year longer.

Because—What is marriage?
It is sharing and caring,
Giving and forgiving,
Loving and being loved,
Walking hand in hand,
Talking heart to heart,

> *Seeing through each other's eyes,*
> *Laughing together,*
> *Weeping together,*
> *And always trusting and believing,*
> *And thanking God*
> *For each other.*

Unfortunately I do not remember the author of this inspirational card, which renewed our hopes and aspirations.

The relocation to Toronto was not as simple and as easy as we had anticipated. Heavy snowfalls had hit Ontario in that unforgettable time in January, 1945. No one ever remembered having such a concentrated snowfall, and nothing like that has ever happened since.

The city was completely paralyzed. There was no delivery of milk or bread for several days, and it was impossible to get to a store. Nothing moved; everything and everyone remained wherever they happened to be at the time the snowstorm began.

I was caught in that heavy snowfall in Toronto, while searching for living quarters for my family, who were still in London at that time. The city appeared abandoned for a few days while I was confined to a very small room I had rented on Brunswick Avenue. I slept on a rollaway bed directly above a terrible noisy coal furnace, which kept me awake all night as I unsuccessfully attempted to get some sleep.

The main streets were cleared after the storm had subsided. They looked like deep tunnels lined with huge mountains of snow. One couldn't see the stores or houses on the opposite side of the street. The side streets were in a state of chaos.

I walked the streets each day searching for a low-priced flat, in order to bring my family. There were many flats available but for adults only. No sooner did I mention that we had a one-year-old baby than the flat had suddenly been promised to someone who had inquired earlier in the day.

I finally succeeded in renting a flat on Palmerston Avenue at Dundas Street. There was a condition, however: "If and when the baby should cry or make noise we would automatically be evicted without notice." I also had to agree in writing never to have visitors, not even close friends. The latter condition didn't bother me too much, because we were moving into a new city and we didn't have any friends; later, however, it became very embar-

rassing and frustrating, because we acquired some friends but
were not allowed to let them visit us.

Our rooms were very small; in fact, my older daughter's bedroom was the size of a walk-in closet. The tiny kitchen was very
confining, to the point of claustrophobia, and the concentration
of mice in that kitchen was amazing. As long as there was move-
ment they were in hiding, but when I sat and tried to look through
the newspaper they would begin their nightly rendezvous; the
gas stove burners were their favorite meeting place. I would raise
my eyes and silently turn. I got the feeling that they were preparing to attack me. Hundreds of little heads were peeping out of
the burners. I would make a loud noise with the newspaper and
they would disappear instantly.

The third floor was occupied by two foreign girls, and soldiers
kept going up and down the stairs like a herd of elephants. Now
that I think back I am almost convinced that the mice owned the
house. This was the beginning of our new life in Toronto.

I sat up nights thinking, worrying, asking myself questions for
which I couldn't find answers. And when the night slowly faded
into morning, the sun came up from the depths of the horizon,
smiling at our window.

The world is beautiful, I philosophized, if it weren't for the
greedy, overzealous individuals who believe that the sun shines
only for them. They are constantly in pursuit of power and the
pleasures of life; they are under the impression that all material
pleasures belong to them, even the wind—the breeze that everyone should enjoy. Such people have no conscience, and above all
no "reason." Reason plays a very important part in one's life, as
William James wrote in his book *The Will to Live*: "Reason is but
one item in the mystery: and behind the proudest consciousness
that ever reigned, reason and wonder blushed face to face."

Life looked hopeless, because we had no business to speak of.
I began to think of some inventive ideas as to how I could gradually bring about an improvement. I realized that a lot of work
and endless hours would be needed if I were going to improve
the operation. Even though the store was very large it was terribly morbid. Hopelessness was evident throughout the entire
dimly lit place. One had to be a superoptimist to find a flicker of
hope in that atmosphere.

I became very nervous when ice began to melt on the roof,
or on rainy days, which, by coincidence, always fell on Saturdays,

when there was some traffic in the store. Water would start dripping from the dislodged, dark gray asbestos ceiling squares. In
embarrassed desperation I would place eight or ten empty paint
containers in a concentrated area, where the dripping of water
was quite heavy. After a while the different levels of water in the
containers created different sounds with each drop. It sounded
like a symphony orchestra tuning up before a concert. All of this
was happening because of a leaky roof, which was in need of
repair. I became very disheartened on such occasions, and re-
gretted that I had invested every dollar we had saved in Winnipeg,
hoping to create a better life for my family, but failing miserably,
or so it seemed at the time.

Only another miracle can save me, I thought, but where does
one find a miracle? This isn't an isolated little village near the
Carpathian Mountains where miracles happened every day; this is
Toronto. I had a feeling that I would have to create my own
miracle.

War plants were still operating twenty-four hours a day. People
were spending money without even realizing it, but I sat in the
store for days on end without a single sale.

At this point I thought of a joke I had heard some years before.
A storekeeper was sitting dejected and worried, when one of his
friends walked in. "Zalmen, why do you look so worried?"

"Oh," answered Zalmen, "I am about to close the store for the
day, and I didn't have one stinking sale."

"Don't worry so much; tomorrow is another day. Think positive
and you'll see things will get better."

"That's what worries me," replied Zalmen. "Tomorrow."

"Why should you worry about tomorrow? It can't be worse
than it's been today."

Zalmen locked the store. They bade each other good night
and parted. The following day the same friend came in to see if
business had improved. He was surprised to hear Zalmen say,
"Don't even ask me how business was today. It was worse than
yesterday."

"How could it be worse? You didn't have a single sale yesterday!"

"That's true, but today I had a refund."

One incident still stands out in my mind. I picked out a hundred
or more dresses and hung them on a special rack with a large

bold sign: "One Dollar Each." I sat and waited in anticipation to
see what reaction it would bring from customers, if by chance
some happened to walk in. Within a few minutes a woman walked
in, apparently a war plant worker, judging by the coveralls she
was wearing. She picked out twelve dresses, handed them to me,
and said, "I'll take these."

I was overwhelmed with excitement and quickly packed the
dresses into a large box, tied it securely with rope, and handed it
to her. She nonchalantly took it and walked out of the store. I
felt like dancing for joy. Imagine, twelve dresses to one customer
early in the day! (I can feel it in my bones that I'll have a good
day today, I told myself.) Then it suddenly dawned on me *Oy a
Broch*! (Partial translation: "My goodness!" or "How unfortunate!"
One must clasp both hands to both sides of the face while
exclaiming the words in order to get the proper feeling of despair.)
I had forgotten to collect for the dresses! This was probably because
of the unexpected sale, which had gotten me so excited. Thus the
beginning of an exciting day turned into a day of guilt, despair,
and humiliation.

Those were sad, hopeless days. Gloom and dejection lurked in
every corner. What am I to do now? I asked. Sit there and watch
our *Kishka* money gradually disappear? (Translations of *Kishka*
are many. It's a Jewish delicacy, a derma made with stuffing. One
would say, "I laughed until my kishkes were sore," or, if one is
in the habit of penny-pinching and would rather go hungry than
spend money on food, such savings are called *Kishka Gelt*.) The
money we had invested in the partnership had been earned by
sweat and blood, saved by going hungry, denying ourselves the
necessities of life on many occasions.

After a few months I began to realize that the inventory I had
was of very little value. I had noticed that some garments were
faded; some were dirty; some had wilted because of age. Perhaps
this might well be the reason that business was so poor? Something very drastic had to be done as soon as possible to transform
the whole mess into a fresh new look. I thought of an expression
by William James: "High thinking in business is an effort to some,
to redeem themselves from the crude form they are accustomed
to, and acquire more understanding than the experiences yielded.
One must increase and make use of various points of view."

Business experiences that I had had in other endeavors over
many years began fermenting in my mind. My motto in business

had always been sound. I believed that if one made a bad buy, it was wise to dispose of the item or items as soon as possible. Still, it took a lot of courage to decide to get rid of most of the old inventory and start from the beginning. Then I got to know some people in the garment industry and was given advice on how to go about creating some business.

After analyzing many ideas, the salesgirl and I decided to get rid of the existing old inventory and gradually bring in fresh new garments. How does one go about disposing of the old? I asked. I was told of a man who was operating a mail order business. I was to call him and have him empty the store regardless of price. By the time I fully realized what I was doing the store was almost bare from wall to wall. I did, however, hold back some of the better garments, more for sentimental reasons than need.

I was aware that I was beginning a new life—a new venture, in a new world. It was a world within a world—a world of fashions, fabrics, furs, specials. I began to understand that women buy on impulse, unlike men, who usually plan and are prepared to make a certain purchase when they walk into a store.

Women are sly and unpredictable, I said to myself. That's why hurricanes are named after them. If one is lucky and happens to say the right word at the right time a sale is made. The unfortunate part of it all is that each potential woman customer thinks and reacts differently to any sort of methods used in making a sale. Their tastes in style and in the color that compliments them best are as different as their fingerprints. Some respond to flattery, especially the stouter figures, although some stouts request a junior style, and then complain that the dress does nothing for them. I think it's just the reverse. Some women reject flattery because they think that the salesperson is insincere. In such cases a light-hearted, neutral conversation may stir one to a word of acknowledgment, without commitment.

Proper, honest selling is as timely today as it was sixty or seventy years ago, although we all act in a highly sophisticated manner. Nevertheless, dignity and prestige still prevail over all other types of selling.

I don't wish to imply that "success belongs to the successful." One must prepare for success before one can reap its benefits. It doesn't come by filing an application or through unconstructive desire. It can be accomplished only in the old-fashioned way, namely, through hard work. In the daily strife for survival or success, in which all of us are so deeply involved, we must remember that success is the place in the road where preparation, desire, and opportunity meet, but too few recognize success because too often it comes disguised as hard work, which is acceptable to very few. Ambitious individuals who are willing to work hard, to achieve some pride of accomplishment, should be on the alert for just such a meeting. Retail ladies' wear may well be the most insecure and complicated of all businesses. If it is nurtured properly, however, without feeling sorry for oneself for working too many hours, even though too many frustrating situations seem to appear each day, a measure of success can be achieved.

I agree that this business is difficult, but it certainly isn't more worrisome or frustrating than practicing law or medicine. Nothing that is worthwhile having comes easily, wrapped in a nice package with a bow on top. One must work hard in any chosen profession. The difference can be in one's point of view. If you practice your daily profession or business by thinking that it's a privilege to be doing it, you'll be happy and succeed. If, on the other hand, you practice the same because of dire necessity and project yourself in your mind as a martyr to circumstances, you'll never enjoy your work and never progress. Your mental apathy will impede your progress and any reward you would otherwise derive from it.

On the basis of purely personal experience I speculate on why we prefer one garment as opposed to another, when, in my opinion, both look equally well. To probe deeper into our likes and dislikes would be of no value. I believe that they are no more than habits.

Color is important, however, because of different complexions. It can be pale, dark, light, or sallow. Therefore, one must choose the color that is most flattering, and yet most women disregard an unbiased opinion of a salesperson, even though it's an honest one. One certainly enjoys selling the color that is most flattering to a customer.

When it comes to fashion, most women are not attracted to a style that is suitable for a certain figure. Is there a certain built-in object that seems to stimulate their likes and dislikes? They are inclined to ignore the fact that what makes a beautiful garment on one is a "fright" on another. It's the importance of one's figure, flair, and posture that should be considered. Customers fail to see themselves as others do. Their way of thinking cannot adjust itself to seeing reality. Many of them live in a dream world. They look at themselves in horror while they admire others. I feel sorry for them; they don't see beauty when it comes to their own wardrobe. I am inclined to believe that self-appreciation is a state of mind, brought about by conditions, mental as well as physical, and is subject to change if given proper direction by an experienced salesperson, thus breaking the unwritten rules of objectivity.

New fashions are as changeable as day and night, and just as extreme. Yet they are resisted, even though one is aware of the unavoidable ultimate results. One must move with time rather than resist. Women, however, are a unique breed, but given the opportunity they gradually fall into line.

If you were to ask me how to define fashion, my opinion would be that fashion is a personal thing. Rather than visualizing the beautiful creatures in fashion magazines, you should wear what suits your figure and personality. You are then in fashion without feeling guilty or restricted in any way. Be yourself, and you'll be in fashion.

I remember an incident that was quite embarrassing to me at the time. A woman who was bold and outspoken had been trying on dresses for some time, but found fault with each of them. I heard her say to the saleslady, "Look what this dress is doing to my bust; it makes me as flat as a board." Not being able to resist the temptation to tell her off, I came over and said, "Lady, don't worry about your bust. What the good Lord has forgotten we will fill with cotton. By the time you leave the store with this dress, your bust will be quite acceptable to everyone concerned, yourself included. How about this lovely creation?" I asked, pointing to another dress. "It was just unpacked two hours ago." "I don't think so," she replied. "I have to fall in love with a dress before I would consider buying it." "Do you believe in love at first sight?" I asked her innocently. "Yes, I do. It has to hit me." "Did you fall in love with your husband at first sight—and did he hit you?" "Are you kidding?" she replied boisterously. "We were dating for over a year until I realized that I loved him." "If you were to buy this dress and wear it for that length of time, you would probably fall in love with it too. In fact, I guarantee it."

When I think back on those wonderful years, I realize how much fun one could have dealing with women. Unfortunately I could not afford to provoke them; my livelihood was completely dependent on their idiosyncrasies.

The bad days and small gains were of value to me. Gaining

experience by listening to customers' complaints and desires, I gradually began to bring in some new merchandise, priced low in order to do some business. This reminds me of a story told to me by a friend of mine, but I have a suspicion that he stole it from Leo Rosten's book, *The Joys of Yiddish*. This friend, he said, was in a similar predicament at one time, so he decided to run a store-wide sale, at less than cost. He came in one day to see how his friend was doing, only to find him lamenting that he was losing money on each item he sold. Each time he rang up a sale he said, "Oh, boy! I just lost five or ten dollars," or whatever price the item happened to be.

"Why, then, do you stay in this business if you are losing money on each item? How long can you keep on losing and operate a store?"

"What questions!" his friend replied sarcastically. "Since you seem to be so smart, tell me, do you know of a better way how I can make a living?"

Now that all my money was invested in the store I had no alternative but to work and to hope to build it up to a level that would provide us with some meager livelihood.

I got to know a Ukrainian man who had come to Canada some years before from an adjacent village in the Old Country. His philosophy about Jews hadn't changed; it had been implanted in his mind while he was growing up. He still had the ignorant peasant belief, that Jews were forever preying on illiterate peasants and cheating them if and when an opportunity presented itself. In spite of this we became good friends. He would occasionally give me a short-term loan of fifty or a hundred dollars when I was in desperate need.

My dear late wife often reminded me of a phrase in the Talmud. Her faith in God was almost equal to that of my mother: "In every place where I cause My name to be remembered, I will come unto thee and I will bless thee." Exodus 20:24.

"Don't worry," she consoled me. "God will help us, you'll see."

What better way is there to reflect upon an era than to tell in detail daily occurrences and frustrations? For us, the forties were marked by the drab realities of our lives. If not for my wife, who inspired me with her strong faith to go on, I never would have made it.

I was terribly worried one night about a loan I was to repay the following day. As a result I was pacing the floor of our small living room. My wife noticed my restlessness and told me about a similar case that had happened to her father years ago.

"So you know what my mother did?" she asked.

"No, I don't know."

"She picked up the telephone and called Mr. Fliegel: 'Mr. Fliegel, this is so and so. My husband owes you some money, which is due tomorrow. I called to tell you that you will not get your money tomorrow because he hasn't got it.' She hung up the telephone, turned around and said, 'Now you go to sleep and let Mr. Fliegel pace the floor for the rest of the night.'" My wife had done the same.

The wartime controls were still in effect, which made my efforts to accumulate new garments more difficult. All retail stores were on a quota basis according to their purchases prior to the controls. I didn't qualify for any sort of quota because no one had a record of doing business with me prior to the passing of the wartime measures. I cannot forget, but reminisce with gratitude about two wonderful individuals who had helped me in every way possible: Jack Miller and Louis Kracover of Junior Miss Garment. I had met them only a few times prior to the day when I asked them if they would sell me some coats. Without hesitation Jack Miller took a few garments from an order that was to be shipped elsewhere and gave them to me, promising me more for the following day. There was a man with compassion, a man of honor and sincerity. This unexpected act of kindness gave me courage to visit other manufacturers, who responded in a similar manner.

The store was in the process of being reborn; it began to take on a new look. Business was getting better with each passing month as more new merchandise was smiling out of the bins. I thanked God for small mercies and hoped for better things to come.

I remembered how intensely Poles disliked the Ukrainians who happened to live in their midst in the Old Country. They were always treated with intolerance. I had even heard gruesome stories about their practices on the few poor peasants prior to my departure to Canada.

Poles forever boasted about their sportsmanship and intellectual superiority. As a result, they would sometimes engage in sick, inhumane entertainment. I was told that on occasion they would force a few peasants to climb tall trees in the forest at the point of a gun while Polish sportsmen were shooting at them. The one that came closest with his shots without hitting the climber would be declared the winner. Although an accident did happen on occasion, it was attributed to sportsmanship, and therefore not punishable. (Perhaps it was no more than sportsmanship pride on the part of the participants.)

Remembering the difference of opinion and their dislike for each other, I had anticipated problems, because my business catered mainly to the two nationalities, who resided in a large area all around my location. Surprisingly, I didn't meet any conflict or resentment in the store.

Some customers were aware of the fact that I could speak Polish and Ukrainian, and some weren't. The ones who were aware made me speak their language. They were like putty in my hands. They would ask my opinion on whether they should purchase a certain garment. Whatever I suggested was Gospel to them. The ones who thought that I could only speak Yiddish and English would converse in their language: Should they or shouldn't they make the purchase? On many occasions one would say to her friend, "The coat looks very good on you, but tell him you don't like it so he'll give it to you at a lower price."

I just stood by listening to their conversation; they thought I didn't understand. When I became a bit more persistent, pointing out all of the virtues in the coat, one would say to the other, "Even though he is a Jew, I think he is right."

This last expression was obviously a carryover from the Old Country philosophy; it hadn't evaporated over the years. That was part of their identity that they had managed to retain.

Knowing my inexperience in the ladies' wear business. my suppliers had become my friends, advising me and suggesting what type of inventory I should carry, with the assurance, of course, that I might return all or portions of it should I find it unsuitable for my clientele. My honesty and sincerity had penetrated the hearts of strangers who had become my friends in a comparatively short time.

My courage and determination grew by leaps and bounds. I was in the process of conquering worry and despair. The time was approaching when we would bask in some success and self-respect.

I had sold myself a dream many years ago, believing that someday it would become a reality. I was standing on the threshold of realizing that dream. I had been looking up to someone for my survival since childhood, always trying to succeed for others, living in constant fear that I might fail. A new feeling began to penetrate into my thinking, and my inferiority complex gradually began to diminish with the hope that tomorrow is another day.

It was a complicated task for me to cope with, but the dream I had lived with for many years was becoming clearer each day, and yet I was very apprehensive to admit, even to myself, that the worst was just about over.

I dare not fail my family now, I thought. They are looking up to me; I am their hero. I have always been their hero, but in a different way. I wouldn't let them down now. I must begin to walk tall and with confidence, perhaps I can make it, although I didn't believe it inwardly.

By coincidence I read a verse by Edgar Guest, entitled "It Couldn't Be Done."

> *Somebody said that it couldn't be done,*
> *But he with a chuckle replied,*
> *That "maybe it couldn't" but he would be one*
> *Who wouldn't say so till he tried,*
> *So he buckled right in with the trace of a grin*
> *On his face, if he worried he hid it.*
> *He started to sing as he tackled the thing,*
> *That couldn't be done, and he did it.*

9

Success and Sales

It took a lot of courage and determination, but my work gradually began to bear fruit. Dramatic reality was in the process of being born. I began to feel and act more rationally. The feeling of insecurity was not as intense as it had been in past years.

What are the feelings of irrationality and what brings them on? According to William James they come from a discharge of certain arrested psychological conditions and emotional inferiority. We are very distressed when certain bodily functions are prevented from operating freely, but we feel no pleasure when we breathe freely without arrest or inhibition. We accept the latter as a natural pattern of daily living.

Some even think that an attitude of faith is not only illogical but shameful. To me faith is a religious dogma for which there is no outside proof, but I am tempted and willing to assume faith for my emotional interest.

I know for a fact that had my mother not carved into my heart and my very soul the determination to have complete faith without question or reservation, I would not have had the spiritual strength to go through the turbulent journey of my life, and be reborn after each traumatic experience. To be right, one must also be fair and gain all that comes from faith and right action toward God and fellow man. I can attribute the small measure of success I have enjoyed in business only to faith, and, of course, to endless hours of hard work.

The following observation, "Organic Molecules," by William James, briefly expresses my feelings of the time: "To act as if we didn't know where our responsibility lies, would be shedding our responsibilities open-eyed. It is best to face it rather than pretend it isn't there."

By this time I had employed three sales girls and was doing relatively well. In order to keep my employees happy and make them feel important, I used a diplomatic approach that made us all interdependent. Interdependence creates a better chance for success, unlike an attitude of superiority, which can be the ruination of any business. One must listen and pay attention to opinions and suggestions and then do what one thinks is best, regardless of whether other parties are in agreement with the decision. They have been consulted; that's important.

In most transactions in life, no one but us has to make a final decision. Do not leave things unfinished or unanswered. If we are undecided in our actions and make an error in judgment, we subsequently pay for taking the wrong path; decisions and paths can be deceptive.

Your employees, your family or friends are entitled to their freedom of thought and action, although you may not agree. Mental freedom should not be restrained. In fact, we should profoundly respect such personalized freedom, thus creating full understanding, which results in interdependence and freedom of thought.

Any type of business must be operated with honesty and integrity. The size of the business doesn't matter; if operated properly it will increase in size over a period of time. If this combination is not practiced religiously, you will have only a false security, which will gradually decline, and defeats will follow. An attitude that thrives only on glory will suffer the defeats that are caused by dishonesty and a superiority complex.

Thought is in constant change; it's a state of consciousness. Once it has passed it cannot recur and be identical to what it was before, although it may refer to the very same subject. "Hearing a note of music in the morning and hearing the same note again in the evening," the mental state can never be the same. Interruptions or time gaps break the quality and the sameness of tone, a crack or division exists. "*Consciousness*," William James wrote, "is like a bird's life. It seems to be made of an alternative of flights and perchings."

Thought is like footsteps in mud or snow. No matter how careful you are to retrack the original step, it will show a sign of disturbance. It can never remain in its original form.

An original idea, when put into words, carries a definite line of thought with it, but if you repeat the same words sometime later the thought can never be the same; your subconscious reflects a different feeling when repeated.

For this reason one should put thoughts or ideas into practice when operating a business. The first instinct is usually the best and most rewarding. But if you think about the very same subject a few hours later you will be disappointed; it will not have the same positive enthusiasm. Thoughts and ideas come subconsciously; use them when they come.

I shall never forget the day I was about to sell my first coat in the store. The fashions of ladies' coats at that time were quite different from the creations of today. They were tightly fitted at the waist, with huge gored skirts that shaped into a wide flare.

I was about to pin the coat in the front to show the customer how it was going to look when the buttons were sewn on. While I was struggling with a thick long pin the woman let out a scream that almost floored me. Apparently in my excited state I had stuck the pin right into her belly.

I was terribly embarrassed. I couldn't even apologize; my voice was too shaky. I broke out in uncontrollable perspiration, and the woman ran out of the store in anger.

I felt that I had failed my first test miserably, but in time I acquired some skill at sticking a pin in to hold the coat together temporarily without hurting the customer.

I was gradually becoming obsessed with an unfamiliar feeling called "happiness." It was not complete, but it began to penetrate into our lives. I had joined the Jewish Folk Choir on Brunswick Avenue, under the direction of the late Emil Gartner. I had enjoyed singing ever since I was a child. On some Sundays I would sing to, and with, my wife, half in Hebrew, half in Yiddish: *"Nisim—Nisim—Nisim—Nisim venifluous, der Rabbi is areingefallen in vaser und is arois a naser."* (Miracles—Miracles—Miracles—Miracles and wonders, the Rabbi fell into the water and came out soaking wet.") It's not funny, is it? It doesn't grab you! Of course not, I don't expect it to. But in Yiddish it's really funny. It's humorous, I tell you, but, on the other hand, who am I to tell you? You must feel it in your brain and in your bones; you must know first why it's supposed to be humorous.

As I have told you many times before, we Jews are blessed with an unbelievable sense of humor. We make fun of ourselves unlike any other nation. This is one of the reasons why all sorts of extermination methods used on us for centuries have failed. I have asked myself on many occasions how such a limited Yiddish vocabulary can be such a dynamic instrument for expression, for cursing, blessings, and humor.

It isn't because it portrays simple people as opposed to intellectuals. Words are our chief weapons, and the way they are put together express feelings distinctively without sensitivity.

A reply to a question comes in a tone of a question. You can only compare it to a stand-up comic who says very little, but who makes people laugh with his one-line delivery.

I think back to the day when my mother bought a black-and-white cow. We called her Rifky. She had large, brown, melancholy eyes, and a tongue like a snow shovel. Watching her devour juicy green grass, I automatically swallowed each time she took a mouthful. Mother told us that she was cooking noodles, which would be mixed with some milk. We danced with joy. Taking each other's hands we started to dance in a circle and make up a song as we circled round and round, fitting the words into a Chassidic melody: "A cow—a cow—a big black-and-white cow, the cow will give us milk, and Mama will make cheese and butter. Yam, Yam—Tara Ram—Tara Ram." This happened long ago, but in my mind it happened yesterday. It's an insignificant sort of childish experience, but it reflects so much on the times and the primitive way of life we lived, oblivious to our misfortunes and those of other people living in the villages in that era.

It's also a simple reminder of "no value" at first glance; upon examination of the lives and times, however, one can derive a heartful of understanding and compassion. For true happiness can be induced only by a gradual change, not by a sudden overwhelming occurrence. In our case it was very late and slow in coming; that's why we were extremely happy when we caught a glimpse of daylight at the other end of the dark tunnel.

To be aggressive and fully devoted in the operation of a business, or in performing in the capacity of a salesperson, you must come voluntarily and eagerly, with eagerness to act aggressively. But there must also be a feeling of confidence if you have willingness to act at all. Or is it much easier, but not as rewarding, to remain apathetic to situations or occurrences? In such cases you don't have to strain your eagerness to act and create; just pass the time away. But if you remain indifferent to embrace and take advantage of an opportunity, you lose. As William James wrote,

"If your heart does not want a world of moral reality, your head will assuredly never make you believe in one."

In selling, especially in retail ladies' wear, which I happen to know best, a person with an extensive vocabulary, who knows instinctively what to say and when, is far better prepared to achieve success than one who has to rely on repetition. Actually, in selling, what is said is not important as *how* it is said—the intonation of your voice, the emphasis on a phrase. You must say as little as possible, but what you say must sound honest and penetrating. A little study in that direction will make you outstanding. You must be fully familiar with the product you are selling, and in turn impress your customer. A repetitious salespitch is self-defeating. Try to lead your conversation in a direction other than the product. Distraction, especially in the early stages of conversation, will later result in a concentrated area. That step should be taken when you feel you are in charge. If you do this, you will have your customer wishing to purchase the garment, rather than you wishing to sell it; there is a difference.

I have tried this method many times, and have obtained very good results each time. For instance: A customer comes in, and, as I approach her with a friendly smile, she informs me that she is interested in the purchase of a coat. My calm reply can come in many forms, but let's use one to gain her confidence and create some curiosity and anxiety. As we converse I use, among other relevant statements, "There is one coat here in stock that would suit your personality perfectly. I only hope it's in your size."

I begin to look for that particular coat. I can see it hanging, but I bypass it, and, all the while I am going through the coats I quietly say, "I hope it hasn't been sold."

The longer it takes me to find it the more curious she gets. By the time I show it to her the coat is sold.

"Oh, here it is. I am glad it's still here; this is the ideal coat for you. I wouldn't show you anything else."

By now she is really anxious to try it on. I help her put it on gently and slowly. She takes a look at herself in the mirror and says, "I'll take it." She doesn't even ask the price until she is handed the bill of sale.

She is, of course, very happy with the purchase, and I am proud of the way I handled it. That's a satisfied customer. She'll be back whenever she is in need of a garment, simply because I didn't sell it to her; she bought it.

Each sale is important only on the particular day it is made, but repeat business is an endorsement of success. One repeat customer is worth forty browsers.

Store hours in the 1940s were endless. Stores stayed open from 9:00 A.M. to 9:00 P.M. on week days; Fridays and Saturdays until 10:00 or 11:00 P.M. It seems that hunger for success knows no limits.

One evening a man came in, casually took a suit off a hanger, tucked it inside his coat and ran. My salesgirl and I ran after him, and the chase continued through dark muddy alleys and rooftops. I kept close to him and was just about to grab him when my salesgirl screamed from the alley below, "It's a courageous thing you are doing, but stop it."

The minute I heard that I suddenly realized that I was scared. I began to tremble and rolled off the roof right into a deep pile of mud. That proves that our emotions can make us do foolish things sometimes if we forget to control them.

Emotions play an important part in our lives. They even warp our way of thinking and rationality on occasion.

Business was good; Saturdays were extremely busy. It appeared as if I had all of the Poles and Ukrainians who resided in and around Toronto, from as far away as Oshawa.

I remember one Saturday selling a coat that needed some alterations. I had promised the lady that I would deliver the coat personally later in the day. When I entered her room I was shocked by the scene I saw. She just waved at me, signifying for me to get out. I sat in the car for a while contemplating whether I should drive back to the store or wait. Then she nonchalantly strode down the stairs, handed me the money, took her coat, handed it to a man and said, "Here, stupid, take it upstairs."

That kind of woman had money, and I was there to get it.

One day a little Chinese boy walked in and purchased an expensive fur coat. He made me write out a check for him. Of course, I wouldn't release the coat before I had the check certified. I asked him whether he was driving. He said no, he didn't own a car. I told him innocently that I would drive him back home to Elizabeth Street. He kept refusing my generous offer, but I kept insisting that I take him home. However, I stopped by the bank and had the check certified before I let him go.

Those were the kinds of times and the kinds of customers, which leads me into a true story about an event I witnessed in

Winnipeg in 1929. I was browsing around in a jewelry store on Main Street, when I noticed an immigrant buying a cheap watch. He was given a five-year guarantee. After the guarantee was signed by the storekeeper I heard him say to the customer, "You better leave it with me. I'll put it in my vault, where it'll be safe. You might lose it if you take it with you." The customer was grateful for the favor.

Complexities in everyday life and in business come in various forms. A reasonably satisfying balance has to be found in order to keep what has already been accomplished. One must strive for progress in a direction that will maintain the balance, which will eventually lead to a more satisfying experience, thus reducing the reasons for frustration. Religion also can and does make anxieties and frustrations easier to bear. "Religious fermentation is always a symptom of the intellectual vigor of society" (William James). I remember that, on the day when I was leaving for Canada, my mother warned me, while weeping silently, "Remember that you are a grandson of an Orthodox Rabbi. Have faith in God. He may not cure your ills or solve your problems, but it will make it easier to bear."

When I think of my mother, my dear late wife, Fanny, penetrates my senses. Her strong faith in God and religion, her sensitivity and compassion were almost as strong as my mother's. From the very first moment I met her I loved her. But it was more than love—more intense, more painful. It was a feeling of penetration of the soul; it was devotion. That cannot be expressed in sensible terminology; one can only feel it to the very core.

I had a feeling that I had known her before that day. Perhaps it was a case of reincarnation; we might have known each other at another time in another existence. When I walk alone I think of her; when I sit in a park and watch birds busily building nests, I think of her. I think of the years we were trying desperately to build a nest for our children.

When I sit alone during long endless evenings I think of her. Outwardly I am completely independent, but my heart and soul weep quietly, seeking someone to comfort me.

I think of her every waking minute, as I count the days, the weeks and the months, and after some time I stop counting.

Each anniversary of her death I commemorate by a special candle. I keep it burning for twenty-four hours, in memory of a light that has passed on, but that perhaps is still shedding rays in another sphere.

Anniversaries are solemn days for me, filled with tender memories: the touch of a hand that has vanished, the compassionate look in her eyes that are closed forever, and the sound of her voice forever stilled.

Memories of past love are like looking at roses in a dark cellar; you can't see them but you can smell their fragrance. I was married to an angel, only I didn't know it. We are in the habit of taking things for granted. If I could only tell her so now, it would heal my soul.

The same feeling applies to bygone years, childhood, youth. We thought they would last forever. You can see the past in your mind's eye but you can't touch it, like hearing melodies but not being able to see the orchestra. It's like looking at waxed fruit and painted trees and pretending that you see the Garden of Eden:

> *Oft in the stilly night*
> *Ere slumber's chain has bound me,*
> *Fond memory brings the light*
> *Of other days around me,*
> *The smiles the tears*
> *Of happy years,*
> *The words of love then spoken,*
> *The eyes that shone*
> *Now dimmed and gone,*
> *The cheerful hearts now broken.*
> —ELIZA COOK

Perhaps meditation can help to clarify imaginary dreams of the soul, or the yearning for a loved one after parting, a dream of being reunited again. Perhaps meditation is also a way of becoming aware of humans and their loneliness. Or is it a searching for the cosmos in celestial endlessness and being filled with joy by being a part of it?

Perhaps it's searching motives, wishes, values, which are obliterated by the daily bustle of life.

Whatever it is, meditation is supposed to be a spiritual medication that heals the soul and calms the spirit.

I have tried it on occasion and my yearning has partially

subsided. Especially now that I am no longer involved in business activities, it's that much more difficult.

Let's get back to business. I have some advice for buyers. A buyer for a ladies' wear store must be on guard at all times not to overbuy. Disregard the usual pressures of the salesmen, who are interested in only one thing—writing big orders—regardless of the consequences you may have to face, and hardships you'll endure to turn your garments into cash. You must be alert to spot a garment among hundreds shown to you, which, in your opinion, based on logic and past experiences, may turn out to be a "runner." This is a garment that for some unknown reason outsells all others that are similar, but that remain stagnant all season long. No one really knows why this is so, but I have a theory.

I have observed over many years that when new seasonal merchandise is put in stock, the sales help haven't the vaguest idea as to which style will sell best. But when the first customer comes in and accidentally purchases a certain garment, it is usually not because of its superiority over many others hanging there. Rather, it is either sheer coincidence or, possibly, the salesperson finds new garments easier to sell than leftovers.

Knowing this, the store staff naturally go to that style on almost every occasion. They get the impression that it's the style that is selling quickly and easily; thus, it becomes a "runner," while the others hang and almost beg to be disturbed, to be tried on, rather than stagnate.

But you dare not say anything or question your sales staff regarding that "runner." You may upset the pattern of a normal operation.

There is also jealousy that often exists in a business, one trying to outsell the other; this is a healthy situation, provided you don't show any favoritism, or try to give special assistance to anyone. That would create resentment; you must therefore adopt a policy of neutrality.

When placing your order for an upcoming season, place very lightly in order to be in a favorable position to repeat the "runner," which outsells all other garments throughout the season, while hundreds of similar garments survive when the season has long come and gone.

I remember the sales tricks used by salesmen showing their lines—how persistent they were, and how I resisted their pressure.

One day in June I was sitting in a showroom watching a continuous parade of models, showing coats and suits, to which I became completely indifferent. After an hour or more, they all began to look the same. One gets terribly confused on such occasions. You either throw caution to the wind and write an oversized order, or you become extremely cautious. Consequently you choose wrong styles.

In June, when business is slow, whatever sales are made are of low-priced items; one is not in the proper frame of mind to order high-priced coats. You are understandably on the defensive, determined to order as little as possible. On that day I thought, why should I order now? He isn't going out of business. I can get coats later on in the season if business should demand it. The salesman was determined to sell me as much as possible, but I was equally determined to order as little as possible. A war of wits developed. I resisted; he insisted. The more insistent he became, the more resistant I became. I asked him innocently, "When is the first shipping date?"

"Are you kidding?" he answered my question with a question. "It's only the beginning of June. Give us a chance to make the garments. In fact," he confided in me, "it's almost impossible to get the goods, and the help situation is hopeless."

After a while I pointed to a coat that caught my fancy. "Is this one selling well?"

"Is it ever selling! I already got repeat orders on that coat."

"How did you get repeat orders when by your own admission you don't even have the goods?"

His face turned crimson and he came up with a shrewd answer: "A department store originally ordered two hundred coats but doubled the order a few days later. I can see that you don't believe me; here is the cancellation," he said jokingly.

Don't be impressed by what you hear; guide your ordering on two basic principles: First, how did you do with a similar garment last year? Second, follow your first instinct and the impression you had when you first saw the garment. If you let yourself be talked and persuaded into ordering it, don't buy it. If you are persuaded or pressured into buying something that your first instinct rejected, chances are that you'll consider yourself lucky if you salvage your cost out of it at some future date.

Buying is definitely closely associated with the expression "Love at first sight." Proper buying determines your profits. If you analyze your projected volume for the year, you must establish a pattern.

The accepted normal standards in the industry are misleading, as far as I am concerned. To turn inventory over ten times during the year is considered good business or a well-managed business. That would in fact mean that in order to do $300,000 gross sales yearly, one would have to carry an average inventory of $30,000, which, in my opinion is much too high. You must carry as small an inventory as possible and do as high gross sales as possible. This is the secret of success, especially in a neighborhood store. Its inventory is compared to milk; if it's not used up within a few days it turns sour. Ladies' fashions turn sour too; there is something new on the market every single day of the year, plus four or five complete changes of lines, according to the seasons. I operated a store for thirty-three years and turned my inventory over eighteen to twenty times each year, which my suppliers considered close to impossible.

My assumption has always been that what you don't have you don't miss as long as you have the essentials—the garments that have a wide appeal and are suitable for the majority of customers; they are the most important.

If one is selling groceries or fruit, one can't sell oranges when the customer asks for carrots, but dresses basically all look alike. One out of many may on occasion come in with a preconceived idea, but a smart saleslady can sell her what there is on hand.

Moreover, I found on many occasions that the larger the inventory, the harder it is to make a sale. There are too many garments hanging, begging to be tried on, which only confuses the customer. The less inventory the less confusing and the easier it is to make a sale.

I would rather lose a sale than get stuck with goods that are not in popular demand. Regardless of how many dresses, gowns, or coats you have in stock, sales will be lost for one reason or another.

How do you *know* that a sale would have been made if you had a larger selection? It's impossible to have every style, every size, every color. If you have green they'll want red; if you have red it will be in the wrong size; the odds are against you all down the line. But if you have a small inventory you can add new items each day or twice a week, so that a customer will see something new on each visit. This especially applies to neighborhood stores, where the clientele is local, unlike a shopping center, where traffic is always heavy and much more diversified.

One who is in the habit of carrying a large inventory sooner or later gets his neck in a noose. You can't buy, because your inventory is large and your money is tied up, and yet you can't abstain from buying, simply because your customers have seen all the garments you have, many times over.

The solution to the problem is simple. Buy as little as possible but as often as business demands, so that your inventory will always be new and fresh and your money will sit safely in the bank.

I think back to my first few years in business. Most of the dresses were old-looking and creased, although they were steamed and pressed, but it's apparently as hard to make an old dress look new as it is to make an old lady look young. You may succeed but only for a very short time; they quickly wilt to their original selves.

I once overheard a conversation between one of my salesgirls and a customer:

Customer: "But this dress looks so old. Can't you show me something nicer?"

Salesgirl: "Missus, if you were to hang on a hanger for as long as this dress has, you would look much worse."

Needless to say, I soon gave that salesgirl her walking papers.

To achieve some measure of success you must be a salesman on the floor, a goodwill ambassador, a diplomat, a psychoanalyst, a baby sitter, a warm-hearted, compassionate individual, and a promoter. Moreover, you must remove or neutralize your nerve center just as a dentist neutralizes the nerve in an aching tooth. You must also be inventive, always take the initiative in order to have the store operate smoothly, quietly, without being directly or indirectly responsible for creating an uncooperative atmosphere among your employees, which can readily be detected when one enters a store.

If and when you acquire some success, don't let it go to your head; don't allow your ego to become inflated. Success has a hundred fathers; failure is an orphan.

Remember at all times that your success or failure depends first on your own behavior; second, on your help, which reacts to your moods in one way or another; and third and most of all on your customers. Honesty and integrity can make you; without them you will fail.

In business you must be flexible and adaptable; you can't apply

the same business rules and regulations at all times. There is
always a situation that demands specific individual attention and
that may not conform to business rules or ethics. There are always
exceptions to rules; rules are made to be broken when necessary.
It's highly important that such cases should be dealt with in a
most tactful manner.

As time passed, my suppliers became my very good friends.
How could I forget an individual who was like a brother to me? I
mean none other than Alex Richman, "a businessman's gentleman."
I owned an old car and on occasion I would pick him up early
Sunday morning and drive to Wasaga Beach, where his parents
and I rented cottages for the month of July.

We walked on the sandy beach before sunrise and watched
the tiny waves singing and lapping silently at the white sand
while the town was still in deep slumber.

I also think of many years of true friendship with Alex Davis,
who is well versed in the Talmud, and therefore possesses a wealth
of Jewish humor. He is my kind of individual. I got to know his
lovely wife, Alice, who is a genuinely compassionate lady. I also
had the privilege of having the friendship of his business associates, Barney Bierenbaum and Louis Tomaselli, two wonderful
people, and, Mr. Jack Goldbach, a real friend, who has a heart of
gold.

My friends Max Bernstein and Harry Silverberg of Melody
Dress are in a class by themselves; they are good, kind and
understanding.

Julie and Al Zaltzman are two shrewd but kind and clever
fellows. It would be impossible for me to elaborate fully on their
virtues. I learned a lot by dealing with them, and they always
treated me as if I were King of Spadina Avenue.

Louis Manley and his brother Jack are two true loyal friends,
and the very fine Mrs. Louis Manley had a smile for me each
time I walked into the office.

I also wish to express my continued admiration for two Orthodox gentlemen who operate a dress factory and remain loyal to
their religious convictions, Mr. Morris Rosenzweig and his partner,
Sam Gluck. They are the only ones I know of who close the
factory early on Fridays and keep it closed until Monday morning.
They observe every Jewish holiday religiously, and yet they are
quite successful in their operation, in spite of the fierce competition

that exists in dress manufacturing. It's amazing how they have managed to retain their traditional way of life over the years, despite the competitive chaotic conditions in the industry, which is most demanding at all times.

I also met some queer characters along the way. I remember walking into a showroom to see a dress line one day. I had noticed a rack of dresses in a corner, they were covered up securely. I asked why they were covered up.

"Because I don't wish to sell them just yet," the salesman replied. I insisted that I see them. He finally agreed, but not before I promised him that I wouldn't buy them.

This episode reminds me of a man who was to inform his friend of the sudden illness of his mother. It was on Yom Kippur (the Day of Atonement) and he had to go into the Synagogue to convey the sad news to his friend, but was denied entry by an usher.

"Please let me in; I must speak with my friend. It's an emergency!" he pleaded.

The usher thought about it for a minute and said, "I'll let you in for five minutes, but you must promise me that you won't pray while you are inside."

"A dark dream on you. I won't pray, I swear. Just let me in for a few minutes."

Only then was he permitted to enter.

10

Return to Winnipeg

I took a sentimental journey to Winnipeg in July, 1975, anxious to see the homes in which we had lived during the Depression years and some years thereafter.

There were many reasons for my wanting to return to "Memory Lane." I was curious to see what inroads and progress, if any, had been made during my absence. By coincidence I met a wonderful individual, Arthur Kushner, who offered me his car, his services, and any information I may have needed and assisted me for an entire week.

To express my feelings upon arrival in Winnipeg in logical terminology would be impossible. I can only try to describe the city, its people, and the nostalgic memories it brought back after I had been away for more than twenty-five years.

The minute my cousins drove me out of the air terminal parking lot I was facing a new world, a world I had forgotten. I felt as if I had been liberated out of a jungle into a paradise. A feeling of serenity came over me as I saw people drive slowly in traffic-free streets. I saw people walk slowly, live slowly, eat and talk slowly, even sleep slowly. Western people seem to have time for themselves and for others. Western hospitality is impossible to describe, much less understand. They are loyal to each other regardless of whether they know one another or not.

The downtown hotel I stayed in was packed with guests and crawling with youngsters. I later found out that they were celebrating a Western music festival. They had come from as far west as Vancouver to participate in a junior musical competition. The hotel elevators were crammed with kids, ages six to twelve, who carried large drums, accordions, and bass fiddles. The hotel was in a turmoil until they finally checked out on Sunday.

I had occasion to speak to many regarding business and the economy of their respective provinces. In answer to my questions about recession and unemployment the reactions were almost identical: We have no recession, we have no unemployment, business has never been better, the crops are bigger and better each year, and oil is constantly gushing out of the oil derricks.

Contentment hovered like a halo on every Westerner, unlike in the East, where everyone is in a hurry going nowhere. We are so engulfed in our own problems and daily frustrations that we don't have the time or the patience to notice anyone around us. At the end of a day we become listless, tired, exasperated, and disgusted with ourselves.

So this is Winnipeg! Downtown hasn't changed much, except that some old buildings have been demolished and replaced by new modern structures.

I came out early one morning, curious to see "rush-hour" traffic and take some photographs, but I failed to see the traffic I expected. I stood at the corner of Portage Avenue and Main Street, which Winnipegers claim is the widest in North America. The streets appeared to be very peaceful, as on a very quiet Sunday morning in Toronto. I waited for the green light and walked across to the north side. Two other pedestrians walked across with me, again unlike in Toronto, where one has to fight his way across a downtown intersection. Those two nice people even stopped to talk to me for a few minutes when I told them that I was a Torontonian.

Twenty-five years had vanished into the chain of life since I had been to Winnipeg. It seemed as though I had never been there, and yet, when I came back downtown, I had the feeling that I had never been away. I was taken to Manitoba Avenue, where nostalgic memories began to penetrate my mind as I continued my visit down Memory Lane.

Streets and intersections were spotlessly clean, and wide, waiting patiently for traffic that seldom came. Portage Avenue was staring at me invitingly. It's as wide and loyal as the hearts of Western people, waiting to share the serenity and unquestionable hospitality. Your pulse begins to beat more slowly. Your life tempo is wrapped in tranquility; contentment takes over; you begin to notice the sky, the sun, the beautiful parks where children play and swim in nice swimming pools. You rest your eyes on colorful flowerbeds and the smiling, winking flowers basking in the sun.

One of my friends drove me to Kildonan Park one Sunday afternoon. We sat in the shade of a huge tree on the banks of the Red River. The sullen murky water appeared heavy and undisturbed. It just sat there like heavy oil, until a pleasure boat loaded with noisy, happy people appeared. It slowly sliced its way down the river, leaving restless waves cradling majestically behind, which gradually subsided into tiny ripples as if disturbed by a breeze, while a soothing wind silently whispered a prayer.

Nothing really happens on such long, lazy summer days, when time stretches ahead in slow motion forever and the hot days melt into one another. The summers are short in Manitoba; they flip past like pages of an open book caught in a breeze, and finally by a brisk cold wind. It seems that the people barely realize that summer is here. In a flick of time they are busily engaged in preparation for the cold winter ahead.

But it's summers past that linger in memory—children making mud pies and decorating them with flowers, the buds and blossoms of spring, the tender rain, the rides on a scooter up and down the silent street, or leisurely riding on a bike in the cool of the evening. The sun coming through the windowpane not covered by the drapes, the splash of color on the floor in all the glorious reflections of a rainbow. The joy of sitting in the back seat of a bus on the way to a park where a family picnic will take place, with cousins, aunts, uncles and friends, where orange juice and Eskimo pies will be served to the children and ice-cold drinks to the adults.

Ofttimes a grandchild wakes up in a strange bed in the house of grandparents, but company arrives unexpectedly and ice cream or a cold drink is served. The grandchild is overwhelmed by all of this and forgets to cry.

What a life! What loyalty! What devotion! It doesn't matter whether the visitors are family or friends; they are accepted just as warmly and are welcomed to the family circle. That's Winnipeg.

Later in the week my friend Arthur drove me to see and take photographs of the homes that gave me some joy many years ago, but also left scars in my heart and soul.

"Here is 509 Dufferin Street," Arthur announces.

"Is this Dufferin Street?" I ask in an unbelievable tone of voice. The streetcar tracks have been removed; buses now operate through the entire city. While we are on the subject, I wish to express my admiration for the Winnipeg bus drivers; they are kind and courteous. When a bus driver sees someone walking fast in the direction of a bus stop, he will wait for him.

I look at the house on Dufferin Street. I remember its sparkle, its boisterous cleanliness. It stood out like a beacon at one time, but that seems like a lifetime ago. I visualize the people who had lived in it; this is where I met my wife for the very first time; this was her brother's house. It now looks dirty and in need of repair. A poor Pakistani family lives there but it looks abandoned, as if it has been sentenced to death and is waiting to be executed.

What a change in the entire street! The tiny corner grocery stores have disappeared; some are boarded up; some have their doors and windows secured with heavy wire. They must have been abandoned by their owners; very few remained in business. The ones that did have Venetian blinds covering their windows, and a small white sign with one red printed word on it: "Open." A stranger would never know that it's a grocery store. It's deserted; no one is walking in or out.

As we proceeded farther up the north end, the names were unfamiliar to me. Time waits for no one.

It was in July, 1944, when I had delivered my last case of soft drinks to some of these stores. The names I had known then are no more; new names have been painted on the old wooden signs.

Our next stop was 504 Manitoba Avenue. This was supposed to have been our first house, but the mortgage company foreclosed and took ownership of it. This is the house with the sloped ceiling and walls up in the attic that wept all winter. Water constantly ran down the walls in the very cold weather and very little heat that came from a slow, grief-stricken fire that festered in a wood stove. The house was built of lumber slabs painted white.

This is the house where the water pipes froze solidly each winter, where bread and sardines were the diet of the week, but tasted better than the finest steak. This is the house where we had a one-way, one-piece toilet. One had to get down on hands and knees to get in and back out the same way. This is the house to which my daughter Sheila was brought from the hospital when she was eight days old. This is the house where we endured hunger, pain, and poverty.

I stand across the street decades later and look at it with deep nostalgia. I can hear echoes coming out of one small window facing the street, echoes of a baby crying within the room of weeping walls. The room is ice-cold, but life goes on somehow.

I am here to see that house again, and relive past memories

that beg to be forgotten. But how can one forget the cruelty of the times?

There is the fence. I see myself standing there leaning on the wire gate in the haze of a humid, hot summer day. I am unemployed. I have nothing to do, no place to go, just waiting for the day to step into the relief line and receive our weekly token.

The house is dirty gray; it probably hasn't seen a paintbrush since we were forced out. Some windows are missing; the verandah door is hanging precariously on one hinge, swinging in the breeze. The whole street looks like a morgue, and the houses smell like old rusty caskets full of decaying corpses.

The deserted street is just sitting there as if it were waiting for an earthquake that will topple the old dirty habitats. I look at my friend Arthur, but he refuses to look at me; he looks down at the dirty sidewalk.

I could hardly tear myself away but, I thought, perhaps it's not a good idea to linger among ghosts. I walked to the car slowly and proceeded to Magnus Avenue, our home of forty-five years ago, where two trunks full of precious books my uncle had given me went down the drain because of a heavy rainfall that occurred the first day we moved in.

I was positive that I would recognize the little hut, but the dark gray stucco had been replaced by dirty-looking boards, so that most of the poor, low-roofed huts looked the same—humble, melancholy, silently meditating in the hot misty air.

After questioning a few neighbors, I finally found the house. Arthur and I walked into the backyard, which was small enough to cover with a tablecloth. We noticed a very old lady sitting in the shade of a small sickly bush. In her hands she had a book that she seemed to be reading. She closed it as we drew her attention. I walked up closer and observed the paperback novel she held in her lap. The cover was dark green, but the title of the book was in bold gold letters: *How to Make Love*. It turned out that she didn't understand English. We were frustrated by not being able to make her understand. If, in fact, she could read a novel, why then couldn't we get her to understand? Perhaps she was only looking at the illustrations.

After a few minutes of no response, we began speaking to her in Yiddish. She showed some interest and admitted that this was the house she and her husband had bought many years ago. She remembered that the previous owner was a young man who drove a huge soft drink truck. I entered the kitchen and retreated quietly, as if I were inside a sacred chapel.

I silently spoke to the humble-looking house: "You are still standing up, sheltering people. I never thought your life span would last that long."

It's ironic to note, and sad too, I suppose, that I have to refer to individuals as the late so and so, whereas houses remain in the present tense. But who can change the pattern of life and its complexities? One must accept it. Although I would be insincere if I were to say that I accept the natural realities of life, unfortunately there has never been and probably never will be an alternative to mortality.

I am not hungry for money now as I had been when I was young. We could have lived better, nicer. We could have given our children more enjoyable times while they were growing up, but that too belongs to the unforgettable past. Money is secondary now; it's my soul that is seeking serenity.

The following day we drove up to see the bottling plant, where I had carried thousands of cases of soft drinks for more than eight and a half years.

I remembered the day when a three-year-old deaf-mute ran out in front of a parked car and was killed by my truck.

The plant had disappeared, as had everything else in that part of the city. The muddy driveway leading out to Main Street, where I had shoveled snowdrifts ten feet high, has become a part of a new subdivision. Beautiful quiet streets, adorned with cool-looking grass and proud-looking bungalows, are standing on the once barren prairie of thirty-three years ago.

I was very sad as I looked at that part of the city, remembering the hard times I had lived through: the unbearably hard work I had to do in order to make a five-cent commission on a case of soft drinks, provided all empty bottles I returned were in perfect shape, without the slightest chip, so that they could be used again. Otherwise they were smashed in a metal barrel, and my five cents were wiped out.

I was also curious to visit River Park and to see the dazzling array of flowers, which I remembered winking invitingly as they basked in the sunshine, glowing in peaceful bliss of delight, and covered with warm dew, embracing each other in the stillness of night where German youths held rallies, carrying large signs printed in red: *"Deutschland über alles."* It seemed that the park had also disappeared, some structures having been erected there. They look as if they had grown out of the ground.

Memories were tumbling in disarray and numbing my senses. Everything I looked at appeared strange to me. Strangers were walking the streets; how disappointing!

I couldn't spot a single familiar face. A variety of ethnic people had moved in to my North End, while the original inhabitants had moved to new homes in Garden City, or had passed on.

I passed by the store where my wife once bought a tweed coat for me for $13, on payments of course. I recall purchasing a winter coat in the same store some years later for $25, but my employer refused to guarantee the balance of $15. I also walked past Kaplan's Jewelry Store, where I bought the wedding ring for my wife for $15, also on credit, and it took us more than two years to pay for it.

Selkirk Avenue, which was called the Jewish Uptown, remained unchanged, except that some small grocery stores had disappeared. The area was like a mouth, wide open, with empty spaces where teeth were missing. Other stores had been abandoned or were operated by foreigners.

I was driven around the McPhillips area, where deep ditches and rough roads had been replaced by high-rise apartments and shopping malls.

I looked up my helper, Mike, who was a young boy when he worked with me on the truck at the time. He is now old and gray, but unbelievably rich; he was apparently forced into real estate. He applied for some sort of job many years ago, but was turned down because of his limited education.

This reminds me of an old story that was told and retold in my village. One of our community Chassidim had decided to move to a city and seek a job as an attendant to a famous Rabbi, but was turned down because he couldn't sign his name. Many years later one of our Chassidim happened to visit that city and met a man who was very rich; he claimed that he had lived in our village some years ago.

"To what do you attribute your good fortune by getting so rich?" asked the Chassid.

"I would say it's due to my illiteracy," the rich man replied. "I had applied for a position with a famous Rabbi but was turned down because I couldn't write. I had then decided to try the world of business and succeeded. Had I been able to write, I would have been an attendant all my life."

The moral of the story is that one doesn't necessarily have to have an education in order to succeed in business, but in our sophisticated society I believe that it helps, even though common sense without education is of more value than education without common sense.

I also visited Mr. Yankowskie's grocery story on Manitoba Avenue. I had learned that he had passed away some years ago. Poor Mr. Yankowskie, it took me more than an hour to convince him that he should allow me to leave two bottles of soft drinks when I first started with the company.

The streets that bustled with people years ago are now dejectedly desolate.

I was told that Hirsch and the surrounding area have become wealthy in the past ten or fifteen years. Oil has been discovered on the very same virgin prairie where I had dug granite rocks with pick and crowbar when I had first arrived. Now one can see oil derricks all over the area, where thousands of barrels of oil are pumped each day. Farmers enjoy good years, crops are growing, and oil royalties fill their pockets. They live in cities and commute each day in their shiny new Cadillacs.

I didn't visit Hirsch as I had intended. I was told that there was nothing familiar for me to see, only two families I had known are still living there.

According to information I gathered regarding the founding of the Hirsch colony, it was in the late 1880s when the Young Men's Hebrew Benevolent Society in Montreal, confronted with the problem of assisting a vast number of refugees who had fled the anti-Semitism and oppression of Eastern Europe, appealed to Baron Maurice de Hirsch, who responded generously. The Society then decided to use the Hirsch grant to purchase a building as a temporary shelter for newcomers and a school for immigrant children. In 1890, the Society had plans for a new farm settlement in the West. The Winnipeg immigration agent, Thomas Bennett, found work for the immigrants among the farmers. These people were also asking the Canadian government to assign homesteads to them west of Winnipeg to start a new colony. A letter was written to John Lowe, Minister of the Interior in Ottawa, asking him about the possibility of obtaining land in the northwest for a new settlement, and the request was granted. Fortunately, Baron de Hirsch had been interested for some time in assisting Jews to settle on land, and in 1891 he established the Jewish Colonization Association.

The following few years are most memorable, having Jewish families take up homesteads in Sonnenfeld and subsequently in Hirsch, Saskatchewan, at which time, or perhaps a few years later, my uncle Mendel Hirt, Mr. Frost, Mr. Zelickson, Mr. Garber and their families (just to mention a few) had taken up homesteads in Hirsch with the help of the government and with the financial assistance of Baron de Hirsch, who had formed the Jewish Colonization Association. When I arrived in Hirsch in 1927 all the above-mentioned pioneers and many more were toiling on their farms and thanking God for their miraculous liberation from pogroms and persecution. They were enjoying democracy for the first time in their lives. On extremely cold winter nights, they would gather in my uncle's house, play cards, and reminisce about the hard years they had endured when they first settled on the virgin prairie.

Until the railroad track was finally built, the nearest store for supplies and necessities of life was in Frobisher, fifteen to twenty miles from where they had lived. A small wooden railroad station was erected in Hirsch and also a grain elevator, a small shack that was used as a post office, and one general store. As shown in photographs from 1909, the white building served as an immigration building, a temporary shelter for new arrivals. There was also one store and a Synagogue. The photos show my younger uncle, Berish Hirt; fourth is my cousin, Fishel (Phil) Hirt, and my cousin, Harry Hirt, the last one on the left who had sponsored me to Canada. He has passed away since, as have my uncles. May they all rest in peace. The others in the photo are unknown to me, most likely "hired help."

One evening I was invited by very good friends to visit them at their home. I looked at Ernie and remembered his young face of thirty years ago; he, too, had driven a truck for the same bottling company. He looked deep into my eyes and remarked, "Looking at you now, I can't believe that you, too, had endured over eight years of hard labor on the truck over a half a lifetime ago."

The following day I taped a thirty-minute TV interview and went back to say good-bye to my friend Mike. He recalled the years he had been in the army; soldiers were given saltpeter to make them lose interest in girls. "You know, Harry," he said, "it took thirty years for me to feel its effects."

He introduced me to a friend of his—a Jewish boy who stuttered badly but had apparently adjusted to his condition over the years and was making fun of himself. In reply to my question whether he had been to a doctor who could perhaps help him, he said, "When I was b-b-born in the Old Country the doctor picked me up b-b-by my f-f-feet, my head h-hanging down. The cir-cir-cum-circumciser m-m-made an er-r-or and circumcised my t-t-tongue instead of my p-p-penis. That's why I st-st-tutter, but it's not s-s-so bad; I only s-s-stutter when I speak."

"What do you do for a living?" I asked.

Mike took over the conversation at this point. "He has many ways of earning a living. He makes counterfeit money among other things, but the last batch didn't turn out too well."

"Why? What happened?"

"Something went wrong in the process. Instead of making $20 bills, the machine went crazy and turned out $30 bills."

"Where can one dispose of such unheard-of denominations?"

"We decided to seek out a small town off the beaten trail, where no one would know the difference. We drove to Winnipegosis, a town which I thought was out of touch with civilization. We approached a lumberjack who lived in a broken-down shack outside of town. He appeared quite eager to do business with us when we approached him with our irresistible offer. We were willing to trade our money at a discount and accept $18 for every $30 bill. He agreed to the deal and said, 'I'll take your $30 bills and give you two 7's and one 4 for each one of your 30's.'"

I was amazed to learn that Mike would be involved in such business practice, and expressed surprise.

"I am only trying to help this 'Shmo,' but it amazes me to find that others are also engaged in the racket," he said. "But my friend here has the brains because he is Jewish. I am honest because I am Ukrainian, remember? We will make out."

"Yes, I remember the days when you stole cherries and grapes from cold basements when we made deliveries to grocery stores."

I wished them both good luck and left.

I may have given you the impression that I like Western Canada. I confess that I do, until I begin to think of the winters.

When you are walking down Main Street and you suddenly get an excruciating pain between your eyes, just above the bridge of your nose, you know it's cold! When I think of the bare frozen wasteland preceding the heavy snowfalls, the endless prairie looks brown as if the skin had been pealed back to show the disarray of frozen ground beneath.

When snow begins to fall, when the nights are swallowed in deafening silence, when the temperature drops to forty-five below zero, when the air is so dry you think it will break if you move, when the shimmering multicolored Northern Lights appear on the horizon, reflecting on the snow-covered, barren, desolate prairie, you know it's winter.

If the winters weren't so severe a Western Province would be an ideal place to retire, rather than fry in the Florida sun and humidity all year round as some folks do. The West promises serenity, a slow pulse beat, a quiet undisturbed life, and each year seems to consist of twenty-four months. Unfortunately, the cold winters are somewhat discouraging.

My feelings for the West are perhaps no more than sentimentality for the unforgettable past and youth that can't be recaptured, or am I missing the hard life we endured without sensitivity? Improvement was unreachable and impossible, and yet we were happy, probably because we were young, and, to be happy with the present, one must reflect on the past sometimes.

Streets in western cities carry a certain humble culture and innocence, like an ancient melancholic melody without words, occasionally disturbed by a passing car. They are humble, and yet noble at the same time. It's the painful innocence that transforms one's thinking into a form of meditation.

Flowers grow in parks in blissful dream, bathe in cool dew during the night, and bask in sunshine during the day. Life is free, yours to create and enjoy. God is the reason for human freedom and for everything that lives and grows. I had the feeling that I was in a wonderland, in a world of unreal dreams that begged for silence and prayer.

Where does one find such people nowadays? Most project a crusty exterior, too sophisticated to be humble or friendly. If one seeks humility one should go out on a farm, see the tall crops grow in silence, and like water waves keep on moving with the wind until harvest time. They overwhelm one's imaginary importance.

"Consciousness is dependent on the brain," says William James. "A strong will and a purpose in life can be a decisive factor in emotional rehabilitation, which is often reflected in instability of positive thinking and hallucination." When one takes time to look at nature as I have, one realizes how insignificant his imaginary troubles really are—how time passes you by, not making a dent in your selfish existence.

Today I was driven by car out into the country. Today I saw the wind playing with the withered, dust-covered leaves of a humble-looking bush, cuddling against tall, half-dried grass and a wire fence. I saw the wind blow up some fine dust on the road leading to a little red schoolhouse similar to the one we had in Hirsch. It stands in the midst of open prairie loaded with ripening wheat that is in the process of turning golden. The red school's arrogant smile in bright sunshine was obviously filled with expectation. The students would soon return, and winter wouldn't be far behind, when play and laughter would fill the yard again, and horses would be nibbling hay contentedly in the barn nearby. The red school is surrounded by endless wheat fields, basking in the sun in unbearable silence, shaking their heavily loaded wheat heads in agreement to the whisper of a silent heavenly breeze.

I saw houses which a paintbrush hasn't touched for decades, horses and cows grazing in luscious green pastures, as they had half a century ago. I watched a bumblebee desperately trying to rest on a tall, skimpy blade of grass. Each time it tried to land it fell off. It finally settled on a twig of a small bush.

I heard birds sing in the clear fresh air of the West, unlike in the Eastern Provinces, where they cough because of the humid air and smelly exhaust fumes created by heavy traffic.

Everything looks the same, except some houses that are badly in need of repair. Perhaps they have been abandoned over the years. Some look sad and dejected; gloom hovers over and around their dark brown frames. They had served their purpose when they were needed; now their doom is unquestionable. Farmers don't live on the farms nowadays; they have all become sophisticated. Life and laughter that filled those houses for a century or more has left them to their own fate. Despite the overpowering beauty created by the glow of ripening wheat, an unexplainable melancholy filled the air under the hot summer sun.

Perhaps my feelings for nature have been numbed because of years of absence, but I can still hear a silent prayer in the shimmering haze, or in the silence of night.

Some windows are missing in the farm homes, which project the appearance of vacant eye sockets; doors are swinging on loose hinges, but there is no one to notice this; crops are growing lusciously and abundantly, unlike in the years of the drought.

There is a theory that good crops come in cycles and so does drought. Instead of having gentle rain falling in June, hot winds begin to blow, taking turns in each direction. One who hasn't lived through a drought can't possibly comprehend how devastating it is to land and life.

I look up at the sky and see a bizarre mixture of mist, pink at the edges, dark orange and brown in the center, while the scorching sun is hidden behind the breathtaking beautiful array of shimmering dust:

I had a visit with nature and the romantic vision of country life. I had lived this kind of life almost a half a century ago. It was intense, genuine, which survived reality. I had a vision of sun-drenched pastures and wheatfields, strolling alone accompanied by a whisper of a breeze. I couldn't take my mind off a farm boy working in a cow shed, the dark brown structure and the sweet-smelling hay. I felt that it was fulfillment of the soul in its entirety.

I remember the time I first arrived in Hirsch and was put to work on my uncle's farm. It was in the middle of harvest. I was given a large-brimmed straw hat to protect my eyes from the sun, dust, and grime. With a pitchfork in hand I began pitching sheaves of wheat, loading a wagon as high as possible; then the horses pulled it to the threshing machine. The first few days were unbearable; I was aching all over. Gradually my muscles became adjusted to the demands; my movements began to express a certain exuberance and confidence as I learned to pitch the bundles gracefully, almost effortlessly. It was all a matter of grace and rhythm. It was almost relaxing to slip the prongs of my fork into a row of sheaves, and slip them over the shoulder onto the wagon.

Milking cows by hand on cold winter mornings, I leaned my head closely against the cow to keep my face warm. It seemed like a continuation of a dream—until my fingers were numb. I found that cows have character comparable to humans. Some stood quietly and cooperatively, while others punished me by swatting my face with their wet tails. Plowing with horses was also an overwhelming experience, as I sat on the plow relaxed and watched the furrows turning over, step by step. It gave me the freedom to soar through time and leave a prayer in the heights of the endless universe, where time is nonexistent.

I miss it all now, since I have been exposed to nature again. Memories of the unbearable and yet peaceful, heart-warming life fill my heart ever so often. But time cannot be recaptured; it belongs to the past.

I boarded the plane for my flight back to Toronto. Mixed emotions and a feeling of sadness penetrated my thinking. I felt that I had lived a whole lifetime in the ten days I had stayed in Winnipeg.

By coincidence I occupied a center seat. On my right was a young man returning to Montreal, and on my left was a lady who was returning to Toronto from an extensive vacation. As the plane took off I noticed the lady held on tightly to the arm rests, an indication that she was not accustomed to flying, while the young man sat relaxed, reading a book.

I am not a drinker by nature but the young man insisted that I have a drink. I didn't want to give him the impression that I was antisocial and agreed to have one. The lady also ordered a drink. I watched her out of the corner of my eye as she shakily reached for it and took a gulp. She turned crimson; apparently she had ordered powerful stuff.

To use a Hebrew phrase, *"Veyayin yesamach levav enosh."* (Wine makes happy the heart of men.) This happened to hold true in this case. After the three of us had a drink of liquor, the silent lady on my left became more courageous and talkative, even though she was a Torontonian.

I asked her where she was coming from.

"From Majorca," she replied. "I have been away on vacation," she added.

"Where is Majorca?" I asked innocently.

"How should I know? I flew there and back," she replied boisterously.

In the meantime my friend on my right began to tell me jokes that he thought were very funny. One of them I remember and will share with you.

The wife of a friend of his was ill and had to undergo surgery.

But preceding the serious operation she had a heart-to-heart talk with her husband.

"In case I don't make it, I want you to promise me that you'll remarry. I wouldn't want to have it on my conscience that I was responsible for your loneliness. Give your new partner in life everything I possess: my jewelry, my tiara, the one that is covered with brilliant sequins, my bracelets, my pearl earrings, my dresses."

"Wait one minute," the husband pleaded. "The partner I am considering doesn't wear jewelry, and he is a size forty-four. Your dresses won't fit him, but don't worry, dear, if you don't make it I wouldn't hold it against you."

11

Productive Selling

We return now to the art of selling—its intricacies, complexities, daily occurrences, people and their idiocyncracies.

According to evolutionary account of life and mentality, the fundamental situation is a relation between an organism and its environment. The situation is fought with struggle as the organism copes with its environment in order to survive. Mind is one of the most important faculties whereby an organism comes to know the environment in order to adjust to it, thereby increasing its chance for survival.

—WILLIAM JAMES

The above quotation can be applied to productive selling. Your mental attitude is very important, and your organism must adjust to situations and environments to function as a team in order to cope with daily living and selling. Your mind is your most important product when organism and environment combine and adjust to each other, thereby facilitating all of your thinking in a positive direction. Worrying how to succeed will be of no help; in fact it will dull your concentration.

I remember when I was on the farm in Hirsch, Saskatchewan. I stayed with my uncle, aunt, and cousins. My aunt, may she rest in peace, would shake each one of us early in the morning.

"Wake up! Wake up!"

"But it's so early, let us sleep just a bit more."

"No, it's time to wake up and begin to worry. You can't do it while you are asleep."

In selling, too, you cannot allow your mind to sleep; one must be awake and alert at all times.

Although there is no such thing as perfection—only the constant search for improvement—one must always try to go forward. Failing to do so is a failure of the mind and mental stagnation.

When you approach a customer and ask, "May I help you?" you may receive the reply "No thanks, I am just looking." Looking for what? It's therefore important that you complete your question: "May I help you look around?" You thereby rob your customer of the usual reply.

Love, ambition, or pride in your work are considered as feelings; they are fruits grown on the same tree. They give you bodily and mentally sensations of pain or pleasure; it depends on your thinking and your accomplishments.

When you mistreat a customer in some way (God knows, some deserve it), don't feel downhearted later and cry; don't tremble because you are sorry; don't be sorry because you cried. An unpleasant situation must be quickly forgotten so that it doesn't carry over to the next customer.

My good friend Jules Shinan, who is as honest as the day is long, never pressured me into buying a garment that I felt was not for my trade. He would often say to me, "When I begin to pay your bills, that's when I'll tell you what to buy." The same theory can apply to a customer.

I hope that many of my friends or business associates whose names I failed to mention will understand that it's impossible to remember and list them all. However, I hand out bouquets of gratitude to you all, who directly or indirectly were responsible for the small measure of success I enjoyed in the ladies' wear business and that I wouldn't have had without you. You were kind, cooperative, and helpful. The years have passed but nostalgic memories remain. A brotherly bond of loyalty has held us together tightly over the years.

I remember a time when I was suddenly in need of a large sum of money. I visited some of the people I had mentioned, and within one hour or so I deposited $40,000 in my bank account. That was in the early 1950s. Such a sum of money would be equivalent today to about $200,000. Those people had trust in me, and helped me without hesitation.

When I think back to those years, it gives me the sort of pride one cannot find in monetary success. I am proud to have been associated with such loyal people.

Words could not describe the friendship I have enjoyed with William Frohman.

Past years become the present when I think back over a span of half a lifetime, or my friend Joe, who emptied his pockets and piled up the money on his desk like hay, turned around and walked out of the office.

I ran after him, begging him to stay while I straightened out the pile and counted it. "Joe, please wait. I don't want to be left alone here with all this money."

"Count it, I'll be back in fifteen minutes," he replied.

My hands were trembling when I excitedly began counting the pile of tens, twenties, fifties, and hundred-dollar bills. There was a total of $8,000.

When Joe returned I asked him to count the money, but he refused. "Your word is good enough for me. You know how to count," he said.

To *believe* that we know the truth and are being trusted is very simple, but to *know* for sure that we know is a blessing.

I don't think I could express my gratitude enough to Rabbi David Monson even if I tried. I consider him my dear friend and a friend of all people who are in need of help and inspiration. He always found time in his busy life to introduce the Chassidic play as only he can, whenever we performed. He continues to influence me with his wisdom and kindness, which contribute greatly to my spiritual fulfillment to this day.

I believe that each individual should be dependent on God. It is an entity that embraces, among uncountable deeds, faith, religion, charity, and morals. It is a universal phenomenon. A combination of many virtues spell that mysterious single word.

I had a friend some years ago who found satisfaction in boisterously claiming that he did not believe in religion or in God. He was faithless and apparently proud of it. We had discussions on the subject on many occasions.

I asked him once what made him think that he was an atheist, or could he prove that he was one. In answer to my question, he expressed his logic, which made sense to him: "I don't pray because I don't want to be disappointed should my prayers not be answered. I have no faith for the same reason. Faith is only an illusion to a warped mind," he said.

"But is it not a satisfying spiritual experience to have faith?" I asked.

"To me it would mean to pretend, but I am not in the habit of doing so. I am a realist by nature and nothing can change it."

I dropped by to see him one day, and was about to leave when his wife came rushing into the house, crying uncontrollably. He turned to her and asked, "What happened?"

In between sobs she managed to say, "Our daughter was in a car accident. She is in serious condition in the hospital."

My friend turned white, pressed both hands against his head, and exclaimed, "Oh, my God!"

I couldn't believe that the words came from one who was a proud atheist only a few minutes ago.

Spadina Avenue was my beat for thirty years. The garment industry was there to serve and protect a loyal account. Most of the lines I handled were confined to me in my area. I had also done business with leather manufacturers, but for some unknown reason I had never established with them the association I had enjoyed in the industry. I attributed their unfriendly manner to the effects of the smelly glue to which they were exposed; this was perhaps responsible for their hostile behavior, plus the nature of their business.

When I think of my friend William Frohman, I think of a story I heard many years ago. I feel that Bill is most deserving of having it dedicated to his good sense of humor.

Hershel and his cousin Burich came over to Canada during the Depression. Jobs were nonexistent, especially to newcomers who didn't speak or understand English. They were having a very hard time, until by sheer luck they met a "Landsman," a man they knew from the Old Country. It appeared that despite the unemployment he was doing well.

After they had met him several times he invited them both for dinner.

"Max, what do you do for a living?" asked Hershel while devouring a juicy steak.

"I operate a bawdy house," answered Max.

"What sort of a business is that?" the two asked with curiosity.

Max explained it the best way he knew how, and they parted, promising to keep in touch.

After some time had passed the two cousins got to understand the nature of Max's business and decided to try their luck.

"Did you see the silk tie Max was wearing?" asked Burich.

"Tie, shmy!" said Hershel. "You should have noticed the cuff links on his silk shirt! I swear they were studded with diamonds.

They sparkled so brightly they were blinding. He must own a very profitable business."

They both agreed that he owned a gold mine!

Hershel opened a business in the east end of the city. Burich found a good location in the western part of the city. After several months had passed the two cousins met one day and found that neither of them had heard from Max since the last time they met for dinner.

"I am going to pay him a visit first thing Monday morning," said Burich. "As a rule business is very slow on Mondays."

About 10 A.M. Burich was standing in front of a house with a clean polished front and heavy draperies covering the large tall front windows. He pressed a gold button and heard musical chimes playing inside the house.

A good-looking young man appeared, dressed in a royal blue uniform trimmed with gold stripes, and pure white silk gloves. "May I help you?" he asked courteously.

"Yes, you can. I wish to speak to my friend Max," said Burich.

"Max? We have no one here by this name."

"But he gave me this address the last time I saw him!"

"Just one minute," said the guard politely. "Perhaps you mean Maxim Lafontane."

"Show me that Lafontane. If it's Max I'll recognize him."

The guard pressed the button, and out came Lafontane, wearing a shiny black silk tuxedo, a pure white shirt, a black silk bow tie, and shoes that shone so brightly Burich couldn't look at them; they hurt his eyes.

"Max, it's you!" he shouted while embracing him. "You look so different since I have seen you last. You promised to call me but you never did. I thought that you might have lost my phone number, or you were ill, God forbid."

"Burich, my friend," said Max slowly, apologetically, filled with dignity as befits a successful businessman. "I meant to call you many times, but we were so busy that I couldn't even spare a minute. Just to give you an example of how busy we are, last Friday night we were overbooked so heavily we were compelled to use my mother-in-law."

"*Mazal Tov.* I didn't know you got married."

"Burich, my friend, forgive me for not inviting you to the wedding. I married a Catholic girl, which would have most likely been against your Old Country tradition, and besides it was a marriage of necessity, which was arranged in a hurry and unexpectedly."

Burich met Hershel the following day and told him of the "gold mine" Max owned. They both sat for hours trying to figure out how Max managed to continue making a fortune out of the very same type of business they were both operating and starving to death.

"Hershel," said Burich. "You always pride yourself on being clever. Having had a Talmudic education you should be quite smart. Why then don't you come up with some logical explanation to his success?"

They both sank into deep silence, thinking, shrugging their shoulders, staring at each other.

Hershel's face began to break into a smile as he tapped his friend on the shoulder, and yelled out loud, "I've got it, I've got it! In fact, I am sure of the method he is using!"

"What's the method? Tell me already!"

"Max collects from his clients on the way in, while we idiots collect on the way out! There is a difference, you know."

"He is a fraud!" screamed Burich.

"So what? Frauds are perpetrated in every human endeavor; he is no exception. Some people are honest in the flesh but thieves in their spirits. Max is an all-round thief."

"William, my friend, find a good location and take me in as a silent partner; I'll only do the promotions."

THE PROPER APPROACH IN SELLING

Retail business, especially ladies' wear, is cutthroat competition, particularly when it comes to price; that's when the haggling starts. On such occasions one must be alert and hear all, or part, of the conversation between customer and salesperson. By circulating on the floor you can be within hearing distance most of the time.

"Well, you are a good customer. I'll make an exception to the rule and let you have the coat for $150. As you can see it's marked $189."

The customer calls me over and begins to remind me of the many years she has patronized my store.

"Do you remember me?" she asks.

"Of course I do! How can I forget such a nice lady?"

"How much will you charge me for this coat?"

"I'll give you a special price."

In order to impress her I continue, but in a very quiet voice, almost a whisper, "You can have it for $165."

"What?" she screams. "The saleslady offered it to me for $150." (As if I didn't know.)

"Do you know why? Because she is giving away my money, not her own."

I walk away slowly, but not before she gets a friendly pat on the shoulder.

"I told you not to call the boss! . . . Mr. Henig!" the saleslady is calling again. She tells me apologetically that she had promised the customer to let her have the coat for $150.

"Well," I say hesitatingly, "you are a nice lady, and we want to see you happy, but don't you ever tell anyone how much you paid for it."

"I won't tell, cross my heart and hope to die if I do."

The customer is happy, the saleslady is happy, and I am happier than both of them.

The customer thanks me many times over for being so nice.

This reminds me of a similar story I read in the book *Enjoy, Enjoy,* by Harry Golden. The title of the story is "How's That Again?"

The hard-of-hearing salesmen flourished mainly on Stanton Street in New York. Here is how they operated. A customer was trying on a few suits and every question he asked had to be repeated three times.

The salesman cupped his ear and distorted his features, trying desperately to make out what the customer was saying: "What did you say? Please repeat it! I am very hard of hearing!"

Finally the customer picked a suit he liked and now for that big moment: "How much?"

The deaf salesman yelled to the back, "Louis! How much for number 2734?"

And from the back came the voice, very loud so the customer heard it clearly, "Sixty-five dollars."

The deaf salesman turned with a straight face to the customer and said, "Thirty-five dollars."

Whereupon the customer pulled out thirty-five dollars, grabbed the suit without waiting for it to be boxed, and hustled off with his big bargain, while Louis and the "deaf" salesman went to Davis's Saloon for a cold beer.

That was a clever, ingenious method of avoiding the haggling over price.

Never ask questions. Never ask a woman the size she wears; she'll tell you that she wears an American size 9, when in fact she wears a 13 or a 15. Some women are vain and are prone to exaggerate a lot.

A woman confronted me one day with just such wishful thinking. She made me commit an unforgivable sin by asking her, "On which side?" After I jokingly calmed her down, my saleslady sold her a size 15. She removed all tickets before she had the customer try on the dress. Upon emerging from the fitting room she triumphantly remarked, while looking at me with some resentment, "You see? A size 9 fits me to perfection. I am wearing it home; put my other dress in a box."

"I am sorry, I was just joking."

"I bet you were!" and gave me a sly look.

The following day the lady came storming into the store, madder than blazes. "You tricked me!" She was fuming. "You sold me a size 15 purposely to satisfy your chauvinistic feelings."

"Doesn't the dress fit you?"

"It fits me to perfection, but the size is clearly marked on the inside of the belt."

Oy! Am I a cabbagehead! I forgot to erase the 15."

The moral of this episode is, even though the dress fitted her to perfection, I was compelled to give her a refund.

After I had listened to the customer's argument, I agreed that she was right. Then I listened to the saleslady's argument and told her that she was right. A friend of mine who had witnessed the entire episode came over to me and asked, "How can they both be right?"

"You know something? You are right too."

A size 9 would have fitted her on one side, as I said. It would have burst at the seams, or squeezed her eyes out of the sockets, but the customer is always right.

Women's vanity is a state of mind; they are inclined to hallucinate in unrealistic daydreams. Unfortunately we can't correct the condition, but only hope for the best.

In case I am giving you the impression that I am a chauvinist,

I wish to assure you that I am not; most of my good customers were women and I don't mean to imply that all women are of the same intellect; there are exceptions of course.

Perhaps my opinion stems from the fact that most of my customers were of ethnic origin and found it difficult to adjust to the Canadian way of life. I am of the opinion, however, that women in general worry too much about their appearance, and never think of how to improve their thinking and reasoning. I say this with all due respect to the ladies. But because I have been involved in selling most of my life I feel that I am fully qualified to make this observation.

Let us now examine briefly the behavior of some salesladies.

A customer enters the store. A saleslady—tall, frosty, gray-haired, like an aristocratic icicle, who appears to be profoundly offended by figures other than hers, with a voice that freezes in midair—approaches the customer.

"I am looking for a nice gown," says the customer apologetically.

"What size, and around what price are you looking for?"

"You are the saleslady, you should be able to judge the size! And as to price—I don't recall mentioning price!"

"Honey, I am here to help you. There is no reason for you to be hostile."

"I am here to purchase a gown, not to argue with you," replies the customer. "Furthermore, I would appreciate it if you would refrain from calling me 'Honey,' with your highfalutin cross-examination. I have a feeling that I am in the wrong store."

Women especially will appreciate this dialogue, when you think of some stores that employ overzealous or completely indifferent sales help who disregard the proper approach or manner.

The customer walks away from the icy creature, only to be accosted by another saleslady who is trying to be pleasant but fails.

At this point it is obvious that the customer has been upset by the icy face.

The frosty, gray-haired creature remarks as she is walking toward the rear of the store, "Another looker. The last of the big spenders!"

Needless to say, the customer walks out.

Because this episode took place in a shopping mall it was easy for me to follow the potential buyer and see where and how she eventually made her purchase.

She entered another store two doors away, and here I witnessed the happy ending, as I stood inside the store pretending that I was a browser.

A charming middle-aged saleslady approached her and surprised me by not saying, "May I help you?" Instead she greeted her warmly and said, "Isn't it a lovely morning?"

"It certainly is," replied the lady smilingly.

The following is a brief report as to what took place.

"I am looking for a real nice gown for a very special occasion."

"Well, if it's a special occasion I will try my best to find a specially nice gown for you. Trust me, I'll not mislead you," said the saleslady.

They chose two gowns and chattingly walked into a fitting room. Within minutes they came out. One gown was put back into stock; the other one was carefully folded into a box. Smiling happily the lady walked out with a gown, purchased in a most congenial way.

It was obvious that the soothing voice and the sincerity of the saleslady were responsible for instant communication and a satisfied customer.

I have often analyzed the vulnerability of a customer if handled properly. Because I was involved in selling most of the time, I began to practice a special type of diplomacy.

Some customers seem to be on the defensive the minute they walk into a store. This may be due to some unpleasant experiences they have had at one time or other at another place of business.

They make statements such as "I am just looking." Looking for what? A woman's subconscious tells her to look in a dress shop; otherwise she could satisfy her curiosity in a drug store or a food store. Or she'll say, "Perhaps I'll see something I like." Now this is more rational.

I show her a dress, which she claims she really likes. I suggest casually, "Go and try it on."

"Oh, no! If I try it on I am afraid I might buy it."

Can you understand such reasoning?

Some say, "I'll think about it," or "I'll bring my sister."

"Where does your sister live?"

"I have two sisters," she informs me. "One lives in New York, one in Buffalo."

Or "I'll ask my husband. He would kill me if I bought a dress without his permission."

"At least you'll die happy," I jokingly say.

They have excuses that haven't yet been invented.

Only the other Saturday a woman came into the store, her face covered with perspiration, as if someone had just poured a pail of water on her head; her pointy chin was dripping like a leaky faucet. "I am leaving for Yugoslavia tonight," she announced, "and I want a nice gown to take with me."

She looked at about twenty gowns, examined them inside out, and without embarrassment said, "I'll come back Monday."

Try and understand women! All one can do is say, "Thank you," and hope she shows up again.

Over the years I have repeatedly tried to impress upon my sales staff that when a customer walks out without making a purchase, you must be as nice to her, or nicer, as when she first entered the store. It gives one a guilty feeling when you take up the time of sales help only to walk out empty-handed. Make her feel welcome by walking her to the door, and invite her to come again, and she will.

Practice the wisdom of the Talmud: "Cast thy bread upon the water, perhaps in the future you'll find it."

Investment in courtesy is in the habit of being repaid at one time or another. It's a good investment that usually bears dividends, and remember, the customer you are talking to is a hundred times more interested in herself and her problems. Her aching corn on her toe, or a boil on her neck, means more to her than a rumor of a coming famine. Show her that you care; draw her out to tell you her problems. People like to find a sympathetic ear to talk to. Think of that the next time you start a conversation with a customer.

One must also analyze each sale, why it was made, or, why it was lost, after a long battle of wits.

My observation, which is based on years of experience, is: When one is trying to make a sale there is always that psychological moment when the sale is made. Failing to take advantage of that moment the sale is lost.

You can also unsell if you don't stop at a precise time and ask for a deposit. Once you have some money in your hands the sale is more secure. You can then take your time and answer all questions a customer might ask.

A customer may wish to ask questions rather than get involved in an irrelevant conversation before the sale is completed. This should be avoided.

Basically, a general principle can be applied to many things in daily living, from selling to credit to illness: The longer it takes the less chance of its success.

There is a Jewish proverb, "The longer the illness, the rarer the cure". The longer it takes trying to sell an item, the less chance you have of selling it.

You can compare selling to a bottle of soda; the longer it's left open, the flatter it becomes. It fizzles out.

The same applies to the granting of credit; the longer it takes to collect, the greater the risk of losing.

I always based granting of credit on the following logic: Today my customer is working and is feeling fine. How am I to know what unforeseeable problems may come to her as time goes by? All sorts of unpredictable possibilities can materialize. She may lose her job, have illness in the family, or even an accident.

One should think of such and other related possibilities when granting credit. It has happened before.

Let us now take a couple of hypothetical situations in selling.

A saleslady is desperately trying to sell a coat to a lady who is completely undecided as to whether she should or should not buy it. She has run out of excuses by now and is in the final stage of making her mind up.

I once watched such a case for over an hour while the saleslady was on the brink of collapse. The customer took the coat off, hung it up, examined it inside out again, and said quietly, "I think I'll take it."

But here is where the saleslady lost her head. Instead of asking her to pay for it, she said, "Would you please put it on again so that I can mark the buttons for you?"

The customer obliged her, while pins were being put in as markers where the buttons should be sewn on.

She suddenly turned and said, "No! I think I better come back with my sister tomorrow."

She took the coat off and walked out.

Where did the saleslady go wrong? By not taking into account the hard time she had to have the lady commit herself. She unsold it by marking the buttons before she got paid. Had she done this she could have turned to the customer and said, "I am sorry, I forgot to mark the buttons. Would you please slip the coat on once more?"

Customers don't know whether pins have to be put in, or where buttons are to be sewn on. Customers don't know whether a coat has to be marked around with a chalk-marker at the bottom in order for it to come out even when it's shortened.

All you have to do is put in a couple of pins for the desired length. After you have all of the money or a deposit, you innocently apologize for forgetting to chalk the bottom, or other alterations you know have to be done of which the customer is not aware.

An inexperienced or gullible saleslady unknowingly incites a customer not to make the purchase that she is trying so desperately to encourage. She works against herself because she lacks logic, diplomacy, and timing, which is of the utmost importance.

Unselling can also result in a saleslady's nonstop dialogue; there is a time when you have to cease conversation until the sale is completed.

You can also lose a sale by simply holding the garment over your arm while writing a bill of sale.

Such pitfalls can be avoided in two ways: First you get the money or part of it before reaching for the salesbook, or, second, you hang the garment away out of sight before you ask the customer to pay for it, or, get a sizable deposit; otherwise you may run into problems. If you are observant you'll remember from past experiences that a customer is examining the garment while you are writing the bill of sale. Many a sale has been lost just at that crucial time.

A second hypothetical unselling or overselling happens when there are several people involved. Jealousy can be a factor when a friend or so-called adviser shows signs of disagreement. On such occasions one can say (in a joking manner of course), "Don't be jealous, I have got one for you too. I'll let you try it on."

When you are selling a dress or a gown it's wise that you complete your sale in the fitting room; otherwise you'll notice, if you are observant, that the customer automatically looks toward all of the dresses hanging in stock while trying to decide if she should settle for the one she has on. She is thinking, "Maybe there is a dress there that I may like better."

Do not give her that opportunity; if you do, you'll most likely lose the sale.

A bride who bought her gown in our store brings in three,

four, or more, bridesmaids. I feel that I should first explain that there is always one rotten apple in a barrel when it comes to bridesmaids; one of them usually refuses to go along with the choice of the others. There is a way of getting her to see our point of view and that of the other girls, provided the salesgirl knows her business and clinches the sale in the shortest time possible. Otherwise chances are that the ones who agreed on a certain style or color will gradually be influenced by the one who rejected their choice at first, but agreed in order to keep harmony within the group.

The minute two out of three, or three out of four, say OK, an experienced salesgirl will call the girl who was most resistant and ask for a deposit. The dialogue can sound similar to what I am writing.

"Can you leave me $30?"

"No, I don't think I have that much on me. I can leave you $15."

"Okay, give me $15."

She hands the money over. The salesgirl then proceeds to take her measurements, and so it continues down the line until the order for the entire group is completed.

Do not ever take measurements or write a bill of sale before you have a deposit in your hands. Should a deposit or deposits be by check, don't have the store name on it. Have her make it to yourself and you can cash it.

Many sales have been lost because payment has been stopped on a check. Because the check doesn't bear the name of the store, it's impossible to have payment stopped.

If you step out of the well-planned system by inadvertently asking another one of the girls to try on the sample gown to determine her size, the group gets into a huddle quickly. By the time the girl comes out of the fitting room a new plan has been decided upon: "Well, this is the first store we have looked. We won't decide now; we'll be back."

The group walks out and the salesgirl carries on as if nothing has happened. She doesn't realize that she had made a nice sale, only to unsell it by her gullibility.

Such situations are daily occurrences and can cost the store owner a fortune during the year.

Shopping malls are not subjected to such losses because of the heavy, endless store traffic, but in a neighborhood store, where traffic is limited, such potential sales should be made, regardless of the unorthodox methods used to make them.

A salesgirl must concentrate on each sale as if it was the last one she'll ever make. One day she'll be right.

As I said before, women are a rare breed. They are never sure of anything when it comes to selecting a wardrobe; they do it on impulse rather than thought.

I have witnessed unbelievable scenes on many occasions. I know you won't believe this. A customer selects a garment that she apparently likes very much, but she is repeatedly asking her friend, "Do you really like it on me?"

"Yes, I do."

"Are you sure?"

"Sure I am sure!"

This went on and on one day until I finally took an Italian dictionary in one hand and some printed material in the other, walked up to her and asked, "What would you have your friend do to prove that she is telling you the truth, sign a statement or swear on the Bible?"

Of course, such subtle jokes are done in a very discreet manner.

Or a woman comes in with a three-year-old, and without a bit of embarrassment asks the child which dress looks better on her.

You do not believe a word you are reading, do you?

I swear on the Italian dictionary (Bible) it's the truth. Unreasonable stupidity is carried too far sometimes.

Rather than get upset you create an entertaining atmosphere and accomplish a lot more. Proper understanding and reason are rare commodities to some; therefore, one must be mentally flexible, and adjust to all levels of mentality.

In order to be successful in this highly competitive field one must analyze and correct situations and ideas. Keep them in proper perspective and treat them as a fine art.

There is another aspect to selling that few people are aware of, or do not think about; that is, to interest a potential customer in a garment which is beyond her financial means. You get her to like it beyond any doubt, only to be informed that it's far too expensive for her. You then make an attempt to switch her to a lower-priced garment, but it's too late; the damage has been done. She walks out, goes to another store, and purchases a lower-priced garment. You must begin with lower-priced merchandise and feel your way along. You can always go up, but it's impossible to back-track. You can compare it to wages or salaries. An increase is gratefully accepted, but a decrease will be rejected.

I have studied selling over the years, the way one studies music or medicine. I have always searched for reasons and analyzed each sale individually and collectively. I have found that the less you say the better. It's not what you say that is important; it's the way you say it. You have to be almost humble in your chosen words, innocent and honest. Never look a customer in the eye and wait for a reaction. You must take the initiative and be instrumental in having the customer say the things you want to hear.

When you see her touching her shoulders or hips, you count to ten not to make it obvious. You then draw her attention to the very same areas and give her a compliment.

"Look how beautiful the shoulder line fits. Look at your waist! You appear to have lost twenty pounds the minute you put this on!" (Women like that.)

If she stands in front of the mirror too long, take a positive approach by saying, "Is this length okay, or would you like it a bit shorter?"

This will force her to react one way or another.

Time is of the essence; don't waste it with what we call a "deadbeat."

Don't be surprised if you hear her say the unexpected: "I'll take it."

This is an expression that sends many a salesgirl running to the washroom. The overwhelming feeling of winning a battle of wits can be almost unbearable sometimes.

Or she'll throw you into desperation by a few simple words: "I'll come back tomorrow" or "I'll sleep on it."

"Oh, no! You won't sleep on my garment. Pay for it first, then you can do with it whatever you wish."

There are literally hundreds of excuses used by women shoppers to get out of a store. Why did she come in in the first place? Ask her! She has no ready answer.

There are, however, exceptions. Some women are practical, fashion-minded, and intelligent, and appreciate value and courteous service.

My experience has been with ethnic clientele most of the time, who are very difficult and unreasonable when it comes to clothes.

I therefore single out the Italian people as the most loyal of all, but price-haggling is their way of life, even if it only entails seventy-eight cents. They are not happy unless they get some sort of discount. An Italian customer has never paid the price as marked. "What is the best price?" or "What will you take off?" On rare occasions I replied, "I'll take the ticket off if you buy the garment."

Nevertheless, I have great respect and deep admiration for the Italian people. They are industrious, honest, loyal to their families, and to the store that treats them right. They are a very emotional people and require special diplomatic personal attention. They used to enjoy seeing me take forty-eight cents out of my pocket and put it in the till, because they refused to pay, but I was most often rewarded with a crunching handshake and a solemn promise to come back and bring new customers.

Although most of them have moved to suburbs in all directions, their loyalty remains at St. Clair Avenue and Dufferin Street. They do not shop elsewhere, especially when they are in need of a better garment.

To extend credit to an Italian customer is like depositing money in the bank, except for a very few who sometimes run into unexpected problems. In spite of that I have never questioned their honesty.

Recessions have never penetrated Italian lives. Most of them own homes; they rent out every bit of space possible to boost the family income. No job is too hard or unsuitable for them; they don't pick and choose.

I have nothing but praise for them. Even though the price-haggling one has to face becomes unbearable sometimes, it is worth it. Not only do they express their gratitude verbally, they also bring in good customers.

Friendship must be controlled, so as not to allow it to develop into favoritism. If and when it goes beyond the established business practice, it becomes a personal relationship, which can lead to embarrassing bargaining, and consequently loss of business, simply because you have allowed people to get you involved personally, rather than dealing with dignity and honesty, which your business image is supposed to represent.

I shall always remember a lady who came in to buy a dress, but couldn't speak English. One of my salesgirls tried very hard to make the sale. Whatever she said the customer kept on saying "Sister." The battle of wits had gone on for almost an hour, when she finally opened her purse as if she were going to pay for the dress. My salesgirl put her hand out anticipatingly to get the money, when the customer pulled out a kerchief, blew her nose loud and clear, said "Sister," and walked out.

Selling can be very easy and quite simple if one uses diplomacy. One must point out the virtues of the garment where the customer is about to find faults. It takes anticipation to react quickly and turn all of the so-called flaws of a garment in your favor, provided you don't wait until the customer gains the upper hand by pointing them out to *you.*

12

Weddings

Our bridal gown business was very poor and I couldn't figure out why. Girls were coming in, inquiring and looking, and then leaving without ever trying one on.

I decided to pay special attention to this problem, and as a result I soon discovered what my sales staff were doing wrong. Wedding gowns are in a class by themselves. Different methods, different techniques, and a completely different approach must be exercised. When a girl comes in and inquires about a gown, do not ask her, "Can you buy one without your mother?" Some of them will reply, "Of course I can! If I find one I like." Others will say, "No! I am just looking today, but if I see something I like I'll come back with my mother."

Don't believe either one! You can sell them gowns if you know how to go about it.

I had also noticed that my sales staff were showing gowns indiscriminately, without a bit of love or tender intimacy. Because all gowns look alike when shown on hangers, customers stood shaking their heads at each gown and finally walked out.

We had a meeting one day and decided upon a new approach.

First, a saleslady must know her gown inventory, which is in the stock room, because bridal gowns are never readily visible in the bins as other merchandise. Second, the following approach must be exercised:

"I am looking for a wedding gown."

"Oh, how nice! When is your wedding?"

In four or eight weeks (or in a couple of days sometimes).

"You don't have much time, considering many other preparations which have to be looked after. Come into our bridal room and I'll show you something very special for this time of year."

You have won half the battle by getting her to come into the fitting room. You bring in a gown and remark, "You'll look like a

141

queen in this gown. You'll see when you try it on; you can't appreciate the beauty of a gown by looking at it on a hanger."

The girl has no alternative, and is also curious to see herself in a white gown. Here you have the advantage because the girl has never seen herself in a wedding gown and is therefore quite vulnerable to your enthusiasm. "Now! Look at yourself! Don't you look gorgeous?"

Should she happen to have her mother, sister, or friend with her, you direct your enthusiasm to the one who is likely to decide whether or not she agrees. Nine out of ten bridal gowns are sold that way.

But remember, get a large deposit if it isn't being paid in full. It's a simple matter while everyone is excited about the purchase they have just made. They may even go to other stores to look. They may even find one they like better and forfeit a small deposit they had left with you, which is unlikely but possible.

As a result of this new technique we began selling hundreds of bridal gowns and within one month increased our bridal business by two hundred percent.

On many occasions when a wedding gown was being sold, my mind would wander back to my village, where weddings were rare, unless our undernourished matchmaker, who weighed ninety pounds soaking wet (twenty pounds of which was his oversized nose), wandered from village to village matching couples who didn't even see each other until the time of the actual wedding ceremony. Matchmaking and wedding arrangements were made by the respective parents and the matchmaker, who made the deals without the knowledge or consent of the bride or groom.

Today, one must fall in love first, before an engagement can be contemplated; then the planning for the wedding begins.

Unfortunately many such modern marriages are based on the one word *love*, which in my opinion is not enough to build a happy family life, and as a result some marriages fall apart at the first gust of a storm. They end in separation and finally in divorce, whereas weddings in the villages between two complete strangers were for life. Perhaps the twenty-four-hour duration of the wedding ceremony had something to do with it. Whatever the reason, marriages were for keeps.

The man and woman swore to respect and obey each other in sickness and in health, in poverty or in plenty. The wife silently and obediently attended to her daily duties and responsibilities while the husband was studying the Talmud, but he was always considered the king of the household and was respected as such. A mutual bond and devotion grew stronger with each passing year.

Entire communities from surrounding villages came to such joyous weddings. In the spirit of our ancient tradition, Yiddish melodies echoed against the mountains in the deep silence of a summer night. Dogs were howling, barking, screaming, as if they were being chased by a hundred devils, because there was a wedding in progress. The whole village was in a turmoil, and the guests were in a state of shock, hypnotized by the overwhelming event. Time stood still for twenty-four hours while the mountains sat silently in deep meditation, witnessing the jubilation.

Can anyone understand the magnitude of such a wedding? Can anyone appreciate the happy melodies the orchestra was playing? Melodies saturated with undertones of sadness, which were left suspended in the air, when they were no more. Such Yiddish music carries a note of melancholy exile and persecution that spans thousands of years.

I was not supposed to have been at one particular wedding. My mother had reminded me each day since the matchmaker had invited us to be ready on a particular day that I was too young to be taken to a wedding. One of my married cousins also warned me not to count on it; his reason was somewhat degrading to me. He claimed that I really didn't care so much about being at the wedding, but I wanted to come because of the food that would be served. He was not entirely wrong. I did hope that I would get some sort of meal by being there.

I was undernourished and forever hungry. How else can a poor, fatherless child feel? To exist in perpetual hunger was good training and adjustment to face adversity without oversensitivity on the journey of life. But I had other plans, which I didn't reveal to anyone.

When an unforgettable night of jubilation had finally come, I was there, hiding behind the musicians so that my mother wouldn't see me. Finally the ceremony was over and the dancing began. I noticed the groom's mother, Zipoirah, standing in a far corner, and the bride's mother, Goldy, sitting down in the opposite corner, while the Chassidim formed a circle and began the traditional wedding dance. Feet were stamping, faces turned upward, eyes closed, perspiration running freely down faces and heavy beards like trickles of melting snow, but the dancers were oblivious to it all—lost in a hypnotic trance.

The two mothers sized each other up for a while as if they were planning an attack. The center of the floor was suddenly cleared as if by magic, and the two of them launched at each other with grim determination, maneuvering for position, hands on hips, a shift to the right and a shift to the left. They suddenly got lost in each other's arms, embraced tightly as if never to part again. I sat and waited impatiently to see the outcome of the furious confrontation. After they had danced a while, they parted as suddenly as they had embraced, without a word or a sign of emotion.

I have never been to another wedding that would equal or come close to that unspoken experience of love, or hate.

That particular night stands out in my memory because of the beautiful melodies played by the violinist. It penetrated my very soul because to be a violinist was my greatest ambition.

I don't know the reason to this day why it was considered so terribly degrading to be a musician in the Chassidic communities of my time. Unlike a tailor, a shoemaker, a baker, or even a freeloader, who were all respected, to be a musician meant to be an agnostic, which was the worst form of degradation one would bring upon himself and his family. It was compared to one who had the education to read psychology or philosophy books in which one could find some explanations or reasons for various human behavior—perhaps find a way to conquer medieval fears and superstitions. Such an individual was considered a sinner. And yet music was the most enjoyable part of a wedding, even though males and females were separated by partitions because mixed dancing was against Chassidic tradition.

Dancing at a wedding was not considered a personal pleasure but an act of piety, an expression of gratitude, thanking God for having been given the privilege of being present at such a joyous event. But to be a musician was out, even though I was fatherless and had no home. My mother hired me out to a baker, where I slept on a wooden bunk, covered with a bit of lice-infested straw.

13

A Bitter Memory

You very seldom have to disagree with a customer regarding her choice, fit, or value of a garment. You must diplomatically prepare her beforehand for almost everything she may dislike.

"If I thought for a minute that this . . . is not for you, I wouldn't have had you try it on."

This phrase however must sound sincerely innocent. As a result you will have gained the confidence of your customer. However, one cannot expect to satisfy all of the people all of the time; there are exceptions to the rule.

I also had a very good fur coat business; customers came from as far as Oshawa to purchase fur coats. I remember an incident when a husband purchased an expensive fur coat for his wife, she being exceptionally short. About twelve inches were cut away from the length to make it look proper.

They left the store very happy but brought the coat back a week later, demanding a refund. When I refused to take the coat back the husband tore the telephone off the desk and in a raging fury threatened to kill me. With the help of customers we overpowered him and had him arrested.

When a muskrat or a mink coat was sold, I was confronted with one question each time: "Will the coat be damaged if I get caught in the rain or snow?"

Rather than commit myself one way or another, I answered their questions with my own: "Did you ever see a muskrat or a mink using an umbrella?"

I had heard this humorous answer many times when I was ordering fur coats and asked the manufacturer the same question.

"Since you are so sure why don't you give me a guarantee?"

"Of course I will; you are entitled to one! This coat is guaranteed for one year, worn under normal conditions." I was in a fortunate position, however. Rarely did I have to issue a written guarantee; my verbal guarantee was accepted in most cases.

I also remember a Ukrainian woman who purchased a dress for $12, had it ripped on a wire fence, and brought it back a week later, complaining that I had sold her a damaged dress. She called me "lousy Jew" because I refused to give her a refund. I picked up a lightweight chair and smashed it over her head. I was so angry I could see stars explode before my eyes—not stars of a democratic country, but of my anti-Semitic village.

Recollections of the past usually come back in a flash when a spiritual or emotional crisis occurs. Something rose up in me in a frantic protest that made me think of my village, my childhood, and the small poor Jewish community I had left behind.

Have I not paid my share dearly by growing up under the pressure of brutal anti-Semitism, hate and ignorance? My whole family had been slaughtered. Six million innocent people had been destroyed. Was it all in vain? Do I have to be reminded of the sick philosophy of warped ignorant minds here in a democratic country?

But how can one blame such vicious, evil people who brought their hate with them, a hate that never ceased fermenting, even in the New World? If they knew better, their way of thinking would probably have changed.

Even in this New World one must understand how to cherish and appreciate freedom of worship and opportunity, equally available to all that reach the shores of democracy, regardless of race or religion. But how can anyone make the evil understand that it is much more rewarding, more humane to strive for equality?

This is not Rypiana, a sleepy little village lost in a deep valley nestled tightly against ominous Carpathian Mountains, where a church stood at the edge of a winding mud road. The church was the pride and joy of the peasants, but a constant threat to the Jewish community, especially on Sundays and Holy Days, Christmas and Easter, when pogroms were planned constantly and hoodlums terrorized the Jews.

This episode made me think of my childhood years, of the suffering we had endured. Those were medieval times and primitive people. Although we never showed any signs of outward bruises, we nevertheless bled internally. The Ukrainian villagers were particularly hostile at that time of year. They claimed openly that the Jews were a menace to their villages and therefore should

*Baron de Hirsch, philanthropist, founded and financed the Jewish Colo-
nization Association, which assisted Jewish immigrants from Europe.*
Courtesy Jewish Historical Society of Western Canada

Hirsch, Saskatchewan, a colony named for Baron de Hirsch, was settled with the aid of his organization. This photograph was taken the year of my birth, 1909. Courtesy Jewish Historical Society of Western Canada

Shortly after my arrival in Hirsch in 1929. Left to right: Esther, my cousin; her husband, Harry Hirt; my aunt holding her grandchild; my uncle; and me.

typical farmhouse in Hirsch, circa 1930. Courtesy Jewish Historical Society of Western Canada

The threshing crew. My uncle, holding the pitchfork, is flanked by his son-in-law, Harry Hirt (far left), *son, Phil* (fourth from left), *and the hired help.*

*Clearing the land on
a homestead in Hirsch, 1914.*
Courtesy Jewish
Historical Society
of Western Canada

*On a recent visit I posed before our attic home
on Manitoba Avenue in Winnipeg where we lived
from 1932 to 1935.*

The Right Honorable John G. Diefenbaker, former prime minister of Canada. Canadians never had and most likely never will again enjoy prosperity comparable to what we had under his leadership.

Major Lloyd Eason and Commissioner Arnold Brown of the Salvation Army. It is impossible to appreciate fully the tremendous scope of their activities and the dedication with which they carry on their noble work.

A view overlooking the courtyard of the Western Wall in the Old City of Jerusalem, with me in the foreground.

Jews praying before the Western Wall.

be persecuted and destroyed. The church had always been most influential in inciting hate and terrorism and was looked upon by the peasants as the Gospel of Truth.

Christmas Eve was a night of fear. I remember my mother would huddle us into a dark corner of the hut, not daring to light the kerosene lamp, to prevent or avoid the attention of young gangs that were on a rampage to break windows, smash doors, or even knife someone.

Easter was another time of year when peasants became hostile and claimed that Jews were about to kill a Christian child in order to have blood for Passover. However, if they were not successful in their malicious attempt to have the police come from Turka and arrest a few elders of the Jewish community for the murder of a non-Jewish child, they would then kill an animal and place a container full of blood in the doorway of a Jewish home in order to create evidence of a brutal murder.

If you were to read *The Fixer* by Bernard Malamud, you would clearly understand my brief observation and the traumatic experiences of the times.

Although Jewish dietary laws were religiously and piously observed in Eastern and Central Poland, the Ukrainians and Poles alike never ceased insinuating that the Jews used blood of a Christian child for Passover.

Nevertheless, when the First World War broke out, Jewish men were conscripted into the army the same as non-Jews. They were maimed and killed in battle on Ukrainian and Polish soil as well as in foreign lands. They had become first-class citizens to die defending the country, but became non-citizens just as soon as the war was over.

After the battle, limbs, heads, and torsos were lying around in the forests or shallow trenches as if a butcher had used a cleaver to dismantle the decaying bodies. The Jew and the non-Jew found peace in death, united without resentment, in a peace never achieved in life.

I can never forget an episode that occurred years later in Canada. It broke my heart and made me weep for days. It was on a Saturday. Because of limited store activities I had occasion to greet a lady who apprehensively entered the store. In order to make her feel more comfortable I greeted her warmly, only to realize that she didn't understand English. When I repeated my greeting in Ukrainian her eyes lit up as if she had come out of a trance. Overwhelmed by hearing me speak her language, she began to cry.

Upon questioning her she unfolded a most unusual heartbreaking story. She informed me that she had come over from Rypiana (the village I came from), and that she had been in Canada for only six months.

When she heard me say that I, too, came from Rypiana, her eyes penetrated deeply into my face and silently she murmured, "Are you by any chance Hershko, the little scrawny child who worked on the field for my father? My name is Marysha. Don't you remember me?"

A shudder of surprise and happiness flashed through my mind. "Are you the little girl who used to steal milk from your house and give it to me when I was ill?"

"Yes," she replied.

"Do you remember the time I was deathly ill with what was called 'Black Cholera,' shortly after the armies retreated from our village? You had brought me some beef soup one day in a wooden dish with a wooden spoon your father made, but my mother refused to let me eat it because it was not Kosher. I survived somehow, while hundreds of villagers, including children, fell victim to that horrible contagious disease. In fact, people with dangerously high fevers wandered around deliriously, aimlessly in the deep snow and below-zero temperatures, until they dropped dead in their tracks, only to be swallowed up by swirling drifting snow; but we had survived."

"That was a miracle," Marysha said.

She suddenly embraced me tightly, put her head on my shoulder and cried silently, while telling me what a wonderful religious mother I had had. She died with the ancient prayer on her lips: "Hear, O Israel, the Lord our God the Lord is One."

She told me that the day the Nazis occupied the village, they gathered the entire Jewish community into one area, lined them up, and a firing squad was ordered to mow them down with a heavy burst of machine guns, which reverberated against the mountains all around, and the weeping village became painfully silent.

"I was there," she said. "That is why I feel sometimes that I am going insane. Darkness hovered over the village, even though the sun was shining and the sky was crystal-clear. Life had stopped, as did the birds in flight. Life and death met head-on, and remained suspended in the sickening silence of the Valley."

While we were embraced in each other's arms, I thought of history recorded in the section "Vayigash," a part of the Five Books of Moses, where the story is told in detail of how Jacob's sons sold their brother Joseph to a band of Egyptians. They were, however, forced to go to Egypt years later to buy some food because of famine, which led to bringing Benjamin, the youngest of the brothers, to meet Joseph, and I quote from Genesis 56: V14: "Joseph fell on Benjamin's neck and wept, and Benjamin wept on the neck of his brother."

At this point I lost control of my emotions and cried bitterly without embarrassment as customers looked on silently.

This episode gave me a partial understanding of why I was forever living with a dream that I would write my autobiography someday. Memories of my childhood years were haunting me constantly, when I thought of the hunger, hopeless despair, and rejection. Memories that I could not erase from my mind tormented my soul.

The past has always been the present to me, and I was obsessed with putting it into book form some day.

Marysha then proceeded to tell me of the tragedy that befell the Jewish people when the Nazis marched into Poland.

"I had seen your family, I had talked with your mother only a few days prior to the complete annihilation of the Jewish population. You should have seen your sister's children; they were so bright and beautiful. They were all shot down like animals in one unforgettable moment. I haven't been able to find peace in my soul since. I came to Canada hoping to escape those terrible memories, but failed."

She broke down and cried uncontrollably. I called a doctor and had her taken home. She never told me where she was living and I never saw her again. I often think about her, perhaps upon seeing me her hidden guilt broke all barriers of her soul and made her react so strongly. I'll never know. Even though that episode happened about twenty-eight years ago, I never got over it. I often think about it and my soul weeps.

I also remember the friendship of the Priest's son I had enjoyed when I was about ten years of age, which I cherish to this day. He invited me to his house on many occasions. The house was always pure white, as if its wrapper had just been removed.

There were huge, vicious-looking dogs roaming about in the yard, but he got them to know me. Each time he invited me to the kitchen to give me some food, the dogs would come by, lick my hand and disappear.

I was fascinated when he took me inside the parlor and showed me a piano, which was called a "Clavier" in Yiddish. We had become very good friends because he loved music and so did I.

We enjoyed each other's company, although we were of different religions. We had a lot to talk about because of his influence and that of his father. I was one Jewish child who was truly liked by the Ukrainians, but even the most friendly peasants were obsessed with a feeling that the few Jews who lived in the village were in some way directly or indirectly responsible for an occasional drought, for an unusually severe winter, or even for a short supply of milk that was expected of a particular cow.

They asked me ever so often, "When do you think all the Jews will go to Palestine?"

"When Messiah will come, of course," I would answer, as a grandson of a Rabbi should.

I am intrigued to this day that illiterate peasants of ignorance and hate, who were completely isolated from the world and knowledge, were nevertheless aware of the fact that Palestine was the home of the Jewish people.

I have never heard anyone say that it belonged to the Arabs. Palestine was for the Jews since the times of Abraham, Isaac, and Jacob. And yet over a period of years Arabs have been trying to claim that land, which withered and died while waiting for the homeless Jews to return, so that it could begin to blossom and prosper for its people.

At this point I am reminded of a story I heard many years later in Canada. Two Arabs on a train sat opposite a Jew, who took his shoes off and made himself comfortable. The Arabs tried several times to draw him into a conversation, but without success. One of the Arabs finally turned to the Jew and said, "Hey, Jew, go to the dining car and bring us some coffee."

The Jew in his stocking feet obediently brought the coffee as requested.

He sat down, cleaned up his shoes, which the Arabs had dirtied while he was away, leaned back and relaxed.

Some time later the Arabs repeated the request. The Jew again brought the coffee. When he returned he cleaned his shoes and sat down. The Arabs could not understand his passive behavior. Finally one of the Arabs said, "Hey, Jew when do you think a lasting peace will come between the Jews and the Arabs?"

The Jew replied, "When you stop defecating in my shoes, and I stop urinating in your coffee, the chances for lasting peace will be much better than they are today."

14

Helping Your Help

In my selling career the word *special* represented trouble and aggravation. Every Friday evening was "D day." That's the day of the week when all specials were supposed to come in for customers promised the preceding week.

It was a day of turmoil and frustration, unlike the Fridays in my village. There, Friday was a day for relaxation in preparation for the holy Sabbath, while here we go insane with specials. Customers are calling; the telephone doesn't stop ringing. What is one to do?

Upon questioning some customers, I found out that most of the orders weren't needed for another week. But I seldom knew that before they ate my heart out and started on my liver.

That is only one of the many complex parts of this business, which I haven't come to understand to this day.

What makes some women so genuinely untruthful and cruel sometimes? A lady walked into the store one day and announced, "I need a long black gown right away!"

"Perhaps a street length would do?" I inquired.

"No!" she replied in a hostile voice. "It must be a floor length! I waited many years for this day, and now that my mother-in-law has finally died, it is time for me to be noticed when I enter the funeral chapel!"

What can one say when faced with such brutal logic?

Business was on the rise and my need for more help was becoming a problem. Where does one get the type of sales help that exists only in one's imagination?

Do sales ladies come in all shapes and sizes? Of course they do. They are a unique breed. Some are neat and possess a fair vocabulary; some are short and stout; some project a happy disposition; some are indifferent and spend the day counting the lights in the ceiling, or hold a cigarette in one hand, a coffee in the other, while the mouth is busily devouring a piece of gum.

Some are inexperienced and resist improvement. When fitting a garment, you may hear her say to the fitter, "Take a look at the dress! Her back is shorter than her front."

I was, however, very fortunate over the years. Most of the original help I had hired some twenty-five years ago are still working in the store to this day. Either they are that good or I have been good to them. Whatever the reason, we adapted to each other over the years despite our differences of opinion on many occasions.

The following brief but true story should give you some indication of how difficult it is to get qualified help.

Mr. Stedman was desperately in need of help. He advertised in a leading newspaper for weeks but got no results. One day he decided to place one more advertisement, but this time he ordered the heading in bold black letters: "*NAME YOUR PRICE*," and listed all the qualifications an applicant must possess.

A young man came in, approached the desk, and asked, "Are you the manager?"

"Yes I am," replied Mr. Stedman.

"I came down to see you regarding the position you have available."

"Come into my office. Sit down, tell me about yourself," Mr. Stedman said, while thinking with satisfaction that one can still get good help if one knows how to advertise properly.

"I thought it only fair that I come and tell you that I don't qualify for the position you are offering," the young man replied.

He got up and walked out.

All Mr. Stedman got from that brief interview was an oversized headache.

A happy saleslady is an inspiration to any business. Happiness is contagious. You must feel happy in your work before you can feel it in everyday life, but, in order to be happy in your work you must give it all, rather than watch the clock ticking away, waiting painfully for closing time.

Both characters are happy at the end of a day, but for different reasons. The aggressive are happy because of their accomplishments; the indifferent are happy that the boring day has finally come to an end.

Looking at such salesladies one begins to feel sorry for them;

perhaps they are ill. Their sour, painful expressions seem to indicate pain, anger, hostility, or perhaps all three, or they might consider themselves martyrs because they have to work for a living. Who knows the reason behind their pathetic appearance? But one cannot be too demanding.

One has to be a diplomat in order to deal with sales help who are subject to bruising very easily. One must handle them as carefully as fragile china in order to maintain a pleasant atmosphere and a high morale; otherwise you are fighting a losing battle.

Retail business in general, and ladies wear in particular, is dependent upon discussion. The more frequently you discuss business and its intricate daily complexities with your staff, the more business you will do.

Answering your telephone in a tone that expresses interest, that you are pleased that the person called, will add to your prestige and success.

Did you ever think how pleasant a telephone operator sounds? Her tone of voice makes you feel welcome. It's apparently important to the telephone company—think what it can do for you.

Upon greeting a customer don't grin. Smile sincerely, which will say, "I am glad to see you."

I would rather have a salesgirl who has little or no experience if she has a lovely genuine smile, than a thoroughly experienced saleslady who forgot how to smile for some years, provided, of course, the inexperienced girl will accept training and direction and adapt herself to be an asset to a business rather than a liability.

You must remember that your sales help are your "bees." They are responsible for your success or failure to a large degree. They produce the honey. "Don't kick over the beehive," says Dale Carnegie.

Some employers drive and criticize their employees without diplomacy and without direction. Words of encouragement are alien to them, while those who are more understanding practice the art of cooperation. As a result they inspire loyalty, enthusiasm, and a spirit of teamwork. Such employers enjoy better profits, and, most important, more happiness during business hours and at home.

There should be a law against overdomineering employers, the so-called nagging overlords.

Never think or try to impress others that you know it all. If you in fact believe that, no one will try to correct your errors; it would only lead to an argument. Moreover, if you resist criticism or improvement in your thinking or behavior, you are not likely ever to know more than you do now, which is very little.

The most precious gift one can have is the gift of human values. People are forever in search of something that will make them feel important, and policemen are no exception, as the following story shows.

My retail business made it necessary for me to drive to Spadina Avenue each day, or at least three times a week. I was driving down a traffic-free street one day when I was stopped by a policeman who claimed that I was exceeding the speed limit.

"But, officer," I argued, "this 1938 Chevy couldn't possibly exceed the speed limit. The best I can do is thirty miles per hour."

"Well," he continued, frozen-faced, apparently indignant at my disagreement, "I clocked you at thirty-five miles per hour."

"But how is this possible?" I argued. "Unless a dozen devils were pushing the car! Here, take the wheel," I offered, "and see for yourself. It's not the $2 ticket that I am arguing about; it's the principle."

I failed to persuade him to let me go and forget about it. He was determined to show his authority and gave me a ticket with a dialogue, reprimanding me for driving too fast.

"I didn't think this car could do thirty-five miles per hour," I said, while reaching for the ticket out the window.

"You didn't think! The law doesn't give a darn about what you think; you might have killed someone!"

"How could I have done that? There is no one on the street, and, besides, I still insist that I wasn't doing more than twenty-five miles."

"You keep on insisting and I'll take you down to police headquarters," he warned me. "Drive off while you can, or you'll have to tell it to the judge!"

I then decided to be on the defensive should I be confronted by a policeman again.

Some months later I was driving down Bathurst Street one Sunday morning, only to see a policeman some distance ahead of me waving me over to stop. I knew I was in for it, so I didn't wait until the policeman started talking, I beat him to it.

"Officer, you have caught me red-handed; I am guilty. I have no alibis, I was exceeding the speed limit. I know you'll give me a ticket."

"Well," the policeman said softly, "I know it's tempting to

drive a bit faster when there is no traffic, especially on a nice quiet Sunday morning."

"Sure, you are right," I said. "But I know it's against the law. I might have hit someone."

He looked at me in disbelief.

"I think you are taking this a bit too seriously," he said. "However, I expect you to be more careful."

The policeman also wanted a feeling of importance, which I lavished upon him when I began to condemn myself before he had a chance of doing it.

But had I tried to defend myself as I had done on the previous occasion, he would have given me a ticket.

Did anyone ever win an argument with a policeman?

Nobody likes to be ordered. While we are on the subject, let us briefly analyze how to handle staff and how to get the most out of them.

If you suggest rather than order certain things to be done in certain ways, you'll without doubt meet with enthusiastic approval. Discuss with your staff how to improve business, techniques of selling, promotions, or other matters relevant to your operation. You lose nothing by asking opinions, they may even be instrumental in suggesting an idea you never thought of.

That will create a feeling of importance in your staff, it will lead to cooperation and a desire to accomplish, rather than have a silent cold war exist and grow. Just because you are the employer doesn't necessarily mean that you know it all.

Eliminate all obnoxious parades of superiority and criticism. "The wrongdoer always blames everybody but himself," observed Dale Carnegie.

If you wish to change someone or improve one's performance in daily living, why don't you start with yourself? "When a man's fight begins with himself," said Browning, "he is worth something."

When one considers himself to be right at all times, he is definitely wrong most of the time. "Don't complain about the snow on your neighbor's roof," said Confucius, "when your own doorstep is unclean."

We must understand the people we associate with, who should be motivated by vanity to material and spiritual gains. There is only one way to get one to do things your way, and that is by making him *want* to do it. Nothing can be accomplished by force, only by reason and understanding.

Professor John Dewey, America's great philosopher, says, "The deepest urge in human nature is the desire to be important." People put forth greater effort under a spirit of approval than under a spirit of force or criticism. Appreciation remains in one's memory, nurturing confidence, while flattery which is construed as appreciation is false praise. William James said, "The deepest principle in human nature is the craving to be appreciated."

It is my opinion that in order to feel self-importance you must make others feel important first.

It was this desire that kept me striving for monetary success and to achieve some measure of recognition. Having been deprived of a formal education because of the era and the dark part of Eastern Europe where I was born, it has been a very difficult uphill struggle, but I never ceased trying; adversity never throttled my mind. I do confess, however, that I resorted to a variety of schemes, hoping to invite sympathy, which I interpreted as "importance."

I remember the schemes I used when I was a fatherless seven-year-old. I actually got very ill on many occasions when my brother-in-law insisted that I leave so there would be one less mouth to feed. I was seeking pity rather than be thrown out of the house, only to wander aimlessly in neighboring villages. His form of persecution toward me was less intense when I was ill. He would let me stay home until I was feeling better, when the battle for survival resumed all over again.

15

The Dignity of Work

I joined the Furriers Union in 1933, hoping to get a job as a trainee in a fur factory. It was in the middle of November, when the Police Department of Manitoba placed orders for buffalo coats and hats for their respective police forces who would not have survived the cruel forty-to-fifty-degrees-below-zero temperatures without them. I was a "blocker"; the definition of the word is quite simple, but the work is very hard and exhausting. You unfold a few buffalo skins and put them in a deep galvanized bucket filled with water mixed with some powerful solution, in order to make the skins softer, so that one can stretch them as much as possible, with difficulty of course.

This procedure was usually done before closing time, so that the skins should soak overnight. You took one skin at a time, spread it on a very large board, and then the struggle began. The board had a white chalk mark, indicating how far the skin was to be stretched. Rarely was I so lucky as to have a skin large enough to come even close to the mark. They were all far too small, as if by design rather than by coincidence. My tools consisted of one pair of "pinchers," which were made in the shape of pliers; only the handles were longer. The front end was flat, with ridges on the inside, so that I could tighten my grip on the skin, and pull with all my strength to reach the designated mark. This of course was done after one side was nailed down solidly; from then on it was *pull*, place a rusty nail at the edge of the skin and *pull*, hit a nail with the pinchers while holding the tightly stretched skin with an elbow and forearm, so as not to let it slip away from the chalk line. It was an all-day struggle, week after week, using the same nails each time; they had become rusty and subsequently carved painful ridges into my fingers, ridges so deep that bare bone was visible. The pain was unbearable, but it had to be endured: after all, to earn $3 for a fifty-hour week was quite an achievement.

To write one's autobiography is also most difficult. It has a certain purpose other than just describing experiences, thus giving the impression that the motives may be attributed to one's subjective feelings. It is an extension of feelings and memories.

My sore fingers reminded me of the horses on the farm. They had open festering sores where the harness collar was placed each morning. Despite the obvious pain, they pulled the plow without complaint. Nevertheless they were whipped by the farmer without mercy. My sore, bleeding fingers reminded me of those poor animals each time a rusty nail touched my bare bone.

I was overwhelmed with happiness each morning walking to work. I would dash into hallways to prevent my face from freezing, while clutching a sardine sandwich in my pocket even though I prayed silently that I would lose my job in some miraculous, indirect way. God must have heard my prayers, for within about three months the union leader called a strike, demanding a $2 weekly raise for all employees. I was really proud and felt important when I was called upon to take my turn in picketing the factory. My importance was of very short duration, however. I received a letter that I had been replaced, and therefore my services were no longer required.

That episode in my life happened about forty-five years ago.

Fortunately, the new generation has been spared such horrible, humiliating times. It is incomprehensible to them: they never had to face the harsh realities of such a life, which wrecked all the dreamboats, when one was considered a very important personality if one had a job that paid $5 a week. Times have changed, and I am very happy they have, even though, in my opinion, they have changed too much. Today, help is treated with the highest respect, with salaries to match, if one is to survive in business. Old-fashioned help is almost nonexistent, the sense of pride in accomplishment is a worthless value of the past, in the opinion of modern society.

I am not looking for sympathy, and I am not trying to create an impression that I am envious. I am merely expressing my disagreement with the injustice of the present. Unemployment and other government benefits are bordering on the ridiculous. They are far too generous and too easy to obtain, while hundreds, perhaps thousands of unfilled jobs are waiting to be filled. Billions are paid out indiscriminately each year to those who claim that the world owes them a living. Pride and the sense of values have deteriorated in the last decade, making it difficult, if not impossible, to exist in business because of lack of help, while newspapers are filled with "Help Wanted" advertisements.

Our economists and benevolent social leaders are far too generous, thus creating unemployment, which has become the lifestyle of this generation. Those who have retained some dignity and self-respect by working for a living are being overpaid, considering the hours and their productivity. One has no choice, however, but to swim with the stream of time. If you resist, you are inviting the very popular and socially acceptable "walk out" or "call in sick" and ultimately a "strike," all of which in my opinion are outdated, like the horse and buggy as a means of transportation.

I am in complete sympathy and in full agreement that a worker must have some protection against exploitation, but strikes should be replaced by impartial arbitration, without having services disrupted. This would be a modern way of settling grievances or disputes, without subjecting the country to chaos and blackmail.

Labor unions should have democratic-minded leaders with a spirit of cooperation, rather than be militant and provocative. Desired results can be achieved more easily by reasoning rather than by demanding. You cannot expect satisfactory results by using malice or harsh insulting dialogues. Some union leaders are intoxicated by their superiority, thus acting as if they were trying to overcome their complex.

If good is implanted in you it will triumph without the need to think of morality, for good grows out of ethical morals.

There is a streak of dishonesty and insincerity in most of us. I am not surprised, therefore, by the endless strikes this country has experienced in the last few years; everyone is trying to catch up with parity. It is like a dog chasing his tail, in vain most of the time.

But it is a permissive society; almost everything is justifiable. Normal human decency and fair play have eroded, and we are engulfed by self-created uncontrollable fires of inflation, and dignity has burnt to a crisp. The winds of greed continually blow the ashes into our eyes, obscuring our vision of reason and understanding, refanning the flames, consuming the very values that carry self-respect, morals, and compassion in a normal productive society. Indiscriminate generosity has robbed the independence and dignity of many, thus creating more employable unemployed.

Did you ever stop and think of what happens to those who enjoy generosity to the point of demoralization? They drift around aimlessly, pretending that they are seeking "suitable" employment; the word *suitable* is more than self-explanatory. They were given the opportunity to lose their self-respect, which was priceless at one time. Working for a living is now considered a "hobby." It is certainly not a necessity, when one takes into consideration the expense and effort it takes to go to work, as opposed to benefits one can obtain so easily by remaining unemployed.

I do not mean to be critical; I am merely stating a fact. I do trust, however, that governments will eventually realize the cruel generosity they have pursued for some time now, and I hope they will begin the long journey back to the realities and the responsibilities of life, bringing back the values of independence and a sound-minded philosophy, which was so cruelly taken away from a once healthy economy and a proud society.

Bigots are worried. Racist propagandists claim that immigrants take jobs away from native Canadians. Show me one specific example of such a case. In most cases immigrants take jobs that have been turned down by Canadians. I admire their desire to work for a living, rather than live off the fat of the land.

It is not business or labor that has created inflation and unemployment. It is the government, which is unduly involved in the economy and free enterprise we enjoyed for many decades. The government saps the very fiber of our society, thus undermining our free and competitive world trade.

I blame the leadership of our country, which lacks sound economic experience to manage affairs correctly. Such management must be sincere and capable. Experienced, successful businessmen can do the job, not politicians, whose aims are "politics" and nothing more.

I have had some correspondence with men in Ottawa during recent election campaigns. They omit commitments, but feed you with promises that vanish into thin air just as soon as the elections are over. Candidates when campaigning become very congenial and eagerly responsive to questions put to them. They have a way of writing a lot and saying very little on issues relevant to the country's economy.

I am not associated with any political party, but as a Canadian I am curious to know their views and to express my own at the same time. I am, however, fortunate in a way, because I am no longer subjected to seeking help. I am in no need of "hobby" employees. I am self-sufficient.

We thought at one time that our government was very generous to us. It allowed us to dig small holes for ourselves, in which we found great comfort. We realize now that the holes have become deep ditches from which we must extricate ourselves if we are to become flexible again and adjust to a more constructive life. It would be a simple adjustment if our politicians would stop smothering us with their indiscriminate attention, which is destructive rather than constructive, and permit us to regain our self-respect by subsidies rather than by direct pay for not working.

Inflation is not a contagious disease. If business is handled properly it is possible to get a good day's work for a day's pay, so that we don't price ourselves out of the world market. If governments would only practice what they preach—"restraint"—our country would make an economic recovery in a very short period of time.

16

Memories and Meditation

Spadina Avenue. This is the name given to the Canadian garment industry. It doesn't imply that the entire garment industry is located on the one avenue. It is only a figure of speech like Seventh Avenue in New York. The industry embraces many other streets and avenues; it includes Adelaide Street, King Street, Richmond Street, Camden Street, Peter Street, Queen and Dundas Streets. It is even located on the Lakeshore, where Dylex has its headquarters. Dylex, as is known now, originated on Spadina Avenue by Poslun Brothers, who were manufacturing ladies' coats and suits under the name of "Superior Cloak" perhaps half a century ago, or more. But the general term Spadina Avenue, regardless of the street one is going to, is "The Boulevard of Broken Dreams." Some, however, succeeded in their endeavors, while others failed. This of course applies to those who are directly involved and dependent on the clothing industry for their livelihood. I have seen them come and go, as I plodded the streets for more than thirty years.

The Toronto garment industry is, by and large, concentrated in one area, unlike Montreal, where it is scattered in many directions and outlying areas. The New York industry is situated similarly to that of Toronto, only very much larger of course. The major part begins on Seventh Avenue at Twenty-third Street, reaching north past Forty-second Street, and to Sixth Avenue and across Lexington Avenue. The skyscrapers are bursting with thousands of ashen-gray-faced, sweaty members of humanity, who waste away most of their lives in the confines of brick, stone, mortar, and asphalt jungle. The people working there have very little time for sleep. Going and coming from work consumes most of their time outside the factories to get a respite from the rat race. Just existing on a day-to-day basis is difficult. Some sleepy delirium is possible in the cockroach-infested tenement houses, if one doesn't live near an elevated train uptown, which shakes the very ground each time it flashes by every few minutes, the wheels screeching desperately as it disappears around a bend.

I rode on those trains many times. They worm their way between buildings, so close you can practically touch them. I also lived in a room of such a building for a few weeks. Each time a train flashed by I was blinded by the brightly lit windows of the train, with the sudden burst of light and sparks blazing by my shabby small room. When I heard the dishes rattling in the kitchen, and the pull-chain light in the ceiling began to sway and the walls began to tremble, I knew that the train was about to flash by. Perhaps the trembling of the walls was no more than a figment of my imagination. They have absorbed years of such punishment and somehow remained standing, although wide cracks have opened in the ceilings and the walls from the never-ending tremor, and will ultimately crumble to the ground in a heap.

If one is to survive the rat race and sleepless nights of a large noisy city like New York, one must adjust one's emotions and accept suffering as a part of life. Spinoza said, "Emotion which is suffering ceases to be suffering as soon as we form a clear and precise picture of it." Dr. Victor Frankl said, "He who has a 'Why' to live for, can bear any 'How.'"

Life at best becomes a minute-to-minute existence. I have been involved in that kind of life for more than two and a half years. It left a feeling of compassion within me for those poor victims of circumstances, and there was no Moses to liberate them. That elusive rainbow—the pot of gold—they are in the habit of hoping to hit it big one day; and this is the only reason for their endurance, until the rainbow is swallowed up in the dark of night. But they know that "tomorrow is another day."

To find a meaning in life one has to attain freedom of the spirit, in which each man alone is master of his fate and molds his life according to his own will to find contentment. Each individual holds the key to implementing such universal harmony when his life will rule the heart. When harmony reigns between mind and heart, physical and spiritual contentment become possible, but in the daily frustrations and disappointments that is apparently impossible.

I had walked the streets of New York one day in search of a job, when I came upon a building that had a sign hanging on the door of the main entrance, "Boy Wanted, on the twenty-third floor." This was on Twenty-seventh Street and Seventh Avenue. I tucked the sign under my arm, as I had been instructed to do by experienced job hunters. "Take the sign with you when you are applying for a job!" they told me. "Otherwise another job seeker may come along and apply for the same position, thus minimizing your chance of getting it."

That particular factory was making and supplying dress manufacturers with trimmings of all sorts. I was hired and placed in front of a machine that had the appearance of a "robot." Changes of intricate cutting forms created various designs of trimmings as required. I was facing a silent monster with two long, outstretched handles, as if frozen by time. However, when I stepped on a pedal, which looked like an accelerator in a car, the handles began to move up and down as if they were ready to attack me.

Being adventurous by nature, I couldn't possibly accept that sort of life, stand on the same spot, doing the very same thing day after day. Every hour seemed like eternity, while I waited each day for the minute of liberation which came with the ear-piercing sharp whistle at 6 p.m. when all machines were suddenly turned off. The overwhelming silence was frightening. People who operated the machines all day were turned into ghosts by the deafening hush, and mechanically proceeded to leave the factory, while punching the time clock, tick-tick-tick. . . . I was then instructed to deliver some of the trimmings I had made that day to certain dress factories, while thousands upon thousands of living corpses were tumbling out of buildings like potatoes out of a dump truck, disappearing into tunnels leading to the subways.

If you were ever to be caught on Seventh Avenue at that time of madness, you would readily understand that I do not exaggerate when I tell you that whenever I took one step forward, I was carried ten steps backward by the mass of humanity emerging from skyscrapers all at the same time. It is unbelievable and of course indescribable. I was told later that I was to walk on the opposite side of the street going north. Even though I was desperately in need of a job, I quit within a few days.

In 1953 I went on a buying trip to New York, and stood in the same chaotic block where I had been pushed around almost a lifetime ago when I had lived in confusion, but survived. Sentimentality forced me to walk some of the streets on the Lower East Side. I walked down Delancey Street and had lunch at Ratner's Restaurant, where I had worked the night shift for a few months many years before and where I had looked pleadingly to the waiters for a tip at the end of each week. The owner was a distant relative of mine and therefore hired me. I filled glasses with fresh drinking water, carried dishes, cleaned tables, and scrubbed the floors after midnight when traffic was at a minimum. I did not get paid. I relied entirely on the tips that the waiters might or might not remember to give me at the end of the week. This time I was the customer, sitting proudly at a table, which was covered with a snow-white table cloth. I was being served by another pathetic-looking boy, who looked exactly as I had. The deep tray he carried, in fact, must have been the same tray I had used.

Later in the day I browsed around Second Avenue, where Jewish theaters flourished many years ago. Then I had not had the price of fifty cents for a ticket. Most of the time I would linger near the entrance to hear a phrase of the dialogue or a few words of a song by Pinchus Levanda, Morris Schwartz, or Molly Picon as people were coming in and out of the theater. The streets I remembered appeared the same, although some old tenements were being bulldozed into high-rise projects. Delancey Street, Rivington, Houston Streets—I remembered the trap doors in the sidewalks leading into basement apartments that were choked in damp deathly silence, and the smell of decay mixed with a foul air outside, activated by a breeze that came from the direction of the murky East River.

Then I browsed around Orchard and Norfolk Streets, which I remembered clearly. I used to buy my socks there, two pairs for a nickel. It was an area mixed with gild, garbage, and fantasy. It was an area where nightmares originated. It was an area of the foul smell of fish on pushcarts, barrels of herring, salami hanging outside and swaying in the smelly breeze. There was also the smell of Italian, Polish, Greek, and Mexican dishes, but in limited varieties. Signs above store entrances were not necessary; smells and vapor told the story. Bargaining over pennies was never ending; you were forever reluctant to say yes, constantly saying no, even if you got your way. You were accustomed to saying no because by the time some mutual understanding was reached, you didn't know what you were arguing about—perhaps an agreement that involved five pounds of potatoes, or a bundle of beets. I have heard people insult each other; "You are a faker, since you called me a faker, which I am not. I can call you a 'pisher,' that you are—for sure! Tell me I am wrong! You are not wrong. When

I feel like 'pishing' I 'pish,' but you fake all the time." A few by-standers would usually move in and separate the two "tycoons."

The horses were more interesting than the people: they wore straw hats and their long ears protruded through the openings; they also wore bells around their necks to attract the attention of the many bargain hunters. It was another New York Stock Exchange, where, instead of stocks, cabbage, potatoes, even borscht, were traded and sold. It was a neighborhood where fire escapes had many uses. The steel platforms were used for sleeping during hot humid summer nights, when the roaches came out in full force and took over the house. During the day laundry was spread out on the platform and on the steel fence around it, drying under the hot, merciless sun. In the winter, perishable food was kept there to save twenty cents on weekly expense for ice. All of that plus an effective Yiddish tradition made reality a sort of mystic existence, the kind one could feel forever present.

Half a lifetime later I wandered through those streets again, feeling lonely and disappointed. The magic, the drama, the excitement, the hypnotic aromas, the bargains, the pushcarts, the children with their runny noses, the dogs caught up in all the excitement had disappeared, in a place where comedy and tragedy shook hands and united in eternal embrace. The ghettos of Europe had made the Lower East Side what it had been, with a sense of belonging and not quite belonging. It was ghettoized by natural design.

The area contained everybody's poverty including its own, and Yiddish humor thrived and expanded there, while cursing and blessing in Yiddish and Hebrew contributed great pleasure to the giver but frustration and half-hearted fright to the receiver. I remember that even stores on Delancey Street projected an exotic and oriental secrecy and the complex, unbearable tunes of Greek music. The stores sold samovars, candlesticks, Sabbath bread, everything that was required for the traditions and cultures of Judaism.

I remember a Hungarian Jewish restaurant on the third floor of a tenement house in Williamsburg. It was a few feet away from the elevated trains that operated day and night. My cousin and I had supper there on a Friday night. We had gefilte fish with horseradish, after we each had a glass of wine in honor of the Sabbath. I don't remember the special occasion that warranted such extravagance, but I do remember the strong horseradish that rendered me speechless for some time. All I could do was think of God for a while. Even though my cousin was an agnostic, he nevertheless liked horseradish, as most Jews do.

Thousands of Jews have apparently left those streets for newer areas—Queens, Forest Hills, where one of my cousins had moved. He lived on Clinton Street prior to the time he became afflicted with the disease of affluence. Second Avenue, which had bloomed with Jewish theaters, cafes, and intellectuals was dead; it gave way to other people, other cultures and other languages.

I walked the Williamsburg Bridge as I had many years ago in order to save two cents' fare from Delancey Street to Williamsburg. I looked down at the murky river below, lying there motionless, unless disturbed by a passing boat. I walked by the house on Clymar Street, where I had stayed for a few weeks when I first came to New York. I also looked up to the seventh floor of a tenement building where I boarded for a few weeks, but moved because I couldn't do a day's work after climbing seven flights of stairs several times daily.

I remembered indelibly the day I climbed up to the seventh floor to see the room, which was full of cockroaches. "Will you fumigate the room before I move in?" I asked. "Boychick," said the lady, "If you are afraid of cockroaches my husband and I will take turns guarding you while you sleep." Despite the cockroaches I rented the room, because it was within walking distance of my job. No one could escape the roaches, which seemed to own and occupy most of the tenements. When they had fully explored one building they moved to another.

My sentimental tour ended with a visit to the paper and twine wholesale where I had obtained my first job only a few days after my arrival in New York. It was on Lee Avenue only a couple of blocks from the corner police station. It was called "Paper and Twine" but in actual fact the inventory consisted of thousands of household items—mops, brushes of all sorts, bolts, screws, paper products, dishes, etc. My employer's name was Mr. Wilhelm, may he rest in peace. He was very religious and very kind. We were open four and a half days a week. Friday at twelve noon the doors were locked, to reopen Monday morning.

To me the Sabbath was the island of peace. I withdrew from the modern world for a day to enjoy some spiritual fulfillment. I hung on to a thread of tradition, which has much to offer when one is in doubt as to one's own identity. You try to decide what you

want to do with your life. You are a fool if you think you are helpless; your destiny can be directed somewhat by your own will and
determination in this free society full of opportunity. All you
need is willpower.

I stood in front of that building, which had become a slaughter-
house, or a wholesale butcher. (I am not sure, because it was
closed at the time.) Mr. Wilhelm was a kind man who was open
to the neighborhood retail trade for two weeks before Passover,
when I was put in charge of the sales during evening hours. That
too had vanished. The Jewish culture and traditions that thrived
there at one time are dead, gone, like everything else that carried
a promise of eternity. Everything had disappeared. A feeling of
pride and sadness confused my emotions. I wondered what had
happened to all the people I remembered, who are probably
battling their way through life to this day, and for the same reason:
"Survival." They are, however, impeded, arrested by circumstances,
like a herd of cattle directed into a corral in preparation for whatever fate has been chosen for them. I saved myself from that fate
somehow, only to be trapped by another. I dropped out of one
thing, only to drop into another. I don't think there is such a thing
as a "dropout."

But I never succeeded in erasing my village from my heart. My
heart shall draw in another direction by now, I thought, and in
my solitude other more recent or anticipated images shall appear,
even though I'll never be freed from eternal sorrow. I remember
how difficult it was to be poor and to be a Jew in an anti-Semitic,
illiterate village among peasants and ignorance. Some of us were
fortunate enough to live and wait until the clouds dispersed and
some sunshine—even though briefly—warmed our frozen hearts
and spirits, before darkness enveloped our lives again.

Ours was a simple innocent world, religious, honorable—large
enough to fit into our village and for everyone to share, I believed,
because the older pious Jews of our community and my mother
said so. We lived in constant fear most of the time. The village
was full of uncles, aunts, cousins, but also hoodlums from adjoining
villages, who were ready to help terrorize the Jewish communities
at a moment's notice. They were related by a common bond in their
activities, to terrorize the Jewish communities.

If by Jew is meant a person with love and humanism, such
people should pride themselves, regardless of their nationality or
religion. If the world is not to march on to destruction, we must

use our ability to think, both in religion and ethics, which are part and parcel of humanism. The Christian world will have to reform and arrive at a true gospel—that of love. Moral reactions are the result of the unselfish human urge to sympathize with, and identify with, all men.

I believe that there is a God, but I am not so sure if there is a personal God, who intervenes in the actions of nations and is responsible for the fate of the individual, and whether prayers are heard, or are an antidote for the pain of the soul. I have my own views on the subject. I don't think that God is responsible for all the wickedness and murders in the world. I am not sure that everything happens because of God's will. I do believe, however, that there comes a time when wicked nations topple. We don't know why, but we know that they suffer the consequences sooner or later; perhaps it is a delayed reaction to God's power.

To think about God and nature must end in the irrational, for there are no answers to questions that cannot be specified or understood. Accept the incomprehensible, heaven, nature, universe, God, whatever it is; it must exist in the hidden secrets of the galaxies. To my way of thinking the purpose of praying is to make it easier to bear one's lot by pouring out all frustrations. Prayer is equal to speaking to a prophet or a sage of old, who were held in very high esteem. They were saintly men who possessed words of wisdom and consolation. Serenity when achieved definitely soothes the soul and uplifts your spirit.

> *I remember, I remember,*
> *The house where I was born,*
> *The little window where the sun*
> *Came creeping in at morn.*
> *It never came a wink too soon,*
> *Nor brought too long a day,*
> *But now, I often wish the night*
> *Had borne my breath away.*
>
> —THOMAS HOOD

For some inexplicable reason I enjoy reflecting on an era that is no more, and yet it is as real and alive in my mind as if it still existed. When I think of my childhood and my village nestled innocently at the very bottom of ominous mountains, I relive my childhood years all over again within a few minutes. My mind embraces the entire area, which was quite limited and very confining to me. I visualized the glistening, almost arrogant narrow, shallow creek that forever purled brilliantly under the hot Carpathian summer sun. I sat there for hours, watching in fascination thousands of tiny minnows busily gliding around between and under dark grey pebbles. I was thinking, yearning to know whether there is perhaps more world on the other side of the mountains. If so, I wondered, what kind of God did they have there? Surely there is a God! Maybe only wind, birds, and flowers. Maybe there is a creek too, just like ours, although I doubted it. To my mind our creek was the nicest.

I asked my mother many questions that tormented my mind, including questions about God, mountains, and valleys. "Little fool," she would answer, "God is everywhere."

"But I bet you no one has the kind of God we have in Rypiana," I answered with satisfaction, and I thought about what, if anything, was on the other side of those mountains and dark silent forests, and hoped to find out some day.

Oh! There is Marysha, my little Ukrainian friend. She knows that I am not feeling well today; she is coming toward me carrying some milk in a wooden dish to ease my hunger pangs. She likes me, I know; she is feeling sorry for me, even though her parents are anti-Semites. Ask them why. They don't know! They are just living by a tradition passed on to them by generations. Marysha will most likely change too when she gets older, but she is a good-natured child for the time being. Childish innocence is pure and painful. I know, because I can feel it.

There were many reasons for my unhappy state of mind. I was pining for a bit of love and affection. I was fatherless and didn't dare to think of ever being reunited with my father. I don't remember ever being, or acting, like a child of my age. We were poor, I knew that. I felt it deeply, but not to the point of being envious of others who were more fortunate. We were forever hungry but indifferent to our adversity; we accepted it without sensitivity. We didn't go to school, because there was no school. We weren't taken to a doctor when ill, because there was no doctor for many miles around and no transportation, except a mud road winding tightly against the mountain like a mud-covered snake. When illness struck one had two alternatives: either to die, or to get well.

We never went to a dentist because we didn't have one. If someone had a bad toothache, the tooth was pulled out with a pair of pliers. I was twenty-five when I saw a dentist, in Winnipeg, for the very first time in my life.

I don't remember ever seeing actual money until 1918, when the warring armies retreated and some communications were restored between the United States and Poland. My mother showed me an American five-dollar bill she had received from my father. In fact, I was not even impressed with it, because I didn't have the vaguest idea what the piece of green paper represented. I do remember, however, the overpowering pleasant fragrance it had, like a dew-covered flower in early morning.

I don't remember ever eating a meal, and yet, I never felt hungry, only a sickening sensation in my stomach, which got better after I had eaten a few carrots or apples stolen from a neighbor's garden. I was a scrawny Jewish kid, dressed in rags, made fun of by Ukrainian kids, but I didn't feel slighted. That was the way of life. I felt unwanted, insecure, inadequate, discriminated against. I was treated and suffered like an adult, forced to live away from home most of the time. How else can it be, I often thought. It seems that I was born into this conspiracy to suffer in humiliation. When I got married I was fortunate to have an understanding partner with whom to share my life, who helped me find myself to some extent, and gradually diminished my inferiority complex, which had robbed me of courage and peace of mind.

I often wonder what gives memories their power to evoke emotion. Perhaps it is their completeness and fulfillment, while it is easy to understand why complete joy leaves us strengthened. It fails to give us a reason for suffering, but anything that is worth suffering for is also worth loving. "Love believes all things, hopes all things, love never fails," said Werner Pelz. My feeling of inadequacy and insecurity began to give way to determination, and I hoped to become a *mensch* (a man).

I was partially successful in reaching the rim of the limelight, which inspired me to strive for some limited achievement and aided me in readjusting, to some extent, the warped perspective in which I had existed. Had I resisted adapting myself to some reality, I would have become an incurable victim of depression and failure. I would most likely have assumed an attitude of rejection, or become an atheist, if in fact such a thing is possible.

I remember an anecdote about just such an individual. Two friends were engaged in a heated but friendly discussion as to which synagogue was more worthy of support. Not being able to agree with one another they turned to a third friend, who had stood by silently listening to the conversation, and asked him which one of them was right. In reply, he raised his hands toward heaven and exclaimed. "Don't ask me, I am an atheist, thank God, but in my opinion one is as nondeserving as the other."

I would have lost the very values my religious mother implanted in me, which I attempted to live by. As Dr. Alfred Adler has said, "Very few individuals are able to change the pattern of their childhood; the childhood experiences remain part of the individual." Only an overwhelming desire can bring about a gradual significant change.

A change of attitude does not necessarily change one's behavior. Even though we try to alter our pattern when we mature, the foundation remains the same. Unless we strive to acquire a better understanding and a riper development, the style of life will not change, only the attitude toward it, simply because the mistakes have become irreversible. Only accumulated experiences can check their progress to some degree, provided the behavior patterns have also been modified.

Incredible as it may sound, however, my attitude toward life has made some progress in acquiring a better understanding of my own existence. I think that Dr. Adler explains very effectively how one can achieve a harmonious adjustment to life if one really tries. Mistakes in business are costly, but can be corrected and perhaps compensated for at some later date, but mistakes in the conduct of life itself cannot be reversed.

There were times when I couldn't forget the faces that blotted out my world so effectively many years ago. I made a halfhearted effort occasionally to reorganize my thinking and my feelings, but retreated into my inner self each time. Nothing inspired me, and I had no desire to understand or justify my actions. My mind played tricks on me, which were also beyond my understanding. Only the impossible mattered, nothing else. Only the vision seemed real; everything else was covered in deep silent darkness. I was completely absorbed in the past; the present had no meaning, and the future held no terror, only a vague promise, and yet everything seemed so simpleminded.

Whenever I listen to a Rabbi delivering a sermon, I realize the man I was meant to be, I would enjoy being, which I'll never be. I would enjoy being absorbed in an invisible kingdom; it would give me much spiritual fulfillment. However, it just wasn't meant to be; I had always known. I have been taught to believe that the things that are impossible with men are possible with God. I had also known, although dimly at times but profoundly, that it has been proven through history many times over that spiritual needs are never ending. Is it a figment of my imagination to believe in such unreal phenomena? Who am I to question the incomprehensible?

I do know for sure, however, and I have thought about it many times, that nothing but faith helped me from being crushed under cruel reality. I constantly visualized my relatives, my family and friends as faceless skeletons huddled in a dark corner, or staring into the muzzles of the guns at the precise moment of destruction. Memories stir within me. I identify myself with them; a feeling of guilt has carved into my conscience. Why was I the one to be spared? Why was I not subjected to crawling as others have been and freed from the impossible expectations, but to live on and carry monuments in my heart? I did not see or hear their last gasps of breath or see their fear, but if one wishes to continue living one must adjust the thinking mechanism to the present by remembering some of the past.

However impossible it seemed at one time, revelation has gradually penetrated my brain. The bitter, cynical feeling of despair that corroded my mind for years changed by degrees. I felt the pain but was determined to accept it in order to salvage some part that still had a spark of rationality. A mystical feeling of realization combined with faith slowly crept into my mind. I began to realize that time is standing still in the deep endless universe; only we, the mortals, are passing by; only we are subject to change, nothing else, and we must strive to bring about that condition that makes the impossible possible.

17

Jewish Immigrants in Canada

One of the first Jews to set up business in Toronto was Judah J. Joseph. He was a skilled optician and jeweler, born and educated in England, who emigrated first to the United States and then in 1838 to Canada. His business was established at 56 King Street East. He was an Orthodox Jew who later became prominent in the Jewish community.

The clothing industry in Toronto started quite early. Two brothers, Goodman and Samuel Benjamin, established a clothing business under the name of Benjamin Bros. in 1835. They contracted with the government of Upper Canada to supply coats to the troops during the rebellion of 1838. They later moved to Montreal. According to a census, there were only seventy-seven Jews in Toronto in 1851. However, Jews who came over in the late 1800s and early 1900, some years prior to the First World War and immediately thereafter, were poor and hungry.

Apparently the clothing industry was the most important occupation among Jews in Czarist Russia and in Central and Eastern Europe. As a result more than one-third of the Jewish population was employed in the Canadian garment industry at that time. Canada was still a basically rural country just moving into urban development. The Jews from Eastern Europe brought their trades to this country, and actually introduced the clothing industry into Canada.

I would venture to say (although I don't possess statistical records) that seventy-five percent of the garment industry was operated by Jews at that time. Employers and employees alike were links in a chain that had its beginning one or two generations ago, among Jews who emigrated to Canada, hoping to escape the oppression and persecution they had endured in their respective countries. Coming to a new land, not knowing the language, they were not suitable for employment in non-Jewish industries; they had no alternative but to pursue a trade they knew, in order to survive. They also hired Jewish help, because of the language barrier. They became cutters, pattern makers, operators, finishers, depending on their backgrounds. Others who were not suitable for that particular industry became peddlers and business-men of sorts on a very small scale. They were like crabs in a basket helping each other to climb out.

I have had occasion to speak to some of the pioneers and also to non-Jews who couldn't take the stress and frustrations resulting from the very complex nature of that business. They gave up after a few years of hard work, unlike the Jewish people, who stuck to it tenaciously, for this was paradise compared to what they had left behind. They all had dreams brought with religious intensity from Europe, with God and Judaism packed in their baggage, and had carefully, lovingly, stored them in the lofts, waiting for the day of salvation when all those holy memories could be revived. But for the time being the real religion was in the cloaks and the geysers of steam created by a twenty- or thirty-pound iron on a soaking wet cloth.

It is therefore not surprising that Jewish immigrants were the pioneers of that vital industry. They were accustomed to hardships and frustrations, but were now free of physical violence, free of pogroms, free to observe the Sabbath according to the Torah and their traditions. It is worth noting that the second or third genera-tion still pursues the trade, on a completely different, modern basis, of course.

Time has bridged the gap between smelly basements and boil-ing hot attics to modern sophisticated conditions. The garment industry's employees now enjoy easy, good lives just like everyone else. It is a thriving dignified industry, which is prospering all over the world, getting larger and more sophisticated with each passing year. Jewish immigrants who had engaged in the industry were frustrated and hopelessly tired by endless hours of hard work. They had no alternative but to hang on to hope in the face of despair. Of course they were accustomed to living one minute at a time; that was in fact the Jewish way of life inherited from their ancestors.

Men, women, and children slaved at their machines. Pressers pushed thirty-pound irons heated by coal. Finishers and buttonhole makers worked furiously. They had to produce to earn some sort of livelihood. It was a pathetic existence, but it was a living, according to the standards of the times.

The tradition lived on despite the hardships they endured during endless weeks. They were worn-out skeletons, tired of living, but there was no alternative. During the week they were pressers, standing twelve hours a day on badly varicosed legs and in constant pain. The smelly, sweaty factories made religious Jews turn to socialism and unionism, living in the hope that they would become citizens some day and thus have the opportunity to vote for a socialist who might be more sympathetic to their needs and exercise his influence in favor of the poor, bewildered immigrants who were looking and hoping that "tomorrow will be better."

They had traversed thousands of grassy and desert years in exile, and thought of Moses in Egypt—and all the prophecies of the sages that would soon be fulfilled, and liberate them from slavery, especially in a democratic country where such miracles could probably be easily achieved. But to help it happen, one had to join a union; there is strength in numbers.

Visualize, if you can, individuals wasting their lives, divided into thousands of days, doing the very same work that they had done for months, perhaps years, sweating topless men, women, and children sweltering in unbearable heat and stifling humidity. They were engaged in what seemed a hopeless struggle for survival, working diligently in the smelly, sickening hot mist of the sweatshops, trying to earn enough to keep body and soul together.

Why did most of them gravitate to the clothing industry? I can only surmise that this was due to immigrants who came over to North America prior to the mass immigration in the nineteenth or twentieth century and found a haven in a democratic country, and who brought relatives, friends, and *Landsleit* (individuals from the same or neighboring villages or towns). The newcomers hoped to get a free meal from a friend or *Landsman* and even to be assisted in finding a job. The new arrivals were subsequently absorbed into the clothing industry. Their numbers have increased with the passing of time.

Perhaps another reason for the rapid increase of Jews into the trade was the nature of the industry and the comparatively easy access to it. All one needed by way of equipment was a sewing machine and an iron. If such equipment was financially out of reach, there were alternatives. There were some who were proud owners of a sewing machine and would take home whatever work they could get. One who had a large family was considered very fortunate. Wife and children would work all hours of the night in order to have the work completed by the following morning. Such individuals were called "contractors." They were paid on a piecework basis

As time passed, small units sprang up, producing a few garments each week. They were cramped into old, unsanitary, rat-infested basements or dimly lit attics, where dark brown roofing and rafters were exposed, adding to the unbearable heat in the summer, and paralyzing cold in the endless winters.

I remember buying coats in such places when I first started in business. We climbed a tall stepladder to reach the attic, which was in semidarkness. I once bought a few coats that I thought were black, but that turned out to be purple; gray coats turned out to be blue, but the cost was much less than market price. That was a time of despair and illness, which was called the "disease of the trade."

I also witnessed many open-air meetings when the industry became a bit more productive, and workers were engaged in the struggle to join a union. One such open-air meeting stands out vividly in my memory. It was lunch hour, and hundreds of people were milling around at the Spadina and Adelaide intersection. A truck was parked in the center of the street. A man was standing on top of it and shouting words of encouragement and provocation, into an amplifier, asking the crowd to stand up for their rights: "Join the union in order to attain higher wages and better working conditions. Let us unite; let's form one big family and fight for our survival and a better life. Let us eliminate all villains from our midst, the basements, and the attics. We want justice. We have nothing to lose, but a lot to gain." The crowd was restless; the mood was hostile; the placards they carried explained in a few red block letters their grievances and demands.

I sympathized deeply with those people. I was familiar with both sides of the parties involved. I have been there and back. Very little has changed structurally in the garment industry in Toronto. One world has almost gone. Another, more fortunate, has taken over. It enjoys much better working conditions and a better life in general. The world of basements, attics, and contractors have vanished forever. Its death is permanent; only the tombstones remain.

The following is part of a song I remember that was very

popular, especially during lunch hours, when the workers were munching on sandwiches in hallways, or outside, in summertime:

> *My name is Shayah detective;*
> *I am always ready and active.*
> *When there is a fight,*
> *I holler, "Stop! wait!*
> *I'll call a cop.*
> *Who can compare with me?*
> *I never carry a pistol;*
> *I always blow my whistle.*
> *Grocers and bakers,*
> *They all look like fakers;*
> *They can't compete with me!"*

Jews have played an important part in the economic development of Canada since early in the French regime, when Moses Hart started his fur-trading business in Three Rivers. The clothing manufacturing industry appears to have begun about the time of the mass Eastern European immigration wave to Canada following the Czarist-inspired pogroms of the 1880-81 period. Many of these refugees were from the Eastern European cities like Odessa, where they had learned trades, particularly tailoring.

William Lyon MacKenzie King, the man who was to be Canada's longest-governing Prime Minister, examined the immigrant community in Toronto for the *Toronto Mail and Empire* and wrote, in an article of September 25, 1897, that the most popular trade among the Jewish immigrants was based on the tailoring skills they had brought from the Old Country.

John McAree, in his two-part article "The Jews in Canada", in the August, 1912, issue of *MacLean's*, wrote that "garment-making is the trade of the Jews, almost exclusively. Ninety percent of the operatives in Toronto are Jews and probably 75% of the Canadian Jews who have a trade are garment makers, furriers or cap makers." His figures are somewhat exaggerated, but the point to note is that the Jews were so predominant in the industry that it appeared to be a Jewish industry.

With the arrival of the Jewish immigrants into the main urban centers of Montreal and Toronto, clothing manufacturers acquired a large supply of willing, cheap labor. Why?

For immigrants with no skills, the industry provided ideal

opportunity. Because of the division of tasks, an unskilled person could learn a trade relatively quickly and become proficient at that line of work. And because the immigrants would work for so little, the existing manufacturers, or contractors, were eager to employ them.

Dr. Louis Rosenberg, Director of Research for the Canadian Jewish Congress in the 1930s, noted in his study *Canada's Jews,* that the Jews introduced the subdivision of labor and the factory system of production into the country. The "sweatshop," symbol of the garment industry, started generally as a room in an attic, basement, or garage at home, where the whole family could work on pieces given to the main wage earner. In this way, you might also note, skills were passed from one generation to the next, and this accounts for the predominance of Jews in the industry until just recently.

The small workshop was the backbone of the developing garment trade. Keep in mind that the factories that exist today did not exist then. In the developing stages, much of the work was "farmed out" to the operatives working out of these workshops.

The workshop system had a number of attractions for Jews. Despite the long and crippling hours of work needed to make a survival wage, it offered them freedom. Most important it offered freedom to keep the Sabbath, which would have been impossible in a Gentile factory, where one worked six days, with Sunday off. This was very important to the Jews. Most of the immigrants were Orthodox or Traditionalists. It was natural, then, that new immigrants would look to their *landsmen* for employment, or go to factories where the Jewish presence had been established.

By the 1930s the industry had grown sufficiently large for the government to start keeping statistics on its development. Prior to 1931 there are no good statistics. A study done in 1939 by Louis Rosenberg gives the best information on the state of the industry in 1931: (1) Jews formed the largest occupational group engaged in the manufacturing of textile goods and clothing. (2) Of the 12,371 Jews engaged in manufacturing of wearing apparel in 1931, 1.8% (1,210) were owners and managers; the rest were wage workers. About this time the small workshops were beginning to amalgamate and consolidate into large factories owned by large joint-stock corporations. The "sweatshop" was beginning to disappear.

In his study, Dr. Rosenberg makes an interesting observation, which I think might be useful to repeat: "In entering Canadian industry, Jews have not replaced workers of other ethnic origins in established industries, but have introduced and developed new ones. Jews in Canada have been largely instrumental in establishing and developing the manufacture of men's and women's factory-made garments and knitwear."

However, everything has changed in the last thirty to thirty-five years. Very few Jewish employees have remained in the industry in the past fifteen years. Hard-working ethnic people now control the production of the garment industry. Most of the employees are Italian. Instead of hearing them sing, "My name is Shayah detective," they sing opera, beautiful arias. Women sing melancholy Italian love songs while the machines hum under their skilled fingers, and the radio constantly interferes with their sad, melodic expressions of longing for their beloved country.

The following is the story of an Italian performer who sang a very famous aria before a very large select audience. He was naturally extremely nervous, knowing how critical Italians are about singing and music in general. He sang the aria flawlessly, he thought. As he turned to make his exit from the stage, thunderous applause broke out, forcing the singer to do the same aria over again. When he finished he thought with satisfaction, they surely accepted me and apparently like my singing very much. However, this repetition was done five or six times and the performer was completely exhausted. He turned to the audience, hardly able to stand up, and said, "Ladies and gentlemen, I thank you most humbly for your unprecedented appreciation of my singing, but, please forgive me, I am not able to sing it again." A voice from the audience screamed, "You'll darn well have to keep on doing it until you learn to sing it right."

Italians are nice people; however, they are highly emotional. This is what makes them so great and loyal. A people without emotion is like a dry riverbed, barren and desolate.

Some years later I had occasion to see similar sweatshops in Miami. Being unfamiliar with the garment industry's location, I called one factory and informed the manager that I was interested in ordering a few thousand dresses. Within an hour or so I was picked up by an air-conditioned car in front of the hotel and driven to a factory. I then learned that, unlike that in other cities, the Miami garment industry was completely isolated from the rest of the world, as if it were embarrassing to have the old wooden shacks exposed to mankind. It was a slum area where underprivileged minorities worked and lived. Some shacks were held together with wire, or slabs of lumber; some were patched up with old rusted sheets of tin or cardboard. They held on tightly to each other to project identity and a message of life within. The factories, however, were erected of cheap rough lumber, one-floor structures with bare unfinished attics where machines were buzzing and steaming, producing dresses at $3.75 each.

Factories were scattered over miles of wilderness without transportation or the necessities of life. The office and showroom appeared quite comfortable because of a noisy air conditioner, which was fitted into one of the two windows. A deafening noise penetrated through the partition. "What is that constant noise that is shaking the wall?" I asked. "Oh, that's from the machines in the factory at the rear," the salesman replied. While placing my order I was led to the factory to choose fabrics and colors. When the sound-proofed door was opened, I almost passed out from the sudden heat wave that hit me. I was fascinated for a few minutes when I saw a hundred or more men and women hunched over machines, and pressers engulfed in steam.

They were protected from the scorching sun and humidity by only a thin tin roof, in unbearable Miami summer heat. There was bitter, sour, stinking sweat, the kind you can see rolling down the faces of half-nude bodies, sweat that looked like smelly, foul trickles from melting dung. There was not a fan or a window to activate some of the foul air, which hung like poisonous gas. Some were humming or whistling as if this were their last acknowledgment that they were conscious. I looked around for a washroom, only to be informed that there was none. "What do you do if someone has to use one?" I asked. "They wait until lunch time," the man replied. I gathered from our conversation that most workers were Cubans. "My God," I exclaimed, "I wouldn't order your dresses if you were to pin a $20 bill to each dress." I felt faint and sick to my stomach.

I made my exit quickly, leaned against a wall, and waited for my taxi which I had ordered prior to entering the factory. I looked around for another factory, but none was in sight. One has to take a taxi in order to reach another one, I was told.

Suddenly, as if by magic, the unbearable noise ceased. The wall I was leaning against stopped trembling. When the machines were turned off, the ear-piercing silence was unbearable. A mass of sweaty humanity poured out of the shack, sat against the walls, and silently proceeded to eat their sandwiches.

An unforgettable episode remains in my memory to this day. As I was walking toward the taxi, I picked up a $10 bill I found in the parking area. I offered it to a woman who was leaning against a wall nursing her baby. "Here, take it," I said. She looked at me intently for a while, then slowly reached out a trembling hand, hesitatingly took the $10 bill, while murmuring quietly, "*Muchos gracias.*" Her voice became louder and more courageous as I was walking toward the waiting car. She kept repeating, "Thank you," in Spanish, until I shut the door behind me. It would be futile for me to attempt some sort of description of my emotions about that painful experience.

On the way back I tried to think or partially understand such brutality, such exploitation. I thought of the word *motivation.* What does it actually mean? What does it represent? I came up with a definition, which in my opinion, is uncomplimentary to the human race. "Motivation" is lust for money, which is used as power by wicked men. It overshadows their rational thinking. They become obsessed with it to the point of exploiting vulnerable, helpless people, who are at the mercy of a tyrant, without the protection of society. "For how can a tyrant rule the free and the proud but for a tyranny in their own freedom and a shame in their own pride?" (Kahlil Gibran). Such tyrants cover themselves with glory and project philanthropy at the expense of the innocent poor. This is evil inclination under cover of hypocrisy and unfilled promises of philanthropy. I treat both with equal contempt. "Man never fastened one end of a chain around the neck of his brother that God's own hand did not fasten the other end around the neck of his oppressor" (Lamartine).

I remember my mother saying on many occasions, "It is not a shame to be poor, but it is undignified and very painful." I had tried to educate myself to cast shame and poverty aside in a worthy manner. I remember a very poor, sickly-looking Jewish man. His name was Yeshua; he was a pot mender. I watched him on occasion as he proudly walked barefoot, his long black kaftan tucked under his waistsash. He carried a ring of soft wire with which to mend broken earthen pots or pans. Peasant boys would tease him about his thin red beard and freckled face, but Yeshua walked on as calmly as a donkey. Only once in a while did he turn and give them a good-natured smile. That smile used to overwhelm me. He was the first to teach me what it meant to keep silent under profanity and persecution. It was this Yeshua with his forgiving smile who taught me how rewarding patience can be in the face of adversity. In him it produced the appearance of nobility without visible sensitivity.

I hurt emotionally when I witness acts of cruelty and injustice. I cannot bear to see the maltreatment of minorities who are helpless to defend themselves in the face of rotten overlords. Unfortunately there is often no one around to notice such acts of injustice. I know the feeling of oppression, when one must perform unbearable labor because of circumstances, and because there is no alternative. Fright turns into despair, then into courage combined with hope, and finally into indifference when everything else fails. Poverty leaves you no strength to deal with anything, but facts—facts of sadness and dejection that have to be borne each day, and the never-ending struggle for existence against all odds of corruption and obedience. It is a kind of battle in the hope of finding liberation at the end of a rainbow.

We are desperately in need of men who are noble in character, wisdom, and compassion, similar to the Right Honourable John George Diefenbaker, leader of the Canadian Progressive Conservative Party from December, 1956, to September, 1967, and Prime Minister of Canada from June, 1957 to April 1963. I cite one sentence from an interview written by Paul Hellyer about the Chief in the *Toronto Star* of September 14, 1975: "Canada's only living former Prime Minister was reluctant to single out the highlights of his career. Certainly the Canadian Bill of Rights, that elusive dream of populists and civil libertarians, is close to his heart." We can draw our own conclusions from this quotation.

Mr. Diefenbaker is noted for his humanitarian attitudes and friendly relations with ethnic groups. He is the honorary chief of a number of Indian tribes, including the Cree Indians, among whom he is called Chief Great Eagle, and the Sioux Indians, who call him Chief Walking Buffalo. He has always been considered a friend of the Jews, and his introduction to the *Canadian Jewish Reference Book and Directory* summarizes his attitudes:

> *The publication of the Jewish Directory of Canada is a worthy contribution to the records of history and will be of benefit to the present and future generations. Canadians of the Jewish faith have done much for Canada in war and*

peace for over two hundred years. The arts, sciences, professions, business, agriculture, and philanthropy owe them a great deal. They brought to Canada one of the two main streams of thought and philosophy and they have served this country well. This publication will provide a fitting memorial to the heritage and better understanding of what they have done in the building of a great Canada.

In recogntion of his attitudes he has been given many honorary degrees from universities abroad, including a fellowship at the Bar Ilan University in Israel.

I have admired Mr. Diefenbaker ever since I had the opportunity to familiarize myself with his philosophy, his understanding of human needs and aspirations, and his humanitarian and minority attitudes. As Prime Minister of Canada he has outshone past and present Prime Ministers in his compassion and wisdom, his incredibly capable leadership, and his prestigious nobility.

Those were good years. Canadians never had and most likely never will again enjoy prosperity comparable to what we had under his leadership. The country had a leader of brilliance and wisdom who made it bloom, grow, and prosper. He was outspoken and acted upon issues that needed attention, unlike other leaders, who fail to act on promises generously glorified by well-written speeches during election campaigns, but never to be implemented.

Is it really necessary to be insincere to be a politician? Apparently Mr. Diefenbaker did not think so, but you must remember that he is a Westerner.

Man's superiority over beast is supposed to be in his intellect. I believe that most people are good at heart, unless they are strongly motivated to do evil, but every effect is only relative to its cause. Socrates believed that men do evil out of ignorance. The assumption that knowledge makes people more compassionate, and that they can be educated out of selfishness and cruelty, unfortunately does not hold true. In most cases you will find that if you give an individual the opportunity to persecute another, he will do so, not so much for the sake of being cruel, but to prove his superiority, a feeling that is motivated by greed and/or by an inferiority complex. He is evil in order to protect his self-imagined prestige. He is interested purely in materialistic values, which are of the utmost importance to him, because of his limited ability to understand his insignificance in the great scheme of life.

18

Selling in
Our Modern World

I believe that many who earnestly seek employment meet with discrimination to a certain degree, like the three friends who were unemployed and pooled their resources by occupying one room while searching for work. One day, noticing an advertisement in the newspaper, "Young strong truck driver required," they drew straws to determine which one should apply for the job. The black friend won the draw, only to be met by a bigot. "We don't hire blacks here," he snarled. The next to apply was a Greek. He came back dejected; he had been turned down because he couldn't speak English. The last one was from the Maritimes. He spoke fluent English and was hired, but the bigot warned him, "We start at seven A.M. Should you not show up at the precise minute, don't even bother coming in." He came back happy and elated by the fact that he had gotten the job. "Boys," he announced, "we eat again." During the night, however, his two friends were overcome by jealousy. It took an Englishman to get the job, they thought, and decided to play a trick on him. They applied black shoe polish to his face while he was sound asleep and waited to the last few minutes before waking him. Then, they began screaming, "Get up! Run! You'll be late for work!" He got out of the room quickly and within minutes appeared at the check-in counter at work.

"Who are you and what do you want?"

"I am the man you hired yesterday! Remember? The name is Smith!"

"I told you yesterday that I don't hire blacks; must I repeat myself?"

"But I am not black!"

"Oh no? Take a look in the mirror!"

186

He walked up to the mirror, looked at himself and said with disgust, "Those two guys never do anything right. This time they woke up the wrong man!"

This episode, crazy as it is, leads to a joke by Leo Rosten. Two jokesters got friendly with a Rabbi one day, and decided to have a little fun with him. They began by offering him a drink, later on another one, and another one, until they got him so drunk that he passed out. They had decided to drive him out to a cemetery and put him down on the grass to sleep off the effects of the alcohol. They sat behind a monument, waiting patiently for the time that the Rabbi would wake up, to see what his first reaction would be. He finally woke up, looked around in amazement, and spoke loudly to himself: "If I am alive, what am I doing in the cemetery? On the other hand, if I am dead, why do I feel the need of going to the washroom? God in heaven, answer me." (This joke has been changed a bit, but basically it is the same.)

"You are not dead, you are drunk," came a voice, which sounded like an echo out of the void. (That voice came from one of the jokesters hidden behind a tombstone.)

The Rabbi later told his disciples that God had spoken to him when he had occasion to visit the cemetery.

The following true anecdote was told to be by one of my friends. A religious man, whom he knew very well, was on his way from Synagogue one Saturday, when passers-by began to bother him with remarks, as if they were prearranged. One woman remarked, "Mister, your business is open."

"What in heaven's name is she talking about? How does she know that I own a business, and furthermore, how does she know the location of my business? I have never had my business open on a Sabbath."

A few minutes later a man walked past and repeated the very same words, "Mister your business is open."

"A *Shwartz Yuhr* [a black year] on you all. Why are they suddenly picking on me? Moreover, they are all strangers, and yet they know that I own a business."

In frustration he began to run back home as quickly as possible to find out why his business was open. When he finally reached his store he was amazed to see that his business was closed. He quickly ran up the stairs and burst into his apartment to ask his wife if the store had been open during the few hours of his absence. His wife, however, beat him to it by remarking calmly,

"Zalmen, your business is open," pointing to his fly. He quickly looked down and pulled the zipper up.

He sat down and thought of the remarks made to him by strangers while he was on his way home. He then turned to his wife and said, "Now I am really curious to know something."

"What's that?" his wife asked.

"Since it's evident that my business was open, tell me, was my salesman inside, or was he hanging around outside the store?"

This brings me to the subject of unions. When I started out, unions were not as powerful as they are today. A cutter, an operator, or a finisher—just to mention a few who turn the wheels of industry—makes more in one day now than the poor souls of the thirties and forties made in a full week. Today, owners of the industry are such in name only, and of course they carry the pressures and frustrations of responsibility. The unions and the employees are in charge now. They tell you if and when they'll work and at what price.

A few years ago I once witnessed a situation proving who is really the boss. I was desperately in need of a "special" for a specific day, which I had hoped to get. After pleading with my supplier for almost an hour, he decided to prove his point. "Let's go and ask the cutter," he said. We approached him in a very humble manner and asked politely, "Would you please do us a favor and cut one coat? It's very important."

Without as much as looking up to us he said, "I am sorry. It's two o'clock and I'll be leaving in one hour. I'll do it tomorrow."

"But I have to have it cut now!" the employer pleaded.

Without another word the cutter took his apron off, handed the scissors to his boss and said, "Here! You do it; I am leaving. Don't expect me tomorrow either."

It seems to me that society is overloaded with power seekers and greedy people who control the lifestyle and the economy of our country to a great extent. I am not anti-union. On the contrary, I have cheered for underdogs all my life. I am for everything that embraces justice for all. But who is the underdog now? It's questionable as to who is running the show.

Now is a time when a supplier considers it a favor to sell you merchandise at ridiculously high prices, and uses the slogan Henry Ford used in the 1920s, when he replied to a question as to the color of a car one could order: "You can get any color so long as it's black." Pressure may be the cause that makes suppliers act in an undignified manner.

Selling is an art. If presented properly it will soothe the soul, uplift the spirit, penetrate the senses of your customers and turn them to your way of positive thinking. People resent what they don't clearly understand, and they don't have full trust in the things you are saying if you overplay or underplay your role. Sales are not made by many words. No matter how relevant they may be, they can be distracting. Sales are made by tact and logical reasoning, especially when you are dealing with ladies. A new dress, a hairdo, or a new hat can and does do wonders for some. Of course you must pretend to believe in the same philosophy.

I recently read a book by Kenneth Forbes entitled *Great Art to the Grotesque,* in which he writes about two miners in heaven. One said, "Let's start a rumor of a gold strike in hell." So the rumor was started and a stampede was on the way. The miner who suggested the rumor said to his mate, "I am going to join the rush!"

"But why?" his friend asked him. "You started the rumor."

"Yes, I did," his pal replied. "But look at all those people! There may be something in it!"

There must be enthusiasm and animation in order to generate attention. "If there is no melody there is no music," Mozart said.

Modern businessmen assert that best results in selling are obtained by saying nothing: "Don't harass the customer." I don't think that courteous help can be interpreted as harassment. Advocates of such beliefs are idiotic. Animation and conversation create curiosity, which become action.

Let us examine the validity of such assertions. Music draws attention and gives you a tranquil feeling of enjoyment. It also draws traffic into a store.

On occasion a browser would come into the store carrying a large Eaton's or Simpson's box, which I assumed contained a suit or a coat. I would then lead our conversation as to what was inside the box. Upon seeing the garment I would remark, "I don't know how much you paid for it, but I could have selected a much nicer coat for you." She would then become curious as to what type and price of coat I would have chosen for her. I inadvertently showed her a couple of coats, which she liked much better than the one she had bought. "I would buy your coat, but I live too far to go back and ask for a refund," she would remark.

"Don't worry, give me your bill of sale and leave the coat with me. I'll give you credit for it, and return it for you."

The deal was made most of the time, and one of my sales staff would take the coat back to where it had been bought and get the refund.

On other occasions the customer would inform me that she had left a deposit in another store. I would then allow her a conditional discount to equal her deposit, which she might or might not get back. If she did get it back, she was to pay full price; otherwise I allowed her a discount of up to twenty dollars, depending of course on the price of the garment. I had to do business by wit and skill, rather than by orthodox methods. I was doing the customer a favor by helping her out of her dilemma.

Animation in any form in a store generates a busy atmosphere where crowds are drawn because of a busy appearance. The idea is to get the traffic into the store. Once that's accomplished, aggressive selling becomes normal and profitable. Intelligent selling is almost as rewarding and satisfying spiritually as soothing music. It has an emotional impact even on browsers.

It is false to claim that hard-core selling is out of date, impractical, and unsuited to modern times. Old-fashioned selling is, and always will be, the most practical and appreciative method in serving customers, rather than leaving them to browse around without help to guide them to particular items. You are lucky if you find someone who will be gracious enough to take your money for the items you chose in frustration and disgust, without anyone asking you if you needed any help. I completely disagree with such reasoning. Honest, enthusiastic selling that glows with sincerity always brings rewarding results. People like to listen to suggestions. They appreciate opinions; they thrive on compliments and personalized service, provided it is not overdone. It is irritating to be exposed to harsh, loud music.

I am not a genius, and I do not attempt to impress you with my views. I do believe, however, that my philosophy about selling is correct, and through the years I have been rewarded in some measure for my efforts. Genuine honesty and sincerity are directly responsible for creating a good relationship with the public, which, after all, is the route to success.

Unfortunately, human values in general and concern for each other in particular, have deteriorated in the last decade. This also applies to customer service. One must remember that the atmosphere and the behavior of staff are created by the executive or head of a department. When you see a downhearted or an indifferent individual performing halfheartedly, put the blame where it belongs.

The decline of North American culture and behavior is frightening. Novels containing horrendous acts of violence are disgusting, and stories containing murder and sex are best sellers. Movies are saturated with blood in true color, gushing from a hole in the head inflicted by a bullet. The sickening sensation of seeing a glistening long knife penetrate someone's back is considered most enjoyable entertainment, even though a level-headed individual wouldn't waste his time on such garbage. We are living in a decadent society, which thrives on cheap neuroses bordering on schizophrenia, and a vulgar style of living. People have become addicted—like an alcoholic who knows that what he is doing undermines his health, but nevertheless contiues the habit until something painful happens to him.

The public is caught up in an endless chain of queer, irrational thinking and philosophy, handcuffed to, among other things, poor taste. Unfortunately, their health is not in danger of being impaired and they don't worry about their mental erosion. They are victims of the mavericks of our society, who accumulate millions at the expense of our low mentality and that of our children. Sick minds seem to thrive on repugnant books and TV programs that are disgusting and that help to degenerate further the minds of the public by exposing them to all sorts of pornography and crime in the name of "entertainment." We are living in a world of madness overwhelmed by our importance, engulfed in egotism and pretense.

Many modern marriages are just marriages of convenience, or desperation. They have no foundation, such as devotion, dedication, respect and trust in each other. Without that solid foundation they fall apart at the slightest breeze. I am a sentimentalist by nature and therefore very sensitive to marriages that fail, particularly where children are involved. I don't feel sorry for the parents. They are grown-up fools. But I know the feeling of a child who becomes the victim of circumstances. I also know the craving for a father in the heart of a child, for I grew up fatherless, envying the children who had fathers. I have seen boys my age overwhelmed by love of their fathers.

Consider the mystery of love—the unfairness of it, the awful freedom of it, and finally the indescribable torture of losing it, or of not having it at all. The ultimate rationality of love lies in loving as only a parent can, and the final justification of hope is in the hope not to lose that unlimited love on account of failures, frustrations, or misunderstanding on the part of the parents. Such an environment or situation becomes very difficult on children. They look with suspicion at the changes taking place around them. They develop a sharp sense of hostility by trying to adjust to a new way of life. Hostility may widen until they eventually grow up and carve out a new life of their own, and forsake the ones who were responsible for bringing about such a drastic change in their secure little world. Unfortunately, we cannot direct our own destiny; how then can we prevent mental cruelty to mankind in general and to children in particular?

Nevertheless, we must take into account that a friendly divorce is better than a double suicide. But, when children are involved, parents should put forth more than average effort to get along with each other. After all, you have attended to them all the way from the diaper stage; you have given unstintingly of yourself so that your children could grow up in the security of a home full of love.

Destiny can be controlled or at least modified only if it is man-made, but most often you are born into it. You are therefore compelled to accept the consequences. You deprive yourself of everything that was and still is very dear to you. It is also a matter of willpower, an extension of your feelings and compassion. You must sacrifice something of yourself in order to prevent pain and sadness from being inflicted upon others by your irrational behavior. Unless your limited intelligence refuses to accept, or cannot penetrate your senses to care, then you are a victim of your own choice.

The spiritual contentment that we seek from those we love is only an excuse, an escape from reality. Fulfillment can be found only in your own heart—it depends on your personal values. If you possess or acquire such fulfillment, your rewards will be much greater in your endeavors.

Should you desire some success in your personal life and in your business world you must work for it and be prepared to pay a price. Give a little of yourself; be prepared to admit your mistakes. Never count your working hours. Deny yourself many pleasures to which you think you are entitled. Look after nickels and dimes, which will turn into dollars and take care of themselves, provided you don't interfere with the progress of their accumulation.

Any fool can make money when opportunity presents itself, but it takes a sensible logical person to retain it. A fool will spend it, forgetting that there may be rainy days ahead.

These are but a few items you must respect, and a part of the price you must pay for some measures of dignity, self-respect, and monetary gains. Without them you will accomplish nothing, for they are reflections and extensions of your personality. Success in any field of endeavor doesn't come easily. Even if achieved only to a limited degree, it is more satisfying than either stagnation or failure. A similar philosophy can be applied to selling. If you think positively and share your contented feelings with your customers, you will be a winner, provided you follow simple rules without making them too obvious. Reaching for a sales book before you get your money is a cardinal sin. So why take unnecessary chances? Remember the system banks use: Even though you are making a deposit and you are not about to change your mind, the cashier does not enter the deposit in your book until the money is in the cash drawer.

I also attach great importance to each sale, regardless of its dollar value. Though it may seem insignificant by itself one way or another, it can be instrumental in a poor, fair, or a good day of business. Remember that out of a little acorn a huge oak tree grows. If you are there to please and serve courteously, regardless of the value of a sale (which should be considered important at all times), you may unexpectedly make a high-priced sale and create a new repeat customer.

Proper management and selling can almost be compared to Jewish humor and its limited vocabulary. A phrase or an observation in a proper intonation may be insignificant, but the facial expression, the raising of an eyebrow, or the innocent wave of a hand can bring the insignificant into focus and create desired results. After a lifetime of direct and complete participation in selling I consider myself an authority on the subject and express my opinions without reservation.

When you hear those hypnotic words, "I'll take it," you are hearing the beautiful music you have been hoping for. But don't overreact with obvious satisfaction or anxiety. Simply say, "Would you be so kind as to leave me X number of dollars?" (depending

on the price involved of course), or "Will you pay in full now?"
By saying that, you accomplish two very important points: First,
you'll get a substantially larger deposit than you would have
received if you had asked, "How much would you like to leave
today?" The more money you get, the more secure the sale, which
minimizes the possibility of a cancellation. Second, the customer
walks out with the feeling that she actually bought the garment
and is obligated for the balance on a specific date. If you were
to ask, "How much will you leave me today?" you would be
shocked to hear perhaps $2 or $5, in which case you would be
compelled to ask for more, thus creating a feeling of resentment
and non-confidence. To avoid such situations you have made a
positive statement of fact at the precise time, thereby clinching
the sale solidly.

One rule that I always impressed on the minds of my staff is
that, regardless of the area in the store where a purchase is made,
the salesperson is to remain there, chatting nonchalantly until she
has the money in her hands. "If you happened to make a sale on
the streetcar tracks" I say, "remain there until you get the money,
even though you see a streetcar approaching." I remember occasions when I stood outside the store and heard different comments
made by various people:

"That dress in the window is identical to mine."

"Did you buy it?"

"No, I just left a small deposit on it."

That's logic, filled with wisdom. Or, "You are not planning on
going into this store."

"Why not?"

"Their clothes are too expensive for us!"

The latter remarks were music to my ears. They knew that I
handled expensive merchandise. That was prestige! My merchandise was handpicked, hanging proudly, projecting complete confidence and superiority, smiling at you, winking, "Come on, try
me on!" That was the image I had built up over many years, unlike
merchandise one sees in some other stores. There is a dress, hanging dejectedly as if it has been sentenced to death even though
capital punishment has been questionable for many years.

Some painters paint a forest, whereas an artist also paints the
heart of the forest. This could be applied to your sales staff. Some
of them serve the customer, whereas others sell with enthusiasm.
Should one act indifferent on any given day, tell her to do the

thing she does best—"sleep" in a comfortable chair. Some are very good at it.

You must constantly remember to retain or expand on the image you have created in the minds of consumers, including prestige, honesty, value, fashion, and courteous service. These and many other intangibles make customers feel at home and keep them coming back. Don't forget that they may also be directly responsible for stimulating extra business for you by praising your fine qualities to their friends.

A store of prestige must also be very particular that garments be thoroughly examined before handing them over to customers, rather than be embarrassed by a complaint the following day.

Repeat business is due mostly to enthusiasm and courteous service. You'll go back to a store because of that. Latest fashions and a new selection at all times make a customer feel as if she is walking into a store that appreciates her patronage and serves her to the best of its ability. As a customer, you'll do this rather than roam around in some store where no one knows you and doesn't care. You seem like just another browser, even though you are out to buy, but who cares? Old-fashioned help combined with old-fashioned service remains a shining example of values that have gone—passed on with the outlandish lifestyle. Maxims such as "Business before pleasure" or "Don't mix business with personal friendship" are very wise and rewarding, but each case must be handled according to the situation.

You must also remember at all times that a business cannot operate successfully in an atmosphere loaded with silent hostility. Joke, mix with your customers. Don't stand and wait for things to happen; *make* them happen: Your personal problems, whatever they may be, should be left outside your business; otherwise they will affect others. Your depressive state of mind will also affect your staff, thus making everyone miserable and apathetic.

In order to create a pleasant atmosphere in a store you must be tactful in handling the sales staff. Never say, "I want you to do this or that." Instead you say, "Girls, what do you think about doing this or that?" Regardless of whether they agree with your idea, you simply innocently say, "Would you give me a hand to change the stock around?" Everyone will gladly pitch in and help. Remember, people like to be appreciated and made to feel important by being asked for an opinion. Don't play the executive role; you'll lose business because of resentment by your staff. I could probably give you a hundred ways as to how costly such an attitude could be.

Aristotle said wisely, "You cannot change one's behavior; you can only make one do things your way because of fear of punishment or dismissal." My experience has been that, even though it is difficult or perhaps impossible to change someone's behavior, favorable results can be achieved by making one feel like a "somebody." A little bit of praise goes a long way, provided it is done in privacy and in a tactful manner, so that pride does not overpower the praise, which is likely to create jealousy when given in the presence of others.

Many years have passed since my initiation into this business, but some embarrassing episodes I faced during those years have remained in the crumpled pages of my mind. Many unbelievable things with which I have had to cope may not sound as hilarious now as they did at the time. Only the other day a mother and two daughters came in to buy a wedding gown. After the bride had tried on several gowns, she was apparently confused as to which gown she liked best. Her mother came to her rescue by saying, "God told us to go out and look at some gowns. We are going home now, and God will probably tell us over the weekend whether we should buy one or not. We will be back just as soon as we hear from Him."

You think that I am joking? No! This is the honest truth. They haven't returned yet. They are still waiting for the long distance phone call. I hope they get it, and it's collect.

I remember one evening while I was alone in the store, a tall girl—I mean tall!—over six feet—walked in, picked out a dress and said, "Can I go into a fitting room and try it on?"

"Why not? Go ahead," hoping that my one and only salesgirl would be back from supper shortly. It didn't, however, work out as I had anticipated.

A few minutes after she entered the fitting room she began screaming for help. She apparently squeezed into the dress, which was much too small for her, but couldn't take it off. I opened the door and saw her standing half nude, her arms reaching to the ceiling. "You'll have to help me take this dress off," she said calmly. She was too tall for me to be able to give her assistance. I climbed up on a chair and began to pull up the dress over her head, but I was still too short to achieve the desired results.

I then took a stepladder, climbed up to the highest rung, and hung on precariously, because the floor was tilted, and proceeded to pull the dress with the other hand, but the dress seemed to be glued to her body. It was impossible to get it over her bust. I was perspiring profusely now, and was scared in case someone walked in. It would appear that I was preparing her for rape. "I hope you are not getting ideas which I may look upon with disfavor," she said.

"Oh, no! I'm trying to help you, as you requested," I replied apologetically.

"How else do you intend to get out of this in one piece?"

"Cut the dress," she said.

It's a terrific idea, I thought. I took a pair of scissors, walked inside the room, and cut the back seam all the way down. The dress dropped to the floor and I went into shock. She was completely nude, like Lady Godiva. All she had on was long hair. I was facing a nude Amazon. I really don't remember by what means I got out of that fitting room, perhaps she carried or pulled me out. I do remember, however, her saying to me, "You don't have to react so repulsively. I am not that ugly. Here, look at me!" She then put her own dress on and walked out.

I laugh inwardly each time I think about that experience and visualize all the details that transpired that evening. That is one experience I will never forget.

Business was getting progressively better, so that I could afford to hire another salesgirl and go to Florida for ten days. My wife of course was devoted to our two daughters, and under no circumstances would she consider leaving them with a housekeeper. She claimed that housekeepers were as bad or worse than mean foster mothers. She would never entrust her two darlings to anyone. "I am the only one that can look after them properly," she would say.

The day I checked into a hotel in Florida remains unforgettable. I was very tired and had gone to bed quite early that evening, only to be awakened by an argument in the adjoining room. Upon coming out into the hallway I saw a lady who was screaming at a bellhop. "Can't you see? Are you blind?"

"I am sorry, madam, but I can't see anything unusual. All I see is a wall of the adjacent hotel facing your window. That wall has been here for many years. Do you expect me to remove it? I'll call the manager," he said in desperation. "Perhaps he can see something."

When the manager arrived on the scene the lady explained in

detail that there was a man in a room facing hers; his window blind was up and he was in the nude. The manager looked out the window and said, "Madam, I am sorry, but I can't see a window, nor can I see a man!"

"Oh, yes!" she screamed. "Climb up on the dresser as I have and you'll see him too. I saw him!" she screamed excitedly. "He was walking around in the room. Later on he rested on his bed for a while. He is Jewish, I swear."

"Why did you climb on top of your dresser?" asked the manager.

"I am a habitual climber," she replied sarcastically. "I was provoked by my instinct, which kept telling me, 'Climb the dresser, you'll see something.' So I climbed just to make sure if my instinct was correct. I also wanted to familiarize myself with the environment, satisfy my curiosity, and relax. That's what I came here for, 'to relax.' Curiosity is the primary motivational force within me."

"Would you wish to move to another room?" the manager asked politely.

"Certainly not, I like this room. Furthermore, I can do some sightseeing within the confines of this room if I should so desire."

"Why then did you create such a commotion?"

"I just wanted to share my secret enjoyment with someone. Now that you and others know, I'll enjoy my stay much more."

I met the lady at the poolside the following day and was told that this was the first exciting vacation of her life.

19

Selling as a Fine Art

When a customer walks in and says, "I am interested in a coat," do not, and I repeat Do Not, proceed to show her coats on hangers. She will most naturally not like any of them. Knowing this, you also know that a garment must be tried on in order to make the right choice. You should therefore, say, pleasantly and calmly, "We have a beautiful selection. I am sure we will find something nice." Have her put her parcels (if she has any) down on a chair, assist her in taking off her coat, and then proceed to look for a coat, all the while telling her that you are looking for one coat in particular that was just put into stock and that will most likely appeal to her.

Now, if you have only one coat of that style, and you are of the opinion that it is her size, have her try it on. But, if you are in doubt, show her one that you have in an assortment of sizes and colors. Carry on a light friendly conversation while you slowly, calmly have her try on some coats. Don't rush her; don't show signs of anxiety. You are not trying to sell her a coat; you are trying to help her make the right choice! Should she happen to favor one that you don't have in her size or color, do not discourage her. Tell her that it can be ordered for her, but that you would appreciate it if she would do you a favor and try on the coat that fits her once more. Now, supposing you had failed to sell it from stock and you are about to order one for her, call the manager and tell him or her in detail what you are about to order. Build up the importance of your customer, so that you'll prevent or minimize the haggling over price.

Normal figures or those near normal are easier to please, but when you get one who has what we call "a duck's disease," one whose rear end is too close to the floor, you are in trouble. They are the most fussy and almost impossible to fit.

I was fortunate during the first few years to have had a girl working with me who was shrewd and enthusiastic. The two of us as a

199

team were unbeatable. We learned the tricks of the trade from each other. When I was about to order a special for a customer I would call her over and tell her as seriously as possible, "I am going to have a coat made to order for this nice lady. Mark down every word I tell you. Pure virgin wool material, the best windproof interlining, and the best chamois available." The reason for making such a big issue was to discourage the customer from haggling over the price, which never failed. It's a tradition with ethnic people to argue price. My sincerity also made her feel very important, so that she had complete confidence in my opinion the next time around.

I would then innocently ask the customer to put on the coat again. "I just want to make sure of the size," I would say. "Now, as you know, I am ordering the same coat for you in brown, but—don't you think that the black coat, which fits you to perfection, is more practical? You can wear it with any color accessories because black is always dressy, but with a brown coat you are limited. You have to accumulate new accessories, which means more expense to you." If it were blue she wanted I would confide in her secretly that blue will fade after she wears it a few times, which is true. You'll notice it by looking under the collar.

We had elevated the technique of selling to a fine art. We were determined to sell from stock rather than take orders, so-called "specials," and acted accordingly. She needs a size 16 in red, but I have a 16 in black or a size 12 in green, but one has to manipulate to sell from stock. I remember when I tried desperately to sell a coat from stock to an overenthusiastic Scottish girl. She walked out on me, promising to come back if she were not able to find that same coat elsewhere at a lower price. About an hour later she came by with a large box, opened it and remarked, "You see? This is an identical coat, which I purchased in another store at a lower price."

I looked at the coat and remarked, "No wonder you got it cheaper. This is not virgin wool material."

"Mister," she replied, "I couldn't care less whether the sheep was a virgin or not, as long as the coat will keep me warm."

"Mrs., this is not pure wool, this is pure *drek*" (dung).

"You have made me very happy by saying that; now I am sure that I got a bargain." She walked out of the store humming, "You take the high road, and I'll take the low road."

I remember an episode when parents brought in a teenage girl to buy her the first coat she had ever owned. It was history in the making, the most important moment of their lives. "How much?"

"Forty-nine dollars," I answered calmly.

"That much for a fourteen-year-old girl? Impossible! Ten dollars is more than enough. If I didn't like the coat I wouldn't give you three dollars for it."

"My dear man, the best I can do for you is give you the coat at cost, which is thirty-five dollars."

Without another word he counted out twenty-two dollars, put the money on the desk and took the coat over his arm. "I'll tell you something," he said. "I could get the very same coat for twenty dollars in another store."

"Why didn't you get it?" I asked.

"Because he didn't have the right size."

"If I didn't have the right size I would have given it to you for ten dollars."

This story is similar to that of a woman in conversation with a butcher:

"How much do you charge for a pound of steak?" she asked.

"One dollar and ninety cents."

"He—Mr. Schwartz across the street sells it for one dollar and forty cents."

"Why don't you buy it from him?"

"He doesn't have any left."

"If I didn't have any left I would sell it for twenty-five cents a pound."

Those were trying times and frustrating days. A woman loaded with parcels walked in on just such a day to inquire about the price and size of a beige coat that was displayed in the window. I told her the price and size and informed her in a subtle way that it was a sample coat, one of a kind, which sometimes makes it more prestigious. "It so happens that it's your size," I said.

"Oh! It's not for me, I am looking for my sister. I want to buy her a gift."

"What size does your sister wear?"

"The same size as I."

"In that case I'll take it out of the window and have you try it on."

She put her load of parcels down, put the coat on, but remained indifferent. She then turned to me and said, "It's too bad it's not in gray. I like gray much better."

She as much as confessed that the coat was in fact for herself. She most likely didn't even have a sister. "It's the same color as you saw in the window; it hasn't changed."

"It's a nice coat," she said. "But there is something about it I don't like. I'll sleep on it."

"But it's early morning. What time do you intend to go to bed?"

"I am really not crazy about it. It just doesn't hit me."

"You should only get hit by a swinging door or something," I thought. It's inconceivable that most women have an abundance of excuses or reasons why they shouldn't buy, but I kept the conversation going and in a joking way I said, "Are you perchance looking for a coat with three sleeves?"

"Yes," she replied arrogantly.

"Okay. Let's make a deal. You show me three arms and I'll give you a coat with three sleeves." I think I shamed her into buying that coat. She has been a loyal customer ever since. Each time I see her I ask her, "Have you grown a third arm yet?"

"No, but I am working on it. One day I may surprise you."

If you were to observe closely the type of "specials" that sales help take, you would fire them all, or take the gas pipe. That is a result of incompetence, gullibility, lack of logic and communication. Sales help confuse a customer by showing too many garments, to the point of promising her some crazy special rather than lose her, while a plain, simple, logical remark could have sold a garment from stock.

Remember, you are the salesperson; the customer is looking up to you listening to every word you are saying. You are representing prestige, experience, and a desire to help your customer in her decision; you are therefore expected to be pleasant, knowledgeable, and helpful. Be friendly and establish a rapport with your customer, but beware of crossing that thin line that exists between all those estimable qualities and useless kibitzing and jokes. If this happens, you have lost control of your customer; all your virtues of experience and prestige vanish. The customer becomes more bold, more outspoken, and ceases to look up to you and value your dignified opinion. You are not a saleslady any more; you have become one of the girls. Your suggestions or opinions no longer count and as a result of crossing over that thin line you have lost a sale.

Women seldom come alone when they are in need of an expensive dress or coat. A sister, a brother, a friend, or the whole family come along for that big moment when earth-shaking history is in the making. One must remember that on such important occasions the likes and dislikes of the one for whom the garment is being chosen are of secondary importance. You must size up the situation as to who is the most important spokesman in the group.

Once you determine that, you should direct most of your selling comments to that individual, but not to the exclusion of the entire group. While the so-called customer is standing still and not uttering a word, the group is busily engaged in examining the garment. "Turn around! Do you like it? How about another color?" They drive the poor woman crazy while she stands innocently waiting for the verdict from her jury. It's obvious that the group was brought along for one specific reason—to criticize.

Now is the time to make your move, by trying to impress the one who apparently will be instrumental in the final decision. The consent to make the purchase comes in the form of a question. It's clearly obvious by the question "How much?" that they like the garment. You must adjust yourself mentally to a long and bitter struggle as to price. When the price is finally settled, a new, although expected, resistance to provincial tax (Sales tax in U.S.) enters into the picture: "I'll pay the price we agreed upon, but no tax." That goes on day after day. Only when I ask, "Do you get checks for your bambinos mailed to you each month?"

"Yes, I do."

"In that case you must pay tax."

They eventually surrender but not before they ask, "How much discount will you give us on the tax?"

After a prolonged period of bargaining, the sale is made. The anticipation and the aggravation are too much for me sometimes, but I have to be the last one to give them the lowest price. If the price isn't right (in their opinion), they'll threaten me by saying, "We'll look around. We may be back."

In such cases, which were normal daily occurrences, I found it impossible to remain calm without having my thinking mechanism thrown out of focus. I would take a walk as a respite from such complexities and gradually bring my anger under control. "I have no time to be angry!" I would think. Some people make anger their careers and have no time left to learn and appreciate the beauty of life, filled with miracles. My work and aspirations were too important for me to waste time on being angry, and I promised myself not to let such incidents bother me. I was caught in the web of life at a very tender age, which made me feel (wrongly, of course) that those who weren't with me were against me. I realize now that my philosophy was a by-product of insecurity. Not having had the experience to cope with complicated daily problems, such as the ones with which my business was beset, and trying to free myself of that web, I got entangled deeper and deeper.

20

Vacation Time

I think it was in 1950 when my wife and I, and of course our two daughters, were on our way to Wasaga Beach. We had saved $150, so that we could afford to rent a cottage for two weeks— not so much for us, but something special for the kids, who had never seen a vacation resort, or a sandy beach, or a lake.

I remember sitting proudly in an old jalopy, traveling at top speed of forty miles per hour between the cooling-off periods. Every five miles or so our car got boiling hot and steam belched out of the radiator until it blew the radiator cap off. We had to stop, let the car cool off, and fill up the radiator with water, which we carried in a very large container for just such occasions. While the going was good we were quite happy and talked about many unforgettable experiences we had endured during the depression years in Winnipeg. There was really nothing that we didn't talk about many times over, but the overwhelming elated feeling of going on vacation made us talk about the importance of the present and the future, which we hoped would deal us a better hand.

It was on a hot humid Sunday, midmorning, when we finally reached Barrie. "Let's go into a restaurant for a coffee," my wife suggested. "It's only five cents a cup. The car will have cooled off by the time we are ready to resume our journey."

As we walked into a restaurant I noticed three middle-aged men sitting at a table. One of them looked familiar to me. I must have seen him some place before. He looked at me for a while and jumped to his feet. "Harry, is that you?"

"Sure it's me. That's my name, who else can I be?"

"Don't you remember me? I was your helper on the truck in Winnipeg."

"My God, are you Joe who helped me load and unload the truck delivering soda pop to the stores?"

"Yes, it's me!" he said, embracing me. Tears of happiness were rolling down his face.

"Joe, you were only seventeen years old the last time I saw you. You are a middle-aged man now!"

"Time doesn't stand still for no one," he replied philosophically. He left his two friends, promising to join them in Collingwood a few days later, and rode with us to Wasaga Beach.

We had rented an old cottage without sanitary facilities, but it had four walls, a roof, and two windows facing the lake. What a magnificent sight! The children were overwhelmed with happiness. I am not a bit embarrassed to admit that the mysterious lake and the sandy beach made a deep impression on me also. I had never seen a lake or a beach before. Everything looked real, but to me it was like a mirage. I had never tasted a bit of life's pleasures, but there I was looking at unspoiled nature, as it had been perhaps forever. I felt a lump forming in my throat. I turned to the kids, my wife, and Joe: "Come on, let's go on the beach! What are we waiting for?"

We were basking under the hot sun on the beach one day, when Joe began to remind me of all sorts of things we had lived through while working on the truck together. We reminisced about bygone years. Memories came tumbling in disarray. We laughed and we cried while we talked about the hard times we had both endured working on a commission basis.

"Joe, my dear friend and thief, how has life been to you in the years past?"

"As usual," he replied. "Very little changed since the time I worked for you. We Ukrainians aren't subject to too much change. We are similar to Jews in a way. We live by our culture and traditions as you do, regardless of changes in society. I was conscripted into the army toward the end of the war and had a hell of a good time. I drove a jeep and made love to more girls than I care to remember."

"Joe! don't talk dirty."

"This isn't dirty, it's a fact of life. I see you are still the loyal puritan as you were years ago. Come on, man. It's about time you put your scrambled brain in order."

"I live by Talmudic morals and principles," I defended myself.

"Yes, I know your philosophy about morals very well. Maybe you are right. Who in the hell knows?"

"Joe, do you remember the cold grapes and cherries you stole each time we carried cases of pop down into the mudhole basements? Especially Mrs. Silverberg, who owned a tiny store in the middle of the block. She had no refrigeration and therefore kept all perishables in the cool, muddy basement."

"I sure do," he said with satisfaction. "But each time I came out of that store my shirt was loaded with all sorts of fruit. We sat in the truck and quenched our parched throats. Poor Mrs. Silverberg. She was most vulnerable to such thievery."

He also reminded me how he used to steal a bottle of pop here and there to make up for broken ones that exploded like firecrackers on the truck under the unbearably hot sun.

"Joe, why did we do all that?"

"For survival man, for self-preservation."

Mr. Zankofsky had a nice store in Weston. It was clean, solid, and prosperous-looking, which was unusual during the Depression years. The shelving, the counter, the floors were built of solid mahogany.

The meat refrigerator, a thing of real beauty, was pure white and shone like a mirror. It was placed across the rear of the store, out of sight of the staircase leading to the basement. He was a good account, sold a lot of our drinks, and never failed to have a few cases in reserve. The profit was nil according to my calculations. He paid sixty cents for twelve bottles of pop, had a large metal box that was always filled with chopped ice and retailed it at six cents a bottle. But because of the heavy demand, most stores handled that particular product. No other bottling company was in a position to compete with us.

I remember spilling some of the pop on the cement sidewalk once. It left a stain as if a torch had been used. It was powerful stuff, but who cared if one's stomach lining was eaten away over a period of time? It was the cheapest drink on the market; nothing else mattered.

"Joe, you were a real thief. You graduated from grapes to cherries to chocolates to stealing one or two bottles out of a case, and finally to one and two cases when the need was urgent."

"I know," Joe said nonchalantly while in deep thought. "Harry, do you remember the dumb blond waitress who worked in a Chinese restaurant on Osborne Street? I asked her one night to meet me at my boyfriend's house. 'But there is no transportation in this part of town at this time of night,' she pleaded. 'Take a cab,' I said. 'But I can't swing it. Fifty cents is a lot of money in the middle of the week; tips are nonexistent. Payday is on Saturday. When I do get four dollars for a week's work I don't know what to pay first.' We did, however, get her to come and broke most of the Ten Commandments in the back of an abandoned old dump truck, and sent her home."

"Joe, I never realized that you were such an immoral tramp."

"You call that immoral? Wait until I tell you what I am doing for a living now."

"I can't wait to hear."

"I am a downright, no-good pimp! I get paid well and I spend it. There is no use saving for tomorrow, for who knows if I'll be alive to enjoy it?"

His remark made me think of an old man who happened to walk down a street in a red-light district. A hooker standing outside asked the man to come inside and share in some of life's pleasures. "Oh, I couldn't do that," said the old man. "My mother and father wouldn't tolerate such behavior."

"Come on! An old man like you has a mother and father? Don't kid me!"

"I am not kidding. I am thinking of Mother Nature and Father Time."

After a couple of days in Joe's company I was beginning to feel that I had made a mistake by inviting him to stay with us. He was corrupting my morals. The day he joined his friends in Collingwood I thought, "Once you turn a certain page in life, years seem to disappear. All the yesterdays vanish into the void, or perhaps link up to time of creation. We all have our hangups and Joe's is no exception." As Kahlil Gibran wrote, "Your thoughts and my words are waves from a sealed memory that keeps records of our yesterdays."

Joe and his friends vacationed about fifteen miles from Wasaga Beach. He came down one Sunday morning and took us in his car to spend the day with him. To this day I can't forget the configuration of the mountains surrounding Collingwood, the beauty of the shaded beaches, and the cool feeling of the sparkling waters. We stayed there for dinner and walked the sandy beach in the silence of night. The luminous beach was mesmerizing—it was like looking into oblivion. While the silent moon looked on and penetrated its calm dim light into an atmosphere of breeze, water, sand, and stone cliffs of a nearby canyon, colorful mountains stood by secretly and serenely, providing unbelievable beauty for the shallow whispering surf lapping at the rim of the beach.

The reflection of the lake and the mountains made me feel as if I were riding the high tide and had been brought down into the depths of an ebb tide. It was an unforgettable night, enveloped in deep secrecy one can never forget. It was fascination combined with irresistible spiritual contentment, walking on the beach and watching the stars, which looked like a large chessboard in the deep blue sky, while the endless lake was shrouded in the dark of night. Only the hushed whisper of the surf licking the shore broke the deep, mysterious silence.

21

Specials Spell Trouble

Unlike a garment that is sold from stock, special orders are prone to create unbearable aggravation, as I have said before. Specials can also bring unexpected repercussions that would be impossible to itemize. In order to bring to light some of the pitfalls to which one is exposed, let's take a normal hypothetical "special." The style number on the ticket of the original garment could have been an error in the factory, or the error could have been made by the employee whose responsibility it is to mark incoming merchandise, or an error could have been made marking the size of the garment. It's also possible that the special order had a slight change or correction, as opposed to the original sample, which did not appear on the ticket, and yet the style number remained the same. The shade might be slightly different if a new bolt of cloth has been used. Sometimes you forget to specify the length of the garment, and if it is fur-trimmed (other than black), you can hardly ever expect to get the identical shade of fur.

What does one do in order to prevent such errors? Sometimes you take the original garment to the factory with you, to make sure that the style number is correct, or have the manufacturer describe to you on the telephone what style number so-and-so looks like. All the other dangers cannot be prevented. When the special comes in, remember, take the original out of stock if it is not identical, to avoid comparison when the customer comes in for it. However, this is only a fraction of the problems, add to it the hope that the garment will fit when it comes in.

Other unpleasant possibilities also exist on the other side of the coin. What can and does sometimes happen between the time the garment has been ordered and the time the customer finally takes delivery of it? You first hope that the material and shade you require are available. You also hope that the garment will come in within three to four weeks (if you are lucky). You must bear in mind that, when dealing in money, the longer it takes the greater the risk. You must consider many adverse possibilities that can occur over that period of time. If you understand the way people think you'll have to take into consideration the following. You must bear in mind that people are reluctant to leave large deposits on something they can't see.

Let us presume that the price of the garment is $150. The customer will feel that a $20 deposit is quite adequate; it's a lot of money at the particular time as far as the customer is concerned. But during the waiting period the deposit becomes less and less important: She is still shopping around, despite the fact that she has already ordered one. She still hopes that she may perhaps find the identical coat in her size and color. She may even decide to purchase one, even though it's not exactly what she had in mind, but she can try it, feel it, pay for it, and forget about the one she had ordered. The $20 deposit is no longer as important as it had been on the day she actually parted with it. Time has made it appear less valuable. The day her coat finally comes in you call her. Here are some of the excuses you may get: I am not well; my husband isn't working; my husband is against my buying a coat this year; I can't afford it. There are hundreds of excuses you can expect as to why she is not in a position to take delivery of her coat.

The net result may well be that you have lost a sale and a customer. Regardless of whether you give her a refund she'll never have the nerve to come into the store again. To me specials, or order takers, are in fact *undertakers*. They can literally ruin or bury a small business.

Honesty in business inoculates people with confidence and pleasure of achievement, in the same way as you appreciate the health and well-being of loved ones, freedom of opportunity, and many more blessings in your life. Honesty is a life of reward and contentment; it's a most wonderful, tranquil entity; it's for you, for us; let's use it. For "humanism" is joy, and this is a part of it. If one is dishonest to a customer, he is dishonest also to himself. I once tried to sell a mink coat to the husband of a customer: "Come on, surprise her, buy her this mink."

"I'll buy her a mink, on one condition, that she shall promise to keep the cage clean!"

He did buy her the coat, although she really didn't deserve it if she "would put up with a guy like me for over twenty years."

The following day he brought in a friend who had remarried recently and was about eighty years of age but still full of life and laughter. The friend bought a muskrat coat for his wife, and while I was holding out my hand to receive the money, he said that he was on his way from visiting his doctor.

"Are you ill?" I asked sympathetically.

"Not really," he replied, straightfaced. "I have a sex problem and thought that the doctor should know about it. 'Doctor,' I said, 'I find that I am not interested in sex any more and don't find it as pleasurable as I once did."

"When was the first time you had noticed that?" asked the doctor.

"Last night and again this morning!"

I shared his joke very enthusiastically, all the while waiting to get the money for the coat.

"How much?" he asked.

"Count until I tell you to stop."

He counted to six hundred and fifty dollars and I said, "Stop."

You are a hell of a nice guy. I'll send my two sons down to see you," he chuckled.

He kept his promise.

22

Advertising and Promotion

Salesmanship is a talent one is born with; you either have it or you don't. It's that intangible something that makes one a champion. Unfortunately champions very seldom change positions. They are well rewarded for their valuable services at all times wherever they happen to be employed.

I basked in the limelight of the garment industry and of course in my own small measure of success. I felt like a slave who had occasion to have a taste of freedom, which strengthened his desire to become independent. I felt that my share of independence was coming within reach. I was respected for my achievements, even by some cynics who were of the opinion at one time that I would never make it, but my relentless efforts began to show definite signs of progress.

Life and ambition can be compared to insignificant streams that over the years carve out small channels, which at some point in life turn into free-flowing rivers.

The fifties were special years, which changed my destiny and brought about new and unbearable hardships and frustrations. I thought that the time was about ripe to expand or relocate to an area that had great promise. We rented a store, had it renovated and opened for business, but as usual if one is to embark upon a new venture one must be prepared to face the consequences. Business was poor and showed no signs of the expected improvement. I then decided to publicize the store on radio. I arranged fifteen-minute programs three times daily, mostly on weekends. Listeners were asked to mail in suggestions for a name for the new store. Whoever suggested the name selected would receive a wardrobe of up to three hundred dollars. Needless to say, hundreds of letters and telephone calls from all over Ontario began to pour into the store and to the radio station. The publicity was reaching thousands who came to the store because of curiosity.

About a month later we drew some names and came upon a most suitable one, "The Fashion Centre". The winner was informed that she had won the promised magnificent wardrobe. A "Thank You" announcement was placed in one of the leading Toronto newspapers, thanking everyone for their participation in helping us choose a suitable name. Business had picked up; store traffic was heavy.

I feel that I should explain briefly the difference between advertising and promotion. Advertising and promotion work on such different planes that it's hardly necessary to state that advertising is conventional truth, whereas promotion is a figment of ingenious imagination, perhaps exaggerated to some extent but highly necessary in its literary honesty. Both are for the purpose of exposure. However, different results are expected. Advertising can be compared to a story in a newspaper, while promotion represents a bold, screaming headline of an important announcement to draw undivided attention to the story that follows.

In 1956, I came up with an idea that to my knowledge hadn't been tried before. I telephoned many places until I found a farmer who specialized in raising and supplying tiny ponies for novel entertainment on special occasions. After searching for about a month, I found two midgets to match the size of the ponies.

I had made two suits for the midgets, which glistened even in the dark of night: bright orange, white, and bright green stripes trimmed with fluorescent red, and of course hats to match. The ponies were decorated in identical colors, and on each side of a tiny wagon, also rented from the farmer, was a sign, proclaiming, "The Fashion Centre! The Gateway to the Fashion World!"

A radio announcer taped several commercials interspersed with lively music. Two amplifiers were mounted on the wagon (one on each side), and the fun began. In those years, walking traffic was very heavy on Friday evenings. It was the only night of the week when stores were open until 9:00 P.M. The procession started at 5:00 P.M. at St. Clair and Dufferin. The June sun was shining brightly and the sidewalks were crowded.

The team of tiny ponies trotted down the street. The amplifiers were blaring; a bright red light was glaring on top of the wagon. What a scene! The rushing traffic had stopped; each motorist or pedestrian was trying to figure out what was happening. Within twenty minutes or so thousands of people lined the streets. It was similar to a Santa Claus parade. I was standing in front of the store, chewing on my fingernails. I didn't expect such over-whelming, almost frightening attention. The same procedure was repeated all day Saturday in various areas of the city. Needless to emphasize, the response was tremendous. The idea turned out to be a huge success. Business also doubled within a few days after that unforgettable parade.

While business was extremely good, I had hired another part-time saleslady. Soon I noticed that, on several occasions, Saturdays in particular, she would vanish down into the basement for a few minutes soon after coming in to work. I began to suspect that she might be inclined to have a drink of the whisky that I kept downstairs. One day I checked my supply and found a few bottles empty and one bottle half full. "She is drinking!" I thought. "This is the reason for her running downstairs every once in a while." I emptied the liquor and filled the bottle with urine. I prepared a drink for her to be remembered for a long time. On Saturday morning she came into work and as usual headed for the base-ment. I waited in great anticipation to see her reaction. When she came back up she was as red as a beet, held both hands to her mouth and headed for the washroom!

When one thing goes wrong the second isn't about to be better. It so happened that there was no light in the washroom that day. A man waiting for his wife, who was in the process of purchasing a dress, went to use the washroom. My saleslady apparently be-lieved in the honor system, or perhaps because of her excited state of mind left the door open. The man walked into the dark wash-room and landed right in her lap. He came running up the stairs and whispered in my ear, "There is some crazy woman sitting in the washroom. I almost crushed her in the dark." It was apparently not her day. About fifteen minutes later she came up, took her coat, and walked out. I have never seen her since. The last gulp of what she thought was liquor evidently didn't agree with her. I wonder to this day if that last drink had cured her habit.

This is where I must tell you a story told to me by a friend. "One evening my wife and I were invited to a very lavish party. When we walked into that home I thought we were in the home of a president of a rich country. The chandeliers trimmed with gold were blinding; soothing soft music filled every corner of that enormous palace. The hostess very graciously showed us around the house. I was bewildered by the wealth I was seeing. The finale of the tour ended by looking at three washrooms. One was decorated in gold, one in pink, one in blue. The hostess also showed us that when you touch any one of the seats music automatically begins to play. One played 'Sha-Sha, der Rabbi Geht' ['Quiet, Quiet, the Rabbi is Coming']; the other played music from *Fiddler on the Roof*. The third? She passed it up.

"During the evening, after consuming many bottles of champagne and assorted imported liqueurs, some guests began the long march to visit the washrooms. A business friend of mine walked into the one that was decorated in blue and came out quickly, soaking wet. My wife and I were terribly embarrassed for him and asked, 'What happened to you?'

" 'I know you won't believe me,' he said, 'but the moment I sat down music began to play.'

"What kind of music, and what does it have to do with you being soaking wet?

"It played the National Anthem, so I stood up in a hurry. That's why I am wet."

"We bundled him into our car and drove him home."

Whether the story is true, I don't know, but in any case, it's funny.

Animation in window display is very important. It generates curiosity, attracts and holds the attention of passing traffic. Promotions must be dramatized and tie in with the entire idea.

In order to keep the momentum going I got in touch with Air Canada and succeeded in getting a display airplane they had in a window at the Royal York Hotel. We covered the window ceiling with sky-blue material and scattered slow moving clouds. Glistening stars made of fabric gave it the appearance of stars twinkling in the dark of night in an imaginary sky. Illusions were created by a few fans concealed behind panels. The airplane was suspended from the ceiling and a large sign on the propeller announced, "Free Luxurious Weekend for Two in New York. First Prize to a Lucky Bride with the Purchase of a Wedding Gown. Second Prize, a $200 Wardrobe of Your Choice. Third Prize, a Beautiful Mink Stole."

Hand bills dramatized the event in detail: "You'll be treated like a star and made to feel like a celebrity. Don't miss an exciting opportunity for an unforgettable vacation or honeymoon." The results were much more than I had anticipated. I was having a hard time getting adjusted to such an overwhelming success created by these unique promotions.

About this time, the first major enclosed shopping mall in our area was nearing completion. It was expected to have adverse effects on many small neighborhood stores. Almost incomprehensible was the magnitude of a hundred or more stores under one climate-controlled roof, which would very likely attract most of the business, especially because of the parking conveniences we didn't have. A customer sometimes drove around the block three or four times, unable to find a parking space, while the wife was making a purchase in a hurry. I was very apprehensive as to our business future and waited for the big day when the mall opened its doors for business. It was a novel, overwhelming experience and very successful. There were business hours—from 9:30 A.M. to 9:00 P.M. except Saturdays. Everything about this new concept of shopping and conveniences attracted heavy consumer traffic, as expected. Our business dropped dramatically, but I was hoping that the novelty would wear off within a few months and business would return to normal as I had anticipated.

Consumers gradually became aware that although we didn't have the variety of goods or the glamour and conveniences the shopping mall had to offer, we did have personalized courteous service, which more than made up for all other novel, modern ideas. However, one cannot accept such giant competition lightly. Countermeasures had to be taken just in case unfavorable conditions developed. Business had to get another boost; but how? We needed another gigantic promotion, such as could be executed only once in a lifetime. "Don't wait for it to happen; make it happen." This has been my motto ever since I began my selling career.

I explored all sorts of possibilities for another promotional scheme. It had to be fantastic, ingenious, thrilling, vibrant, exciting, inviting—something that would shake the very souls of the consumers. It had to have instantaneous impact like an unexpected thunderbolt out of a clear blue sky or an earthquake. It had to be dramatic, draw immediate attention and curiosity from all walks of life. Something sensational to be remembered for years to come. But what? I'll think of something! I want to give away a prize that will stagger the imagination, but one also has to do things within the law, which is not easy if it's to be that impressive.

I got to know a man from New York State who had had years of experience in promotions, and many other gimmicks used over the years. That was not what I wanted. "How about giving away a car as first prize?" he asked.

"No, I don't think it'll produce the results and aftereffects I want. It must be something tangible and yet unbelievable. Something that is alive."

"Like what?" he asked.

"I don't know. You tell me."

"A calf," he said. "We will put it in the window, create a proper atmosphere. It'll draw attention. It's original; no one has ever tried it before, especially in a ladies' wear store."

"But we are not dealing with farmers; we are dealing with city dwellers. Who is going to take the chance of making a purchase while being aware of the possibility that she may win a calf? It'll be more of a deterrent than an encouragement."

"Maybe you would like to give away a baby?" he asked sarcastically.

"A baby? Where are we going to get one? That's insane. Let's think about it. In fact, it's against the law, even if you were to succeed in getting one."

"Don't worry about it for the time being. Let me think about it. I'll get a blue-eyed baby."

"What a distasteful idea, it's revolting, but a piglet is a blue-eyed baby!" I thought.

Some days had gone by until we met again, at which time I revealed my idea to him. "I have kicked it around for a few days," I said. "And here is a perfect substitute for the blue-eyed baby. We will drive out to a farm and buy a newly born piglet. It's a baby and it has blue eyes. We will distribute sixty thousand handbills describing the sale and the prizes in detail. We will cover the windows and door completely with bright-colored signs announcing briefly what is taking place inside the store, and of course the first prize for the winner—"Be the Winner of a Blue-Eyed Baby. No purchase necessary.'"

The day had come for distribution of the handbills, which outlined all details of the sale: "Just come in and drop your name, address, and telephone number into the box. The winner will be notified immediately when the draw will be made after the sale. The winner's name will also appear in the leading Toronto newspaper."

The idea of the blue-eyed baby was torturing my mind with guilt while preparations for the "Sale of the Century" were being made. Intermingled with loud Latin American music, a strong, provocative message announcing the sale and first prize in a loud, boisterous, instigative, persuasive dialogue blared through a loudspeaker hung up on the ceiling outside the store. The store door, which was locked, had a large sign announcing that we would reopen on Wednesday at twelve o'clock after all the merchandise had been marked down, some at thirty percent discount, some at half price and less.

All of this was really true. I was determined to have this unbelievable sale leave an indelible mark for years to come. Crowds were trying the door, peeping through some tiny openings. Curiosity was mounting by the minute.

A layette that had all the needs for a baby—including a baby bottle, diapers, and blankets—covered the bamboo crib that had been placed on a chair at the rear of the store. Everything was there but the baby. A sealed box with a slot was placed next to the crib for names that would be deposited there during the sale.

Within a few hours, however, after the glaring signs had been put on the windows, the telephone began to ring. Churches of all denominations, priests, community leaders, and the child welfare called. They all wanted information regarding the "Blue-Eyed Baby." Some of them threatened legal action if I didn't remove those distasteful signs at once. One man called and screamed into the telephone, "If you don't remove the window signs within half an hour, I'll come down and break them to smithereens." Some people called to inquire if it were a boy or girl. Others wanted to know if the baby were white or black. Some inquired if they could see the baby if they were to come to the store. It was apparent that I had an insurmountable problem on my hands, which was not about to get better. In fact, the sensational news was spreading across the province like a prairie fire.

A truck with large signs and an amplifier was on the streets, concentrating on the heavy traffic areas. Everything was very promising, while I was scared sick. Had I realized that a promotion of this sort would create so much interest, emotion, and curiosity, I would never have agreed to go through with it. But it was too late to call it off. The stage had been set; the drama had unfolded. Regardless of the consequences I had to see it through. Each time a caller threatened me, I would take the sign off the door, which so colorfully dramatized the "Blue-Eyed Baby," only to put it back on again a few minutes later upon the insistence of my promoter.

I didn't get a wink of sleep the night preceding the day of the sale. I was pacing the floors thinking, "I am really not doing anything that's misleading. I am giving the people tremendous values; every garment in the store has been marked down. I want to sell out as much as possible and leave an impression that no one will ever forget. The name of the store will be remembered for many years." The only thing that really bothered me was the "Blue-Eyed Baby." I could have put in very small print, in parentheses "(not human)," but, as I consoled myself, there are various kinds of blue-eyed babies among the animal species. How was I to foresee the gullibility of people who would actually believe that I was giving away a human baby? However, tomorrow was another day. Moreover it was the kind of day that I was very apprehensive in facing, and I was just plain scared of the consequences when I opened the store.

I vaguely remember the first day of the sale. I was in a daze of fear and guilt when I drove up to the store and entered through the back door. A hostile mass of humanity three blocks long was waiting for the store to open. They were standing there like vultures waiting for a victim, ready to tear it apart with vengeance. My promoter and I decided to let in twenty people at a time in order to prevent a total riot. My guilty feelings had gradually subsided by now, because I was impatiently waiting for the anticipated results, which had taken more than two weeks to prepare.

When my sales staff arrived I said a prayer quietly and opened the door. A mass of humanity rushed for the door like a sudden eruption of a volcano. Everyone headed toward the baby crib, which was empty of course. "Where is the baby? Where is the baby?" came the screams from twenty or more women.

"We do not keep the baby here while the sale is on," I answered as calmly as I could.

"Why not?" came the question in unison.

"Do you think it would be proper to have the baby here, subjecting it to hundreds of people? When the sale is over and the draw has been made, I assure you the baby will be here on that day."

"Is it a boy or a girl? Is it black or white? Where in heaven's name did you get a baby to give away?"

"I'll give you a complete explanation and let you see the baby as promised."

The mob then turned to the pencils and forms, filled them out, and dropped them into the box slot. Business was booming. People were so agitated by all of the publicity, and by the most unusual atmosphere and anticipation, that they were buying indiscriminately without thought or reason, as if they were venting their emotions by spending money. The line of humanity down the street was endless all day long. Everyone was flustered with curiosity to get inside the store and see what was actually happening.

My wife sneaked into the store through the back door, watched the turmoil, the questions, the revulsion some people expressed and said to me, "You shouldn't have done this."

"Why not?" I asked. "Just because people are so gullible? I didn't think it would go that far when I first decided on the idea. Should I have deprived myself of a successful sale, which will be remembered for a decade or two, just because of people who reacted so strongly?"

I told her a humorous story by Harry Golden. A country man came home from the city and told his wife, "Listen, love, I saw a fine young man in town. He is a gem, and I have decided to take him for a son-in-law. He is coming here tomorrow and we will give him board and room for nothing."

His wife answered, "Have you lost your mind? How can we have a son-in-law when we haven't got a daughter?"

"Who cares?" he answered. "Because of that I should lose such a son-in-law? He is a diamond. I like him."

We finally hired a guard to let people in and out. The store was packed. Where did all these people come from? Many came from Oshawa and district, from Oakville, from Hamilton. At 8:00 P.M. we locked the door for the night. "This is enough," I said. "Tomorrow is another day."

The following day was a nightmare. It was unreal. I visualized myself standing on a midway with thousands of people milling about me, but I was too confused to be fully aware of what was actually going on.

In the evening two huge, husky men entered the store and produced detective badges. They informed me that the police had received numerous complaints that we were giving away a baby and they wanted to know where they could see it; otherwise they would have no choice but to arrest me. I asked them to come with me downstairs and showed them the little piglet. "This is the Blue-Eyed Baby," I said. They were unpleasantly amused and instructed me to change the signs, and print thousands of handbills, inserting "Not Human." I complied the following day.

Coincidence plays many roles on many occasions, and this was one of them. While the detectives were writing up a report, two reporters and photographers came in to do a story on that indescribable sale. Upon hearing the conversation they didn't take photographs. However, a story about the sale appeared in a Toronto newspaper. I can't recall whether it made the front page, but I do remember reading in a prominent part of the paper a detailed account of a storekeeper at St. Clair and Dufferin who so ingeniously arranged and executed the "Sale of the Century." The story was also carried in the Brantford newspaper. About a week later the *Toronto Jewish Journal* reported the story in Yiddish, saying that a crazy storekeeper on St. Clair was giving away a pig with each dress. It was inaccurate, of course, but was treated as news of importance.

Although we sold out to the bare walls, I must confess that I feel a pang of guilt each time I think about that sensational sale. Now I can reflect upon some of the humorous episodes that took place during and after the sale. A poor naive woman came in one day while the store was bursting with people, edged her way up to me slowly and apprehensively, looked at me sadly and said, "I am not buying anything, but would you allow me to fill out a slip and put it in the draw box? You see, it's not for me, it's for my daughter-in-law. According to her doctor she can't bear children. Maybe I'll be lucky and win one for her."

Another sad episode of that day, which I cannot forget, comes from the unfriendly conversation I had overheard when two women entered the store. I presumed they were mother-in-law and daughter-in-law. I heard the younger one saying, "I was stupid to marry your son. He can't even provide for the two of us, how is he going to provide for a baby?" They filled in two forms and deposited them in the draw box. By that time they were engaged in a heated argument. The mother-in-law insisted that should one of them be lucky to win the baby she would raise it. "As you said," she admonished her daughter-in-law, "your husband would not be in a financial position to provide for the child." The disagreement developed into a loud argument, which drew the attention of many people who were in the store. I approached the two combatants and said,

"Why do you argue now? You didn't even win the baby yet, and if you do, we will try to find someone with the wisdom of King Solomon and let him decide which one of you is best suited to raise it." I calmed them down and they left the store. As they walked out, I thought, their longing and love for a child are like air—invisible, intangible, and yet it encircled their souls with impossible expectations. Poor gullible people! I can't understand their reasoning or deep-rooted, impossible faith.

The episode made me think of an event that occurred in Winnipeg many years ago. I recall a street and an attached house we had lived in. The verandah had a low partition dividing the two families. I remember sitting there on a very hot day in July, while on the other side of the partition the occupants of the other half of the house sat discussing the possibilities of purchasing a second-hand car. "It would be so nice if we could go out for a drive on a hot day like this," said the husband. "Where are we going to get the money to buy a car?" asked the wife. "Well, I could get a used car for about fifty dollars and pay it out over a period of a year."

Their three children sat silently listening to an unbelievable conversation about a dream that might become a reality. The youngest boy, who was four years old, jumped up, hugged his father, and screamed excitedly, "Papa! I'll sit in the front with you." The older boy joined in, arguing, "No! I am older than you. I'll sit in the front with Papa."

The eight-year-old girl protested to her mother: "I am the oldest. I am going to sit in the front with Papa!"

The mother turned around and without hesitation planted an open-handed smack on the face of her young daughter, turned to the two boys and said, "All of you get the hell out of the car right now! None of you is going, only Papa and I. You are all staying home. We don't want any arguments; we want to enjoy our ride."

The sale had finally come to an end. I felt relieved and began to breathe normally again. One late Saturday afternoon my bank manager came in and drew the winning ticket in front of a packed store. The winner of the "baby" was a single girl who lived in the area. I called her to tell her that she was the winner. There was a melodramatic scene as she pleaded with me that she was in no position to look after a baby. I finally persuaded her to come and pick up her prize. A taxi pulled up in front of the store. She stepped out loaded with baby blankets and other necessities, walked into the store ready to take her baby to her married sister, when I slowly came up the stairs and handed her the piglet. She took the pig, kissed it, and said, "Thank God it's not the kind of baby I thought it was going to be." She turned and planted a kiss of gratitude on my cheek while a store full of people stood by, bursting with laughter. Thus ended a Sale of Sales, which for several days had excited, provoked, stimulated, stirred emotions, incited, and irritated people in all walks of life.

A couple of neighborhood hoodlums were quite upset during the time of the sale and threatened me on one occasion. I told my wife about it. She took it seriously and worried about it. "Don't worry," I said. "You know that God watches over us."

"It's true," she said. "But do *they* know that?"

"I'll tell them the next time I see them."

My sales staff (the old warhorses) were falling off their feet by the time the sale finally came to an end, and I was in need of extra sales help. A friend of mine suggested that I hire a girl he knew who had years of experience and was also loyal and conscientious. Even though I was not impressed when I first interviewed her, I did hire her, only to be sorry later. Instinct is a feeling that should be respected most of the time. She was exceptionally tall and very clumsy-looking. Her appearance represented something that was made of a variety of discarded parts; one part didn't match the other. Her hair looked as if she had been met head-on by a hurricane. She had all the qualifications and grace of a barracuda. However, it would be unfair if I were to omit her commendable qualities. She was a really good saleslady and very conscientious indeed. In fact she sat and cried on occasion when she failed to make a sale. Such unorthodox behavior quite often created an unfavorable atmosphere in the store.

I tried to dismiss her many times, only to find her standing at the door in the morning waiting for me to open the store. We got quite accustomed to each other and had one thing in common: I told her to go to hell; she in turn told me the same thing. She was not a bit discouraged by my insistence that she should leave; she always turned up like a bad check. One day I offered her a two-week vacation: "Why don't you take two weeks off and visit your sister in Baltimore? You deserve it. You have been working very hard. Don't think that I haven't noticed!" She took my advice, went to Baltimore, and, believe it or not, she got married.

23

Feelings About Life

The years 1958 to 1963 were very good. The country was led by one of the most capable governments, headed by a brilliant Prime Minister, John Diefenbaker, whose name carried dignity, integrity, prestige, logic, and wisdom, which was directed and properly guided by a born leader for all of the people. He had been elected by the people without the influence of young gullible radicals who haven't as yet reached the age of reasoning. He understood the needs and aspirations of the Canadian people who elected him. He stood for loyalty and justice for people everywhere and especially in Canada.

Today, we watch as one error is followed by another. Half-hearted, indecisive, inconsistent attempts are being made pretentiously to right the wrong that should have been prevented in the first place. Of course the word *inflation* in those years was used only when one needed air in a tire or had a punctured tube. No one realized then that such a simple, innocent word would plague nations one day. Other unexpected complexities of a more complicated nature have appeared on the scene, plaguing our country and other countries in the world.

These problems require a special leader combined with a special government, to *lead* a country rather than ignore important issues, which obviously need prevention and intervention before they explode in a blaze of fire and feed on inflation, a byproduct that creates hardships for all. No one ever thought that a government would or could be capable of mismanagement or would fail to give responsible leadership. It was inconceivable to think that millions of dollars would be wasted in coming years on costly experiments, imported consultants, and architects, only to scrap it all and throw it into a wastepaper basket.

We didn't have to throw out millions of rotten eggs in order to keep prices up, or slaughter cattle and bury them in deep excavated ditches to keep the undernourished and underprivileged hungry. We didn't have to set up commissions to watch over each other, so that each one does the right thing: namely, create shortages so the prices will remain high and probably go higher. Moreover, millions of tons of food had never been wasted then. We were not as affluent but we had priorities. Necessities came first; luxuries came later, if one could afford them.

Luxuries have become necessities over the years. Two or three cars in a family is certainly not a luxury today. How else can one get around? Walk—as we did, or use public transportation? A twenty-six-inch color television is now a necessity." What would one do without it? We are sick and tired of reading sex and horror novels, but we don't care or are unable to understand a literary book. So what's left? Pornography and body-rub places. We are searching for cheap thrills, which are also wearing thin.

We are blessed with the word *inflation*. We are a sophisticated society; we understand the meaning of the word. That's why we strike. There is hardly a day in the year that some sort of strike is not in progress or being planned. It is my opinion that union members in general are getting a rotten deal because of the in-difference, hesitation, and indecisive action by the government. I also hesitate to agree with union demands, which are unreasonable; however, I believe that if government would be more attentive to the demands of unions, regardless of how unreasonable they may appear, strikes and hostile feelings could be prevented.

The government should think positively and deal with antici-pated problems before they erupt beyond control or reason. No sooner is one strike on the verge of being settled than another is on the verge of being called. The Minister of Agriculture sheds crocodile tears over the plight of the farmers. "Poor souls," they are not getting enough money for their wheat; they are selling it at three or four dollars a bushel and more. Our clever government sells wheat to the Russians and then the price of bread goes up. Why? Because the Minister of Agriculture happened to have men-tioned through the media that a shortage of wheat may exist unless we have a good crop this year. If not, we can always buy our wheat back from the Russians—if we pay them the right price, of course.

We give up in desperation and spend every dollar we make. Why not? The dollar will be worth less tomorrow. Unemployment is rising by leaps and bounds.

I think it is about time that strikes should be banned and re-placed by more modern ways to settle grievances without inter-rupting services and damaging the economy of the country. Strikes are settled by arbitration most of the time anyway, so what pur-pose does a strike serve, other than to create hardships and unem-ployment? We must have unions to protect workers from greedy employers. Democratic-minded leaders must guide them, lead them —not with malice, but by reason and understanding. We must also be protected from the rich, who are the spawning grounds for mistreatment. To me a rich man is a symbol of greed, despite his public display of philanthropy.

Inflation is a condition created by poor management and strikes, which paralyze the country and reduce productivity to a point where we lose our export trade because of competitive world prices.

In government, as in operating a business, you must see to it that overhead doesn't exceed profits. Thus it is unfortunate that governments don't possess the elementary knowledge of how to operate a business. They are forever incompetently pursuing the easiest and most wrongheaded experiments, which are baseless and ultimately useless. Just take Pickering Airport as one example of error and misjudgment. Millions of dollars have been wasted on planning, consultants, engineers, demolition of homes, expropria-tion of property, only to abandon it when public protests mounted.

I don't subscribe to the theory that some people support: "If you can't change it accept it." We don't have to accept anything if a majority disagree with certain policies a government tries to implement. We are not employees; we are employers. Our wishes should be honored by those we have chosen to run our economy. Did our chosen representatives ask us to vote as to whether or not a raise in their salaries was justifiable? Nevertheless, laws of all sorts are forever being forced upon us. Some are very good laws; others should be decided by a plebiscite of the people. I am not a politician or an economist, and I am not an authority on matters pertaining to government spending. However, one doesn't have to be either to see the errors, the inconsistencies that exist, and to speak up as a Canadian concerning economic and political issues which are being mishandled. They go to the very essence of our society.

The federal government's Manpower Agency is a useless and highly expensive giant. From my experience I would prefer to see the old-fashioned unemployment insurance branches reestablished.

They served the people well and enjoyed a close relationship with those who needed employees, as well as those who were seeking jobs. On occasions when I needed extra sales help, they would send me an applicant within a day or so, although some applicants who showed up were interested only in working part-time and wished to be paid by cash rather than check. Nevertheless, those branches were quite efficient in locating applicants for unfilled positions, unlike the oversized Manpower, which in my opinion is a waste of money and serves no visible or practical purpose. The only communication I have ever had with Manpower has been the occasional telephone inquiry to learn if they had someone on file who would suit my requirements. I have never heard from them in reply.

I don't claim to fully understand the complexities of politics; I am merely expressing my opinion. I feel it's a citizen's duty to criticize those who are responsible for the conditions facing our country today. One cannot elaborate too much on political issues because of their complex nature. Nevertheless, I am as certain as you are that a sound, consistent policy would rectify some of the self-induced problems we endure unnecessarily. We love Canada. I think it is a country of opportunity, unlike any other country in the world. The social and economic structures have improved dramatically over the past two decades. Mismanagement, however, is partially responsible for its deterioration.

Many years ago I read a story about an ancient tribe who had set up camp at the foot of a very tall mountain. According to their custom a leader was chosen by primitive methods. It was customary on such occasions that three tribesmen be ordered to climb the mountain. The one who would bring back an object or detailed information from the top of the mountain would become the new leader. The first man was gone for several days and brought back a twig, which he got halfway up the mountain. The second tribesman brought back a small tree and some flowers, which had been growing close to the peak of the mountain. He was not able to reach the top because he became very ill. He returned sick and dejected because of his failure to achieve the necessary results. Now was the third man's turn. He was away for several days and presumed lost. One day he reappeared happy and excited, without a scratch—unlike the other two, who returned sick, bloodied, and exhausted. "Why are you so happy?" asked the old Chief. "You haven't as much as brought back a twig or a flower as the others have. Did you not reach the top of the mountain?"

"No, my chief, I did not," replied the tribesman. "But for the first time in my life I saw the sea, the most beautiful sight I have ever seen. Have any of the others seen the sea?"

"No," replied the Chief. "They did not see beauty. They were mainly interested in gaining the leadership."

And so the tribesman who saw beauty that impressed him very deeply became the new Chief and leader of the tribe.

Some politicians are drowning in their own egos. They can't see themselves in their true form. They never see the beauty of the sea; they are too egotistic to see others. They remain blinded by their own imaginary importance. Some people read books but very often fail to find the basic message the book contains. As a result, they don't find it interesting, for they failed to see the restlessness of a creative soul and the majestic turbulence of the sea. The same can be applied to art or music, which is enjoyable to some and penetrates the soul with its beauty, while to others, who can't see or hear, it is very boring. I would think that sensitivity is greatly responsible for one's reactions.

Happiness was meaningless a lifetime ago; no one ever gave it a thought. Life was lived naturally and innocently and no one ever delved into its pattern or mystery. A generation passed and a generation came without question or remorse. Today, everyone has a lot of questions to which answers cannot be found. Everyone wants to be happy without earning it. No one can explain what in fact happiness is supposed to represent. I don't believe that there is such a thing as happiness in reality. The word *contentment* is likely to be more rewarding and tangible. Happiness is for dreamers who dream while fully awake. Happiness, if and when it penetrates one's heart, is but for a fleeting moment. It means different things to different people; it changes momentarily and vanishes to make room for another moment of a different nature.

Here I am, a businessman, a promoter, enjoying some material success. This is a far cry from my peddling days at a very tender age. Reflections always affect me deeply. I like to delve into the past—it makes the present more meaningful—rather than to dismiss and forget experiences just as quickly as a day passes.

Having grown up in a very religious environment, I became unsettled by my new experiences of hypocrisy and deceit, yet I remained faithful to my beliefs, traditions, and religion. My thinking has always been inclined toward realism, seeking in vain to regain an equilibrium in order to promote some realistic thinking. Mutual distrust developed into mutual antipathy, which troubled me deeply. "You have persecuted me long enough. Now let me persecute you for a change." Such acts are against my morals and principles. I therefore adopted a feeling of indifference toward people in general and the so-called philanthropists in particular. There is so little difference between a coward who persistently tries to cover his weaknesses by constantly seeking some sort of glory, and a hero to whom such triviality is meaningless. It isn't so much what one is doing as *why* he is doing it. I don't pretend to be an exception, and I am not qualified to philosophize. I am merely expressing my feelings about life, time, unethical behavior, memories, as they affect me personally.

My mind wanders to the Statue of Liberty I cherished very dearly when I first arrived in New York. That statue stands majestically on a solid pedestal on small Bedloe's Island outside the hustle and bustle of New York City. A massive arm is raised high, holding a torch in the direction of the open, mysterious Atlantic Ocean and to the world, inviting refugees who miraculously escaped the dens of the tigers from their respective countries. The arm signifies a welcome to the homeless and persecuted. It is a commemoration of the birth of the United States and the continuing friendship of the French and American democracies. On the pedestal is inscribed the sonnet "The New Colossus" by Emma Lazarus, which reads in part:

> *Give me your tired, your poor,*
> *Your huddled masses yearning to breathe free,*
> *The wretched refuse of your teeming shore.*
> *Send these, the homeless, tempest-tossed to me.*
> *I lift my lamp beside the golden door.*

The statue relates to you silently but assuredly the promise of protection without reservation. It is the statue that over the years has welcomed people who were gaining their first taste of freedom and security. Such and other memories cannot be erased. They are the essence of one's sense of values.

24

The Need to Grieve

In July, 1956, I decided to take a few days' vacation after the sensational, nerve-wracking sale. I went to Dansville, New York, where McFadden's Health Spa was located; it was very popular at that time. It was ideal for relaxation and also quite famous for its reducing methods. It attracted overweight people from all over North America and Europe. That health spa is now called "The Castle on the Hill." McFadden made the last of several parachute jumps over Niagara Falls at the age of eighty-nine. He had proved to the world that man can retain health, longevity, and resilience by proper diet and exercise regardless of age.

It was an old building standing majestically on top of a hill, embraced by huge evergreen trees and lavish beds of multi-colored flowers contentedly looking up at the deep universe. The building, although more than a hundred years old, projected indescribable grandeur.

One evening at the spa I couldn't help overhearing two ladies discussing their vacations. "The evenings are quite cool," said one lady. "I should have brought a couple of mink stoles or jackets with me." Not to be outdone, her friend replied, "One never knows what to take along on vacation. My fingers feel so bare; I left all my diamond rings in the Chase Manhattan Bank." One innocent-looking lady who sat in a rocking chair by herself a few feet away suddenly fell out of the chair and passed out. I ran to get the doctor who had his office inside the building, and called out, "Help, doctor, help! There is a lady on the verandah lying face down. I think she is unconscious." After the doctor revived her, she was asked what happened: Why did you faint? "I am allergic to 'B.S.,'" she replied.

On another evening I sat under the roof of the verandah, watching fine rain falling, forming water puddles around the building. My heart gladdens at the sight of rain. I love rain especially in the late spring, as it showers the thirsty earth and seeps silently deep down to make green grass grow.

Mrs. Shlep, a guest of the spa, insisted that I listen to her story; I had no alternative but to join other listeners. She hadn't been in good health for some time, and it showed. "I have a very good and understanding husband," she boasted. "I approached him with an idea recently which was on my mind for some time."

"Dave," she said to her husband, "do you know Isaac, who is a master in painting beautiful portraits?"

"Of course I know him."

"I would like to have him do a portrait of me!"

"So—go and have him do it, but why do you want to have him do your portrait all of a sudden?"

"I don't feel too well, so I would like to leave you one to remember me by."

She went to Isaac, the portrait painter, and sat patiently while he was doing what was to be a real masterpiece. On her third sitting the portrait was finally finished. She examined it very carefully and began to demand that he should add some extra glitter.

"You see," she said, "make me a nice diamond necklace, a nice large sapphire bracelet on my right wrist, and rubies on the front of my dress."

"Mrs. Shlep," said the artist.

"Wait, I am not finished. I want a large gold watch on a chain studded with large diamonds around my neck and long diamond earrings."

"Don't you think that all that jewelry will sort of take away from the beauty of the portrait?" Isaac asked in astonishment.

"I know it will," Mrs. Shlep replied, "but when I pass on I know that my husband will remarry. I want his future wife to have a heart attack searching for all this expensive jewelry."

A variety of similar stories were quite common in The Castle on the Hill.

After my vacation I went to New York to see a Miami dress line and called upon my childhood friend, Saul, with whom I had worked on a farm in Hirsch until his father succeeded in bringing him over to New York in 1929.

He met me at my hotel one day and, after reminiscing about our childhood and our memories from the farm, I said, "Let me take your hand, my friend, and lead you to Central Park." It was a stifling hot summer day and we had some idle time to recapture nostalgic memories, which we had left there for safekeeping more than four decades ago. Saul and I revisited a familiar world by which we had been fascinated many a time when we were both young. It was a beautiful sight to see the trees where we had carved our names one Sunday afternoon, a million years ago. The grass, the ponds, the flower beds seemed to be in deep slumber under the hot sun in the midst of oblivion. It was the kind of day when sitting and touching the green grass brought joy and serenity to our hearts. The silence was almost unbearable, and yet so soothing one could sit down and weep for joy. The trees were standing still; only a wisp of a gentle breeze caressed the leaves on the treetops. When the sun had gone down and a crimson glow was still suspended at the edge of the horizon, twilight descended in hypnotic silent prayer. Birds perched on tree branches were still; the swans and ducks in the pond curled up their necks and hid their heads under the wings in preparation for the night. Silence and tranquility covered the park and its creatures. Nature had gone to sleep; only the klip-klap of horses' hooves could be heard in the distance.

Muggings in parks were quite prevalent. I had heard some gruesome stories about Central Park in particular prior to my trip. It didn't, however, come to mind to return to the city at nightfall. We were mesmerized by the overwhelming beauty of nature and the darkness of night. We had much to talk about. Twenty-five years had passed since we had seen each other, and we were reminiscing about the hard times we endured in New York during the Depression, and about the nice girls who were trying desperately to have us propose to them, while we were both young and available. I remembered one girl in particular, who had said to me one day while we sat on the Williamsburg Bridge, "My father owns a furniture and mattress factory. He offered to furnish a beautiful apartment for me; we own the building." Poor soul, she was a good-looking girl, young and innocent (I think), but I rejected her proposition, simply because she was rich and I was poor. I think about her to this day, wondering whether she finally did get married.

My friend and I fell asleep under the huge branches of a tree, while twinkling stars and the smiling moon kept watch over us. It was two o'clock in the morning when we finally returned to the city. We bade each other good night and parted. Such a night can never be erased from one's memory. It remains indelible.

Upon my return to Toronto I found that the store was doing very poorly, particularly in summer dresses. The season was coming to an end and a promotion of some sort had to be prepared. I knew of a man who specialized in unique displays for the Canadian National Exhibition. Rummaging through heaps of junk he had stored in a garage, I found a life-sized doll made in the form of a stout black woman—he called it "Aunt Jemima"—which operated mechanically in a variety of animations. I put her in the store window and dressed her in a red-and-green dress with a bandana around her sweaty head to match her outfit. We placed a laundry washtub and washboard in front of her, put an old dress on the washboard, and turned on the motor. She bent over, took hold of the dress with both hands, and proceeded to work. She stopped every few minutes, straightened her back, and her electric-bulb eyes lit up. She looked to the right and then to the left, raised an arm, wiped the perspiration off her face, bent over and proceeded to work.

This display drew more attention than expected. Dresses were selling as if they were a dime a dozen. Well! Business is good, I thought, but "tomorrow is another day"; let's hope it continues to be good!

Some people call good fortune luck, but I define it as preparedness for unexpected opportunity, which one has to possess in order to reap life's rewards.

We also used film and live playettes on the screens of a few theatres in Toronto and at drive-ins. I imported the films from Colorado, and a local radio announcer taped an impressive message. While soft music was playing, moving live models were gliding and turning across the stage. All these things combined were responsible for building up prestige and a sound business.

Our dream was slowly being fulfilled. My wife and I had put a lot of work into it. Cleaning the store and basement on Sundays and on holidays was a weekly chore for both of us. For years we worried about tomorrow. Will it be better than today, or will tomorrow be worse?

Memories are like waves of an ocean rushing constantly toward the rim of the shore into endless time, but no one knows the exact place of their origin. Waves apparently emerge from the depths of huge bodies of water, somewhat as do memories from a very insignificant part of the brain, which is capable of retaining the thousands of memories and experiences of a lifetime.

I am still a little boy at heart. I visualize heroes little boys dream about. Yurko, our Ukrainian neighbor's black, shiny horse, was my hero. My uncle Eliah was my hero. He was a tall, huge man with a beard to match. He was a horse dealer, and had a number of horses in an enclosed small pasture at all times. I was petrified of my uncle because he never smiled, but I admired him at the same time, especially when he sometimes pinched my cheek. Even though it was painful I loved him; I knew that he had noticed me. He was the closest father image I had.

I am also a dreamer by nature. My mind takes an excursion on occasion, shows me my village and its people as I remember them. I fantasize about our forefathers, sages and prophets about whom I learned and read in the later years of my life. They claimed that the world is based on religion, which is Torah, divine service, practice of charity, ethics and morals, rules of conduct and reason. To neglect them would bring about the downfall of civilization. The injustice and evil we witness today seem to be leading to catastrophe. Greed, hate, and deceit are spreading rapidly, but no one is interested in impeding their poisonous progress.

Perhaps one of the thirty-six saints who, according to the Talmud, roam the world, will show up, restore some sanity to people at large, and save the world from self-destruction. We know from history that whenever the Jewish people were threatened with complete annihilation, a miracle happened that saved them each time. The whole world is in danger of being annihilated now, without exception. We need one or more of the thirty-six saints; we need a miracle to save the crazy, mixed-up people of the world.

Even though intermarriages have become quite common, division, racism, and anti-Semitism exist. I attribute this to society's ignorance, to individuals who are inclined to believe and practice the philosophy of past generations. Such evils also depend to a great extent on one's background and intelligence.

I think it is appropriate here to relate a story I was once told by a dear friend:

Yosel was born and grew up in Toronto, but subsequently moved to Hollywood, where he became a famous movie producer. He called his mother one day, and excitedly shouted into the telephone, "Ma, congratulate me! I got married last week!"

"Oh, my dear Yosel, you have made me very happy!"

"Ma, my name is not Yosel, I am called Joseph."

"All right, my dear Josephil."

"You know, mother, I married a beautiful Asian girl who has two children. Aren't I lucky to have a beautiful wife and a ready, growing family?"

"You sure are," said his mother enthusiastically.

"We have decided to move to Toronto. Will it be all right if we stay with you and Papa for a few days, until we find a house?"

"What a silly question! Of course, you'll stay in our house, not only for a few days, but for as long as you want," shouted Mama into the telephone.

"But, mother, the house is too small for all of us."

"Don't worry, my dear Josephil, you'll have the whole house to yourself."

"How about you and Papa?"

"Oh, that won't be a problem. Your father will jump from the top of the building at Spadina Avenue and Adelaide upon hearing the news, and I will turn on the gas, put my head inside the oven, and leave it there until I am dead. So you see, my dear son Josephil, there is nothing to worry about!"

The poor aggravated mother confided in her neighbor that her son was a film producer and was coming to live with her. "Ethel, I am worried," she said.

"Don't be silly, you should be very happy. I wish my son was a producer!"

"What is your son doing for a living?"

"He is a chemist."

"A chemist, that's a very good profession!"

"Oh, sure," said Ethel, "the trouble is he specializes in one area of the profession. He takes money and makes *drek* out of it!"

It is unfortunate that the overprotected never mature. Parental generosity and unguided discipline usually result in parents losing the respect of their children, because they are forever denied the opportunity of facing the realities of life, or making decisions on their own. They are forever dependent on others; they were never given the opportunity or encouragement to become self-sufficient. Such overprotection can be very harsh when life and responsibilities meet them face to face. Experiences of worrying and coping with responsibilities are not only to be accepted as a last resort, but are necessary in order to make one understand and be prepared to handle the problems of living.

I will skip a few years at this stage to describe a familiar scene that touched me very deeply. It drew my attention and made my soul weep. It brought on unforgettable memories of many years. A middle-aged woman, led by a younger one, was in the process of trying to cross Bathurst Street at College Street, while I was in my car waiting for the traffic light to change. It took five light changes until the struggle of crossing the street came to an end. The older lady was apparently paralyzed on one side; her foot appeared to be nailed to the asphalt. Her assistant finally carried her across. I sat and visualized all the painful years I had endured with my late wife when I tried to lead her to bed from her sofa corner, but she couldn't take one step. She would look at me pleadingly with her watery eyes as if she was saying, "Please carry me into bed," which I did. I can still see the fear in her eyes to this very day.

Twelve years of soul-searing pain cannot be erased, although it is a part of the complexities of life, which are difficult to bear. All one can do is mourn and grieve. It helps if one remembers to notice other people's misfortunes and find some consolation and a possible answer to the ever-present question: Why me?

This reminds me of a man I knew some years ago. He was forever complaining and seeking sympathy because he was poor and couldn't afford the price of a cheap pair of shoes.

Then one day he unexpectedly saw a man without legs being wheeled by a friend. That apparently shocked him into reality and he stopped complaining.

When you are looking down you can always see someone less fortunate than you are, which makes you aware that you have a lot more to be thankful for than you realize.

Mourning as understood by Freud also serves a profound need in human beings; we need to grieve. The loss of a loved one should not be something we shrug off; it reverberates under our conscious awareness of the pain. Mourning is far from being sentimental; it is vital to the lives and the very existence of the ones left behind. Mourning provides time during which we can become adjusted emotionally to the loss we have sustained, so that we can, in time, heal again.

Eventually the time comes when a person realizes that he has mourned long enough, even though deep down the bleeding has not stopped. I felt like a conspirator, guilty for being alive after what we had both gone through—hope, deprivation, and despair. I couldn't hide some crucial episodes of the unreal tragic years. How can I possibly forget the feeling of hopelessness? I thrive on it; there is something tangible in things that are unforgettable.

25

Selling as a Career

The retail ladies' wear business is most insecure and unpredictable; one never knows what to expect—it can change each day from bad to worse. You are forever worrying if tomorrow will be a better day. Most of the time you are treading on thin ice, which can crack, and you can drown as a result; but it is a business, a career. Some people choose selling as a career because they think that they are born salespeople. However, I don't support this theory. I have seen too many poor salespeople, even though they claimed years of experience and considered themselves talented in the profession. It is only an illusion, which hardly ever meets the requirements. To be successful in selling one needs more than an engaging smile. One must be focused on attitude and skills derived from training and self-criticism.

Some salespeople on the retail level do not speak enough to a potential customer. Others speak too much. As a result both parties are guilty of creating a feeling of hostility. A salesperson can be compared to a swimmer; a poor swimmer splashes around in the water, going nowhere, whereas a professional swimmer glides smoothly across the pool without making a sound.

I also compare a professional salesperson to a surgeon, who had his basic training and also extensive experience, but a refresher course is essential in order to keep up with new techniques and improve on the old.

Sales personnel in general, and of ladies' wear in particular, can be compared to attractive, colorful wrappers on chocolate bars. Had the same product been wrapped in plain brown paper, it would sit on the shelf without being noticed. It is the attractive wrapper or container that draws attention. A good saleslady can make a "nothing" dress look like a gown fit for a princess; others can make the same dress look like *drek*. Repeat business depends on the wrapper, the presentation of the product, and the product itself. Duties and challenges are demanding and stimulating; if handled properly they will be rewarding.

Sales personnel should also be committed to self-improvement, which would be profitable for all parties concerned. One must practice self-analysis and be one's own critic; remember the things that were said that may have been responsible for losing a sale. You therefore try to improve and correct your technique, making sure that a similar situation does not occur again. When a sale is made quickly and easily, it too should be analyzed. Was it the customer who was cooperative (a pushover?) or vulnerable, or was it something you had said in a soothing, convincing voice? Make a mental note; it will serve you well next time around. Productive salespeople never brag about their achievements; they accept them as a matter of course, whereas ineffective salespeople are prone to brag. Knowing their inadequacies, they overreact and overdramatize situations.

Selling demands concentration and imagination. The secret to productive selling is very simple: a keen desire, honesty, and a strong will culminate in success. But before you can expect miracles, you must first find the most effective way to approach; after that it is simple.

Customers are people like you, and, to understand them fully, you must understand them with your heart. They are always on the defensive. Some carry a chip on their shoulders, some are as cold as icicles; it is up to you to melt the icicles slowly and methodically. When you sell a garment that sells at more than twenty-five dollars and needs to be altered, don't ask the customer to pay in full; on the contrary, ask for a sizable deposit, in order to avoid the haggling over price or sales tax. Of course many unforseen situations remain for you to decide. You have to be flexible, rise or stoop as the occasion demands, and act accordingly.

I confess that it was difficult to work for me. I was forever seeking improvement. Sales help who had had ten or even twenty years of experience had to undergo a re-training course when they came to work for me.

The following qualifications are required in order to be a successful saleslady: She must work like a horse, think like a man, chew gum and blow bubbles when serving a gum chewer, light a cigarette and blow the smoke in the customer's face when she can't make the sale, go to the back room and swear like a drunken sailor, call her an S.O.B. and come out smiling, talk dirty when serving a hooker, but keep on smiling, act like a lady at all times, and be in tune to deal with all challenges.

Proper selling is smooth soothing music to my ears instead of irritation, unbearable noise, and obvious pressure.

"Dear", "honey", or "darling" can be overdone; call a customer by her first name, and if you don't know her first name, greet her by saying, "Hello, Mary." "My name isn't Mary; my name is Jean" (or whatever), she'll reply. "Jean, oh, I am sorry, you look exactly like one of my customers whose name is Mary. Okay, Jean, can I help you look around?"

"Dear" and "honey" remind me of a mother who pampered her little boy by pouring praise on him each day. In North America it is Mama who prolongs childhood by not giving the child a chance to practice independence, until one day she realizes that her baby is starting school. All of his life he was called "Tatalé" (little father), an expression of endearment, and now he trots off to school, where he begins to discover a new world, unlike that which he had in the confines of his home.

Mama is nervously waiting at the door. "Tatalé" is on his way home. The minute he opens the door Mama embraces him and asks, "Tatalé, what did you learn in school today?" "I learned that my name is Irving" (Harry Golden).

Similar situations can be created between sales personnel and the customer. One has to know when and where to draw the line; otherwise you will spoil them. They will expect you to give them discounts, alter garments each time they gain or lose weight, and this can go on for years.

To me salesmanship was a daily challenge. I liked to influence people and be the victor. Think of a customer as you would think of one who is on his best behavior, persuading you to marry him, and of course the strategy changes. You must strive to be liked not only because you are a bubbling personality but because it is your attitude combined with sincerity and honesty; you make the customer confide in you. Each one of us is seeking a sympathetic ear, and a customer is no exception. Once you accomplish that, you cannot miss. Don't get too chummy with ethnic customers who never give up bargaining. Their favorite expression is "Aren't you going to take something off?" If it happened that an old lemon (meaning old garment) was on the verge of being sold, I would give in, by saying, "You are such nice people, I'll try and help you and sell it for less."

In ladies' wear one must depend on moods, on idiosyncrasies, and on impulse buyers. Failing this, you are on *Gehakte Tzures* (you are in chopped trouble), which is very damaging to one's dignity. One must learn to accept it as a part of life when one operates a business in the heart of a people who thrive on bargaining. It is their way of life brought over from their respective countries. It is traditional to bargain, even though it is unnecessary and unreasonable. It is ghetto style, as in the Jewish ghetto that flourished on the lower East Side of New York half a century or so ago.

There, bargaining was a way of life. They were honest but unwordly people who lived by their emotions rather than thought. They found adjustment to a new democratic world very difficult. They projected naiveté, distrust, and hostility all at the same time, primarily because of years of insecurity.

Ethnic customers in general have given me a hard time over the years. I have found, however, that Italian people accept more readily a genuine smile. Italian unorthodox behavior can be attributed only to emotional frustrations because of the language barrier. They find it difficult to express themselves, and are supersensitive to the Canadian lifestyle.

One day I watched a woman try on twelve dresses while her husband sat in a chair sound asleep because of an overdose of alcohol. She finally chose one dress, left a deposit, got as far as the door, turned right back and said, "I have changed my mind; I want my deposit back. I don't think I want the dress after all."

It was a great day despite the woman who didn't know what she wanted. It was a splendid cool morning with a light milky haze lifting slowly, disappearing in front of a wisp of a breeze. It will be a good day; I can feel it.

There is the prevailing notion that you've got to keep women thinking about themselves and how pretty they are. This can be helpful, but it is also harmful, because not too many women are aware when they are really pretty. Most of them think that they are being flattered into something that is hideous. Of course that is their opinion; they are not accustomed to seeing themselves dressed properly, because they constantly resist an impartial opinion. Nevertheless I shall cope with them, and not let them spoil my inner serenity.

They act as if they want to spite the saleslady when choosing a garment. They reject the things that really make them look pretty, and select something that is absolutely uncomplimentary. But the customers are always right! If they would only realize that a saleslady is their best friend and adviser, they would be dressed smartly, as opposed to their set ways and poor tastes. I know for a fact that the most satisfied customer is the one who takes the advice of a salesperson, rather than disagree. No one can see oneself as others do, especially when wearing a new garment. As for sales help, you must remember that even if your customer does not speak English too well, she will understand and respond to a genuine smile; that is universal.

A woman who interprets "fashion" the way it suits her, rather than thinking of fashions that make headlines in fashion magazines, will always be dressed smartly on a minimum budget.

If you were to ask me what type of woman I favor as being best able to wear fashion and create beauty, I would have to say that, ideally, I prefer one with a nicely balanced figure and a sense of herself. The wearer must inject her personality and individuality and make them come to life. Clothes help, but only a person can give them that certain pizazz.

I definitely feel that, if a woman has taste and good judgment, she will never allow herself to look stupid or foolish, no matter what the fashion of the moment may be. She will wear what suits her figure and personality best.

A woman must try to be individualistic in her choice, to carry off a certain look, depending on her figure and personality. It is not what a woman wears that counts; it is the way she wears it. What may look smashingly smart on one, will look hideous on another; it depends on how graceful one moves about.

Women are also a very jealous breed. They walk around for weeks in search of a gown, which we call "one of a kind." I have had complaints on occasion that another woman wore the identical gown at one affair or another. "I thought that my gown was one of a kind! After all I paid $89.95 for it."

"It was one of a kind in my store, but it is apparent that another store also had the same 'one of a kind' gown."

I failed to mention one part-time saleslady I had hired, who was supposed to have had years of experience. I had noticed, however, that while she was in the process of selling a coat she would eventually come over and say to me, "I can get ninety dollars for this coat; do you want to sell it?"

"What is the regular price," I asked.

"$140."

"How then can you sell it for ninety dollars?"

After the customer walked out, she would go to the back of the store and cry her eyes out. "What are you crying about?" I asked.

"You didn't let me sell the coat after I worked so hard to persuade the customer to buy it."

"You weren't selling it; you were giving it away!"

At closing time she would take her working shoes home with her, an indication that she was quitting, only to turn up the following morning.

I trust you will appreciate to some degree what life is like in retail ladies' wear: the daily aggravations and complexities one has to face, the daily problems one has to cope with and keep on smiling.

Self-discipline is a very important factor in the art of selling. Do you meditate for a few minutes each day, not because of religious beliefs, but only in order to tranquilize your emotions and get rid of hostile feelings that you may or may not have when morning comes as dull and as morbid as all previous mornings? Do you apply creative thinking when you are selling? Do you wait to be told what to do or how to improve in your chosen career, or do you plan your own activities and improvement? Do you remember names of customers? If so, do you speak to them on a first-name basis? If you can answer yes to the above questions, you are a salesperson with promotional abilities. Otherwise, you have apparently no ambition or enthusiasm for your work. Unfortunately there is no substitute for work. It is the price of success.

As James Bender says, "Markets are created by businessmen, and profits are created by enthusiastic experienced sales help." It is to your advantage to create a loyal customer and, of course, the profits that go with that relationship.

To me it was a challenge. I was trying to improve my technique each day in order to gain or maintain prestige. Logic, common sense, and diplomacy, combined with honesty and daily experiences, can do wonders for an individual who is forever searching for improvement. I have been fortunate through the years to have had the same staff working for me from the day I opened the store for business. Some were less enthusiastic than others; some were naive, gullible, meek, lazy, indifferent; some created waves unnecessarily; some pinned medals upon themselves; others were docile; some were rebellious; some wrapped garments before they got paid, resulting in the loss of sales (the customer changing her mind by the time the garment was wrapped). But generally everything went as close to a planned system as possible. My sales staff were considered the best in the garment industry, and so were my alteration girls and fitters.

I had analyzed, criticized, lectured, in order to improve selling techniques. Productive selling must be a spontaneous reaction, and logical dialogue must be convincing and understandable. This applies to inquiries, resistance, or a simple explanation, which are potential sales, depending on your ability to express yourself and on your tone of voice.

Remember that most women—especially when choosing a garment—are very sensitive because of their insecurity brought on by the ever-present inferiority complex.

I find it difficult to forget one part-time salesgirl who was sloppy, unattractive, and due for her third "Bar Mitzvah". She worked like a horse and looked like an ass. She never had a date, and was therefore satisfied, even elated, when she had the opportunity to work overtime. One day a salesman walked in, not overly bright or neatly dressed, as is the unwritten law in the garment industry. He was a *shleper* (which means in Yiddish a drag and a failure). *Shleper* also means a jerk, unkempt, untidy, one who does not invite the proper standard of respect. This kind of individual never has an opportunity of getting an expensive line; he has to be content with whatever is available, usually what is rejected by more capable individuals. Such salesmen carried the samples in their cars and canvassed stores for business. In this particular case my ugly saleslady struck up a conversation with this "sex symbol," and in a coy manner half-teasingly said to him, "I am holding a handful of beans in my right hand, and if you guess how many beans I have I may consider going out for dinner with you."

The salesman turned crimson and played it safe by saying, "You have three thousand, nine hundred and fifty-nine beans in your hand."

"You are close enough; you got yourself a date," she said.

"Give me a picture of yourself and I will think about it," answered the salesman apologetically.

"I don't have any good pictures," she replied. "Every picture

I have looks like me. Sorry, but we are going out tonight as arranged, she said triumphantly.

"I don't believe you, I want a second opinion, I want a recount," he said, looking at me for my support.

I turned away because I was sorry for both of them. I did, however, come to his rescue by calling him to join me for coffee in the restaurant next door. He then told me among other things about a friend of his, a widower, who had just returned from vacation in Miami. The stories about his friend's problems would have touched the heart of the most hardened. His friend was very lonely while he was away; he couldn't make friends in the same way as other widowers had. The widows—who are plentiful in Miami—ignored him, even though he did his best to attract their attention, while they clung to other widowers most of the time. "Perhaps your friend uses the wrong deodorant," I said jokingly. "I don't think that this was the problem," he said seriously. "He is a very nice man, but overly reserved." "That must be the answer to your friend's problem," I remarked. The conversation reminded me of a story of just such a character described by Leo Rosten in his book *The Joys of Yiddish*.

Let me first explain that in Yiddish the word *schmuck* means a penis, and is often used to express one's feelings about someone who is disliked. It is also a form of self-reprobation by one who realizes that he had been taken by a liar. You would say, "What a schmuck I have been to believe him!"

Mr. Lefkowitz, sixty-five and a widower, had a faceless face— the kind you remember, not because it has any character, but because you see it on many other bodies every day. He was having a lonely time in Miami Beach. He observed a man of his age who was never without a companion. People forever streamed around him extending invitations, swapping jokes. So Lefkowitz screwed up his courage, leaned over and said to the popular paragon, "Mister, excuse me, what should I do to make friends?"

"Get a camel," sneered the other. "Ride up and down Collins Avenue every day and before you know it everyone in Miami will be asking, 'Who is that man?' and you'll have to hire a social secretary to handle the invitations. Don't bother me again with such a foolish question."

So Mr. Lefkowitz bought a paper and looked through the ads, and by good fortune read of a circus stranded in Miami needing extra money. Mr. Lefkowitz telephoned the circus owner, and within half an hour he had rented a camel.

The next morning Mr. Lefkowitz, wearing khaki shorts and a pith helmet, mounted his camel and set forth on Collins Avenue. Everywhere people stopped, buzzed, gawked, pointed. Every day for a week Lefkowitz rode his trusty steed.

One morning, just as he was about to get dressed, the telephone rang. "Mr. Lefkowitz. This is the parking lot attendant. Your camel is gone—stolen!"

At once Mr. Lefkowitz phoned the police. A Sergeant O'Neil answered. "What? It sounded as though you said someone had stolen your camel."

"That's right! Er—a form? I'll fill out a form."

"How tall was the animal?"

"From the sidewalk to his back, where I sat, a good six feet."

"What color was it?"

"What color? Camel color, a regular camel-colored camel!"

"Male or female?"

"Huh?"

"Was the animal male or female?"

"How am I supposed to know about the sex of a camel? Wait! Aha! It was a male!"

"Are you sure?"

"Absolutely!"

"But Mr. Lefkowitz, a moment ago you didn't . . . ."

"I am positive, officer, because I just remembered every time and every place I was riding on that camel, I could hear people yelling, 'Hey! Look at the schmuck on that camel!'"

26

Serving the Customer

The sales staff in the store today is as it has been over the years; some are fluent in Italian, which is an invaluable asset to the store, especially since the Italian people began their exodus from around College Street northward to St. Clair and Dufferin Avenue and beyond. A variety of ethnic people have settled in the neighborhood during the last fifteen years, replacing old customers who have moved to out-of-the-way areas up to fifty miles away from the store. Surprising as it may sound, they have never stopped coming back, regardless of how far they have to travel—an indication of the loyalty they have to the store and the image I have built up over the years.

In another part of this book, I mentioned that for some unknown reason customers are always on the defensive from the moment they enter a ladies' wear store, whereas in a food store that same consumer is most aggressive. I believe that I have the answer: They resent the sales help in spite of the fact that they demand personalized service. They feel free and knowledgeable in a food store or a large drugstore, whereas in a ladies' wear store they get nervous, even embarrassed, because of their limited ability to judge their own likes and dislikes.

A customer's behavior, I think, is due partly to her insecurity. When a well-groomed, smiling saleslady approaches her, she automatically develops resentment and says, "I am just looking." She is on guard not to be told what type of garment she should wear to make the most of what she is or has. My advice to salesladies is: Do not push your knowledge or opinion. Leave her be, talk about the weather; she'll come around. I have had complaints on occasion that another lady wore the identical gown at an affair as the one she had purchased. Firstly, I said, bear in mind that $69.95 will not purchase an original; secondly, it only proves that you have good taste.

People in general, and some women in particular, let their imaginations wander beyond the limits of their understanding. They continue to live in a world of make-believe, illusions, and imagination. I agree that they are important, but only to themselves; no one else cares whether you reach your dream goal to be considered rich and important. If you are not important money will not change your image; it will only buy respect, which will be camouflaged by hypocrisy. To stress my point about people and their ways of thinking, the following is an excerpt from a letter I received from a university graduate a few weeks after my first book, *Orphan of the Storm,* was published.

Dear Mr. Henig:

I was born and raised in Canada. I had served in the Air Force during World War II. I consider myself to be of average intelligence and socialize with many Jewish friends. However, after I had finished reading your book I realized that I had lived under a false impression during my adult years. Your book opened up a new world that I hadn't known existed. Let me also mention that I am a devout Catholic and believe in equal rights regardless of race or religion, but I cannot comprehend your picture descriptions of the Jewish communities who lived in isolated villages in hopeless poverty which you describe so dramatically. I have always been under the impression that all Jews were rich until I got around to reading your book that describes so vividly the adversities and the suffering of your people.

I congratulate you on such an excellent descriptive account, it opened a new world to me. It has changed my way of thinking, and my lifelong belief to the contrary. I realize now how wrong I have been.

Yours truly,
Mr. X.

This letter is an example of people's beliefs. It tells us a lot. It tells us how some non-Jews think, but no one knows why. What makes them think the way they do! It is the same inexplicable question as to why ladies think the way they do.

Let us analyze a storeowner in a neighborhood area, as opposed to one who operates chain stores in shopping malls. Let us also examine the successes and failures of stores located in neighborhood areas. I must also stress, however, that hard work alone may not be enough if it is combined with other tangible and unique ideas of promotion.

A hard-working enthusiastic businessman accumulates his profits in the bank at the end of a year, unlike the lazy or incompetent one who shows a profit in the books, because all his profits are tied up in worthless inventory. One must also be completely involved in a business, plan and promote constantly in order to attain some success.

Some twenty years ago an acquaintance of mine went into the ladies' wear business and he made very good progress within a few years. However, his ego apparently got overinflated. He acquired new friends who did not respect him, but accepted him because of his generous spending. He was "Mr. Big" and acted his role. He devoted less and less attention to his business; his buying became sporadic but in large quantities, as befitted a "Mr. Big." He was in the store very seldom and was under the impression that the store could be operated by remote control. The success story was short-lived, however. As time passed the neglect began to show. His sales dropped, his inventory was old and unsalable, and the bank discontinued his credit.

One day he came to see me, seeking advice and a miracle to get out of the mess he was in. In order to find a solution to his problem I drove out to see the store and his merchandise. It looked like a disaster area. The store was packed with useless, old, faded, decrepit goods. All I could think of was lighting a match and thus resolving all of his troubles. The coats and suits were completely unsalable. I can't understand to this day where or how he managed to accumulate such an unsightly collection. The dresses were weeping for the better years they had seen, and customer traffic was practically nonexistent.

"You don't need me, my friend, you need King Solomon. You need a miracle to get you out of this mess."

I looked over the whole mess and asked him, "Are you by chance from Chelem?" (a town in Poland).

"Why do you ask?" he questioned.

"Because Chelemer residents were known to be the country's outstanding fools, and you seem to be one of them."

I felt sorry for him, even though he had divorced his wife during the good years, as a big spender is expected to do; when success comes, the wife is the first to go.

I nevertheless outlined the type of "sale" he was to prepare. "One free coat with each dress at regular price!" I said.

"I have never heard of such a thing in my life," he protested.

"I haven't either, but in your case there is no other way. It will be a first."

We organized the junk for the sale and had great success in selling out to the bare walls. "What am I to do now?" he asked.

"Now, you begin from the bottom again. Have the store decorated, lift up the spirits of your two salesladies, and bring in new merchandise. Buy as little as possible and as often as required. Resign from your highclass club and friends. Pay attention to your business and don't play the role of 'Mr. Big.' You may in time build up a business again. I hope that you were taught a good lesson."

"But to give away a coat with a purchase of a dress was criminal," he lamented.

"You created the criminal act," I said.

Unfortunately a Good Samaritan always pays for his good deeds and I was no exception. I had given him a list of manufacturers he should visit to build up a valuable inventory gradually. He did as told, but invoiced all of the merchandise in my name. Within a few weeks statements started coming in for purchases I had never made. A few phone calls gave me the information I required. I drove up to see him one day and confronted him with his unethical and downright criminal act.

"Benny 'Ganef' [thief], what in hell are you doing?"

"I am doing fine," he replied innocently. "Business is picking up."

"Benny, don't avoid the issue. I want to know why you are buying goods in my name?"

"Don't worry. I'll pay the bills; just bring me all the statements.

I pulled out a bundle of them from my pocket. "Here they are," I said. "I'll stay here until you make out checks for all of them and mail them. Furthermore, we are going to the bank to see if you have enough money to cover these checks, or I shall have no choice but to have you arrested."

He paid all the accounts that were charged to me, and I was in the clear. "Benny, you are a big schmuck! What made you think you would get away with it? I have done you a favor, I have put you back in business, did I deserve that?"

He looked down and said, "Necessity has no dignity; there was just no other way."

"Look who is talking about dignity! Where was your dignity and prestige when you were ruining your business, divorcing your wife and playing 'Mr. Big'? Your ego got overinflated until it burst. I am sure you will understand humility, starting today."

My involvement had apparently gone too far. All I intended to do was to help that yokel out of his predicament, but not to create complications for myself; I had enough of my own!

This is an unbelievable story, but true. To this day I cannot figure out why I got involved in such a mess.

No one can do justice to selling properly when the store atmosphere is loaded with silent hostility. Cooperation is most important to all concerned. To feel free of pressure is to have poise and project tranquility in order to excel in one's endeavors. Unfortunately the indifferent attitude in selling and in services has become progressively worse; one must appear humble and apologetic in order to be helped or served. The modernists call it modern selling; I call it stupidity. Attention brings response; indifference brings rejection and resentment. Motivation is the reason for higher and more rewarding accomplishments. What better motivation can one have than to be nice to a customer? I am perhaps supersensitive to proper methods of selling, having been involved in it most of my life.

A brief personal experience I had only a few months ago will give you an idea of what I mean when I use such words as "modernists" and "indifferent." I was browsing around in the suit section of a department store, trying on jackets, but couldn't find my size, while two salesmen stood a short distance away engaged in an apparently joking conversation. I finally walked up to them and said, "Excuse me for my intrusion, but do you work here?"

"Yes, why do you ask?"

"Because you do not seem interested in looking after customers."

"We didn't think you were interested in a purchase!"

"You don't think that I tried all those jackets just to model them for you?"

I walked out in disgust, cursing the world.

It is important for one to take criticism, even if it is unjustified (in your opinion). Listen to anyone who offers an opinion. As worthless as it may sound, you might nonetheless learn something

worthwhile. It is written in the *Pirkey Avot* (The Sayings of Our
Fathers) that the son of Zoma said, "Who is wise? He who learns
from all men."

As a professional salesperson, one must plan on many moves
and have alternatives. You should not rely on sudden inspiration
or divine assistance to win a battle of wits. Rather, you should
study your customer, her needs, her motives, and how you can best
serve her and meet her needs to make your time productive. The
best way to accomplish this is to plan, to be mentally ready to
make your sales pitch on a sound psychological basis. While your
customer may think of you as an outgoing personality, you are
actually playing the role, going through certain established, well-
practiced motions, while the customer is fighting her own feelings
of inferiority and uncertainty. You are on the daily firing line,
and concerned with one question only: How can I influence my
customer to buy this garment? Your ability to deal with that question determines your capabilities. Psychology holds the answer
to your problem.

If you give the customer a sound, valid reason to make the
purchase, she will do so. Psychology comes through experience if
you are able to absorb different experiences in your mind and
analyze them. Should you find a flaw in your approach or in your
general selling behavior, correct it. Appealing to the customer's
common sense and reason is not enough. You must also remember
that a customer is not always what she appears to be; she may have
hidden motives, or deep-rooted past experiences that make her
apprehensive in deciding whether to buy from you. You may remind her of someone who gave her a hard time by persuading her
to buy something she did not like. Should you meet such a customer, and feel that you are not getting through to her, call the
buyer or the supervisor of the store, introduce her to the customer,
and walk away.

"Turnovers" are very important if they are done in good taste
and the timing is right. Low-pressure selling is sound. It creates
integrity, but it does not deposit money in the bank. You must
show interest in your customer's welfare, her problems, and her
right to accept or reject without resentment, but it is up to you
to choose the proper garment, which she will appreciate. Your
capacity to meet your customer's needs depends on how well your
sales presentation is made. It has to be sincere and innocently

convincing. And don't ever forget "motivation," which plays a big role in your vocabulary.

Once Confucius was approached by a student who thought that he was about to outsmart the master. The student held a live bird in the palm of his hand and thought, if he says the bird is alive, I will smother it; if he says it is dead, I will let it fly away. I cannot lose either way. "Master," said the student, "I hold a bird in the palm of my hand. Can you tell me if it is a live bird, or is it dead?"

"The answer lies in your hands," Confucius replied.

Your customer's likes and dislikes lie in your behavior, in your presentation, and in your power to make the customer think your way and believe you without reservation, for no one with a sense of integrity will knowingly mislead a customer.

In selling one must learn to accept potential customers or browsers warmly, and give them a feeling of welcome, even though the browser is not worth a dime; but that is your opinion. You size her up. She does not have a purse; she does not have a wallet. You assume that she has no money. Don't be surprised if she pulls out a roll from her stocking or brassiere. It has happened many times before. I have sold coats to such individuals who dug deeply into the bra and pulled out red-hot money to pay for it. On many occasions I was perplexed by such simple innocence. They did give me the runaround quite often, such as by saying, "I am going to ask my husband."

"But you don't even have a wedding ring!"

She would admit then somewhat embarrassingly that in fact she was single, and the sale was made.

You must ask yourself each week, "What defects can I find in my selling or in operating the store? How can I improve my selling, merchandising, public relations, and of course my behavior as the leader of all things combined?" Defects can be found and attributed to conditions that do or do not exist; it is always easier to put the blame on someone other than yourself.

Building up a successful business depends on the leader; to improve it is as slow as evolution. It comes very slowly, so that one can look at reality at some future time and believe that it actually happened.

Views and ideas that come to you from your sales staff are very important. James Bender writes about an owner of a toy store who gives his two children credit for his success. When he opened his first toy store his boy was eight and his girl eleven. He took them on his buying trips and was guided by their preferences. He advertised toys chosen by his children. He continues to consult youngsters before making his purchases. His business has grown faster than any other of its kind.

So should your purchases be based, at least partially, on the opinions of your sales staff. You may reject their ideas or agree with some, but you will accomplish a great deal by giving them the opportunity to express their views, which will give them a feeling of participation and responsibility. Even a small measure of success in a business is based on trial and error. Never sit idle and wait for the Messiah to come walking in to make your day; be on the move; experiment with various methods, which can only improve conditions. It certainly cannot hurt to be active. As long as you are moving, someone may decide to move along with you. Never allow a store to project the appearance of a morgue. It must be alive and vibrant.

In order to have the capacity to excel in any endeavor that is based primarily on public relations, one must be adaptable to any and all situations; the challenges are endless, and each individual thinks and feels differently. Following this line of thought one can achieve monetary as well as other gratifying rewards. I must emphasize, however, that many good selling ideas can be created if they are thought out collectively, (that means interdependence). It is only by exchange of ideas and discussion that new thinking comes into focus, however insignificant it may seem at the time. Isaac Newton unexpectedly discovered the force of gravity while sitting under an apple tree; it was a minor thing at the time, but with the fall of an apple he revolutionized the world.

At the risk of repeating myself, I feel that a general observation is relevant at this point in order to explain briefly the episodes, anecdotes, jokes, and the reason for revealing some of the business tricks and the constant battle of wits. It is my hope that they should be instrumental to some extent in promoting a better understanding, a closer and more trusting relationship between consumer and sales personnel. Some consumers are under the false impression that they are being victimized by high-pressure help; they also believe that sales help employ unethical methods in order to make a sale. I admit that such a method may be used on occasion, but only on those who come into a store with chips on their shoulders or act defensively, as if expecting to be robbed or attacked. But if one deals with a store that has been built on honesty and integrity, such fears are groundless. As a customer, you must also remember for your own peace of mind that most sales personnel are always on your side, because they hope you will come back again if you are satisfied with your purchase and the service, for our business depends on repeat customers.

A satisfied customer is one who is willing to listen to a saleslady's opinion or suggestion when selecting a garment. She can be more objective and therefore can select the one to suit your personality. I do not mean to imply that you, the consumer, should have nothing to say in the matter. You are the one who is paying for the garment and will wear it; nevertheless, an objective opinion is important, because you do not see yourself as others do. Trust the saleslady. A satisfied customer is of great value. She will not mislead you; she is trying to please you. Give her that courtesy if you too wish to be satisfied.

People are our specialty; we are here to serve you and to make a profit in the most honest way possible. Do not judge salespeople by their formal education but only by their honesty. They are here to make a living, and the only way they can achieve this is by honest selling. Sales help know that people don't act; they only react. Personal magnetism combined with a jovial facial expression is worth a thousand words; people respond easily and communicate with such individuals. Add courtesy, which is a reflection of empathy, and you will be in a better position to achieve good results. Do not try to make a "quick buck." Success in selling is simple; it is obviously a deep desire to succeed.

When I reflect upon those turbulent active years, I have to confess that I enjoyed dealing with ladies after I got to know their ways of thinking and their idiosyncrasies, their unpredictability and their pattern of impulse buying. They patronized me through the years, which made it interesting, fascinating, and rewarding. My observation leads me to believe that I have lived in a complex world far beyond my understanding. Was destiny really responsible for my traumatic experiences, or was it a combination of errors and honesty?

Now that you know my background, you will readily understand that I was indoctrinated with Chassidic culture, traditions and, of course, the chauvinism of the time, although we never knew

that such a word existed in any language. It was nevertheless practiced through generations in Orthodox circles and communities who
lived in a world of isolation and inhibitions. Females were not permitted to mix with males at synagogues or any other functions. It
was chauvinism; only no one knew that it had a name. Those
were traditions that I had to shed upon coming over to Canada.

I was obsessed with a strong desire to work hard and succeed.
As William James said, "Selling is common sense, and not sense
common to everyone, but sense in common things in contact with
customers." I could probably write two books on the subject of
selling, buying, promoting, and so on. There are literally hundreds
of ways to success. Hard work is one way known to us. It may not
make you a genius, but if you do not try you will never know. I
hope that my book may be of some assistance to someone along
the way.

Now that I am no longer active in the business world, a complete transformation had to take place in order for me to find
a new perspective. I have a lot of time on my hands to reflect
upon many places I have been to and on many people I have
known who meant so much to me; I remember them all with a
feeling of nostalgia. Old age "winter" suddenly glares me in the
face, but you know that, after winter, summer will surely come
again. The young, the bold, and the brazen will be on the scene,
thinking that youth lasts forever, but they, too, will eventually
face November and surrender to winter as I have. Your thinking
and fantasies will change; only your memories will carry your
picture of the past. The dawn was beautiful and promising, filled
with dreams, aspirations and anticipation, during a lifetime of
brilliant sunshine. But the twilight is dim, even though serene;
you surrender to the night shadows, which are moving in slowly
until dawn reappears and brings back memories of years passed.
Memories—what are they? What do they mean? They are like
traditions of ancient times, which were passed on through generations in their original form; not a speck of them was lost over
thousands of years.

For as long as there are oceans there will be waves. For as
long as there is life, there will be memories. They are carved deep
down into the brain, to be used when your mind subconsciously
begins to wander. They are indelible. That is the way memories
should be, because the past is gone; there is no worthwhile present,
and the future is dim, but memories are retained for life.

27

I Give Up My Business

The years 1973 and 1974 were the most traumatic and painful of my entire life. Pain is the loneliest companion in the world; wherever you go it goes with you. The twenty-third of June, 1973, was the day when all miracles, all faint hopes and expectations had come to an end—my wife passed away. My huge home had suddenly become desolate, silent; only echoes of the past remained.

The tragedy and grief made me lose my identity; humility and an inferiority complex had taken over. I was in no position to look after my business any longer. I began to plan an escape from that unreal life, searching for a way out, but not wanting to have the feeling that I had retired. I rented an office within walking distance from my home, and began preparations to turn my business over to one of my sons-in-law. By February, 1974, I was out of business and tried very hard to adjust to an entirely different life in a one-room office, a life of isolation and confinement I had not known before. It was the most difficult transition period in my life.

I began by coming to the office for twenty minutes a day and walking out without even taking my coat off. I wandered the streets aimlessly, trying to find myself in a silent world that was completely strange to me. I walked the streets I had known for years but I actually never saw the streets or the buildings. Now from a walking position everything looked entirely different. I felt as if the sidewalk were slipping away from under my feet. As the shadows deepened and night was gradually approaching, I thought, "God, I have lived in this area for over twenty-five years, I drove on this street thousands of times, but never did I feel so lonely and forlorn."

I don't remember walking purposely in any specific direction, but I found myself walking along the bank of a fast-flowing river. The rush of rippling water made me feel as though it were dancing with joy, holding secrets that were never revealed. The darkness was caressing my face, and everything seemed expanded, endless in the moonlit night, bathed in dim radiance. The breeze seemed to carry the secrets of a million years. My heart was in the process of being dissolved, trickling away into deep pain. Ideas got tangled up in my mind. At such a time there are so many strange images and ideas, they enmesh like a thousand cobwebs.

When I recall those days now, I regard them as the shattered ruins of a burnt-out building. I was seeking the gateway of deliverance until I lost myself in silent contemplation. No one can share your sorrows; no one even remembers or is aware of your grief, unless you meet someone you know face to face. Everybody is involved in his problems, which leave no time to afford some comfort to others.

You look at the wondrous brilliance of stars that flood the universe, and you catch a momentary glimpse of eternity. Isn't there something akin to divine mystery in the blessed sweet light that emanates from such a tiny point as the human eye? Is there not a split second of God Himself?

When morning came I raised my eyes to the heavens: the sky was crystal-clear, the sun was shining brightly, birds were perched on heavily leafed branches and the grass was breathing serenity. I put my hand in my pocket and found an old wrinkled piece of paper I had copied from a magazine some months before. The following is a partial excerpt:

> *This is the beginning of a new day; I can waste*
> *it or use it for good. It is important to me because*
> *I am exchanging a day of my life for it. When tomorrow*
> *comes today will be gone forever. I want it to gain*
> *good, not evil, in order that I shall not regret*
> *the price I paid for it.*

The grand simplicity of our lives had cracked. When that happens, we become aware of things and feelings we never knew existed. We become conscious of our existence. We also become aware that we can no longer follow our accustomed pattern of life. We must undergo a transformation process and be content with the impossible; that's the nearest option.

Winter came and I was free! What an unexpected limited thing freedom is; the world is wide open but one has no place to go. The February rain, snow, and wind were slapping my face like wet rags as I wandered the streets aimlessly, without reason or purpose. All I knew for sure was that my shrines had turned to ashes, and that there was no possible way or reason to cling to them any longer.

It is not easy to endure mental torture when our emotions are completely involved in hopeless despair, tied up in the dread of what appears inevitable. We brace ourselves emotionally and spiritually; we live through it even though we did not think it possible and we surrender because we cannot redirect destiny.

Nothing seems important for one to do except let one's mind wander over a span of years and experiences. My mind finds me in a cold but more or less secure spot on the farm in Hirsch, Saskatchewan. I had worked very hard in forty-to-fifty degrees-below-zero weather, which penetrated the very marrow of my bones. I listened to music from an old gramophone with a huge horn protruding from the sound box, note following note without hurry, waiting for each one to drop into my lap, and reverberating in my ears like soft raindrops in the spring preceding the full velocity of a storm. It is ironic to think about things of a lifetime ago, but memories topple in disarray, without reason.

I had met several women friends in the past few years. I was not impressed, nor did I try to be impressed; it all seemed so juvenile, almost repulsive. I remember some who had bottomless watery eyes and strong guilt, perhaps because of their existence. It was difficult to understand whether the eyes were overflowing with wisdom, intelligence, or emotion; some faces portrayed an overabundance of sincerity that almost deleted inhibitions beyond natural reality. I have also met nice, compatible women, but I withdrew each time. It was against my better judgment to entertain, or be aware of their existence. Perhaps their feelings about me were similar to mine? If they were, I do not blame them. I do not mean to sound ungrateful to those who were seeking my companionship, but how can one recapture the past, or even a small part of it that has vanished as yesterday, never to return?

There must be something intangible between a man and a woman who can sit silently together, not utter a word, and yet feel the mutual deep dedication hovering like a halo over them. I often wonder if remaining alive compensates somewhat for lives that have ceased. It would be of some consolation to us if it were so.

Ages have passed since I experienced the fright of a pogrom in the dark of night. It seems that ages have passed since I had had someone to talk to who would understand me. I have locked myself in a cell of my own, broken all contacts with the world and reality, to avoid or minimize sadness and despair. This is the final affirmation of overwhelming mystical experience, and the realization of its unquestionable results. I have had a sort of vision that kept returning at certain intervals, a vision of hopeless hope, a lucid framework of my thinking, but thinking only intensified my anxieties, which lasted for a while, vanished with yesterday, and turned into fear.

I have been haunted by fear of such freedom, which I could not accept logically. Such a feeling is indefinable; you cannot describe it or come to terms with it. One has no alternative but to believe in the old cliché, "God helps those who help themselves." But one should have faith when life seems unbearable; your afflictions will be easier to bear. Such therapy is most helpful when your world falls apart. We think that each "I" is the most important individual on this earth. We are important to ourselves, of course, for each one of us is an "I". Once you are born you are caught in the cycle of life. You must live it; you have no alternative. The world is flat, after all, and each one of us falls off the cliff one day.

It is absurd and yet so tragic to be constantly frightened of our own mortality. A little man struts and fumes upon this earth, equal to a tiny ant crawling in the grass. A clock keeps ticking away in each one of us; it is the ticking that carries a perishable sound. Time accumulates into years, and melancholy sets in when you realize that you have gotten old without noticing and are getting older; you feel complete abandonment. Because the process is irreversible, one becomes indifferent when the peak of old age is finally reached.

Sometimes in life you will find yourself surrounded by problems created by uncontrollable circumstances; when that happens, do not cry or worry to the point of frustration, which can lead to deep depression; carry hope and faith in your heart, and everything will fall into place somehow. Your tolerance will make it less painful, for without hope you would be like a ballet dancer with only one leg.

If a day comes when you feel that you are drowning in the rough sea of life without hope or purpose, when everything seems to indicate that you have nothing worthwhile to live for, turn to silent prayer of your soul, and you will find a purpose and courage to accept the unacceptable. As I so vividly remember my mother's words of wisdom when I was leaving for Canada, "My son, remember to pray eloquently even though silently. It will help you to overcome obstacles you may meet on life's journey."

I prayed many times. Did I expect something to happen dramatically as an answer to my prayers? I do not know. I only know that I had found consolation in the past, learned to tolerate the present, and was capable of finding some purpose in life. Let us pretend that we are on top of a tall mountain looking down at the world, at the weakness and fear. We will endure our disappointments more easily, and we will look back some sunny day in the future and count our blessings; we will see some of our dreams being fulfilled, standing, glistening in the sun, because we never lost faith. Any worthwhile dream can be realized if you believe in it, nurture it, fertilize it; even though it is hard work it can be achieved by self-discipline.

After the passing of my wife I disciplined myself to turn my affliction of loneliness into a bit of serenity. My life was now fraught with conflict and strife, and yet in a feeble way it shed a new ray of light, which conveyed a faint, consoling message. The publishing of my autobiography, *Orphan of the Storm*, by Pitt Publishing Company in 1974, served to shake off some of the dust of time from my memory. It was a difficult task to dredge up from the depths of time the joys and sorrows of the past; moreover, it was almost impossible to reaccept them without a feeling of guilt. I know that what is shattered cannot be mended, and what is destroyed cannot always be rebuilt. When I think of my first book, I compare my situation to that of someone who is fortunate to have a son who represents immortality; because I do not have a son, *Orphan of the Storm* will have to suffice.

I sold my home and sought silence and tranquility in the confines of my apartment. I finally took to writing; I find it very satisfying. It fills a vacuum in my life.

Even though I try to forgive and forget men who have done great harm to me in years past, my attempts fail. How can one forgive and forget acts of brutality? I can only feel deep pity for the wrong doers.

An honorable man is more likely to apologize for a wrong deed when he may have caused pain to others, whereas an arrogant illiterate finds satisfaction in being responsible for the pain inflicted upon others. Such individuals are to be pitied rather than censured. Adopting such a point of view is quite difficult, especially when one is involved in business from early childhood and has lived by instinct, indoctrinated with the Chassidic philosophy of morals and principles.

People derive great pride when they talk about their home and what it means to them. It is their shrine; it is a place one belongs to, and it belongs to you. It is a place that knows you; it is related to you and to your life; it welcomes you each time you come in (unlike an apartment, which is strange regardless of how long you have lived in it).

Pride is derived from something that is well done, or from someone who has good qualities or achievements. My overwhelming pride was in my home, which I sold in a brief moment of weakness, as I regret to this day.

Pride in my village consisted of strong, unending religion. We did not understand what we recited, but the heart understood. Life was grim but no one complained. It was simple and pure; our hearts were stirred by the realities of our innocent existence. Talmud, religion, tradition, and faith walked hand in hand, which made the unbearable proudly bearable. Everything is relative, I suppose.

When I think of my village I also think of the peasants who considered respectability toward saintly men of the utmost importance, and they were proud to be of service to them at all times. In this connection I remember a story told by a *Baal Aguleh* (a driver of a horse and wagon) who was traveling with a Rabbi from one town to another. As he was crossing a narrow bridge, another driver approached it from the opposite direction. They met in the middle, but couldn't pass each other. It was evident that one of them had to back up to let the other cross. Both drivers were stubborn and refused to back up. The Gentile driver yelled, "Do you know who is sitting in my wagon behind me? It is our holy Priest!" "And who do you think is sitting in my wagon behind me? A piece of manure? It is a Rabbi, that's who!" shouted the Jewish driver. "A holy and saintly man, righteous, religious, a mystic! If I were to tell him that you refuse to let me pass, he would make you and your horse disappear, vanish into thin air!"

The Ukrainian driver became petrified by such super powers. He propositioned the Jewish driver to swap passengers, and only then did one of the drivers back up and let the other come through.

As a result of the exchange, Rabbi and Priest returned home. It took weeks for their respective disciples to figure out how and why they had not gone on to wherever they were going.

Pride comes in various forms, depending on one's status and philosophy about life in general. Pride means different things to different people. I had great pride when I purchased my first car, an old Essex with a tar-covered canvas top. I bought it for $75, on payments of course, but I was proud to be the owner of it. It was mine and I knew that if I were to have told someone that the car belonged to me, nobody would have believed me.

Pride can be derived from achieving success, or one can be proud of one's family. There are countless experiences in life that can make one proud. I have had occasion to be proud of many things over the years as they slipped by unnoticed. Pride came to me through humility, obedience, and self-discipline most of the time, as with an Arabian horse trained to travel and endure countless days in the endless barren desert; such endurance is a source of pride to the trainer too.

But none can compare to the pride experienced when my first book, *Orphan of the Storm*, came off the press. I derived pride and satisfaction from a lifelong ambition—a dream that became a reality when I held in my hands my whole life and was actually reading my autobiography.

When I think back to February and March, 1975, I am very proud, and grateful. Major and Mrs. Eason of the Salvation Army were tremendously impressed with my book, and one evening arrangements were made for me to meet them at my publisher's home.

I have been a friend of the Salvation Army for many years, simply because of being somewhat familiar with their nondenominational activities and the noble work they are doing. They certainly deserve support for the unselfish assistance they provide to those who are less fortunate than we. Their assistance reaches out to many countries and is constantly increasing.

I have become very much interested in their activities, their concerns, and their philosophy. I got to know more of what true humanism is all about, and learned a lot about the organization, which I had hardly known.

Their assistance reaches out almost to all corners of the world: to the sick, the helpless, or to those who have lost their way in life because of some traumatic experiences. They operate hospitals and homes for the homeless; wherever catastrophe strikes, the Salvation Army is there to help. They try to cure alcoholics and rehabilitate the hopeless who have surrendered to a harsh, degrading life.

It is impossible to appreciate fully the tremendous scope of their activities and the dedication with which they carry on their noble work. A message by Commissioner Edgar Ginsted in the 1965 brochure "Our Army on the March" says in part:

> *To meet the challenge of the times is our constant concern. We seek, therefore, to be elastic in our thinking and adaptable in our methods in the spirit of compassionate outreach to the needy—distressed and lonely. It has been said, "Happiness is a great love and much serving." Salvationists are indeed a happy people, because love is still the main spring of our service for the people.*

I have learned that the Salvation Army operates hospitals, nursing homes, rest homes and institutions for the care of the aged. Indeed, wherever there is sorrow, distress, loneliness, or suffering, the work of the Salvation Army can be seen. Men and women alike share in this service of love and compassion.

As a Jew I heartily agree that we have a lot in common in this area and in humanism in general. We Jews believe in God, as all good Christians do. Humility is the central core of belief.

> *"Normal life consists not only in promoting harmony in society, or in actualizing an abstract cosmic order, but in doing the will of God. He is the creator and that is the reason for acting with compassion towards the needy.*
>
> E. W. Heaton—*Solomon's New Men.*

28

The Dreams
of a Lonely Man

What are the dreams of a lonely man? Actually he does not have any dreams. Aspirations and enthusiasm of past years are but memories—memories that can make one proud, or make one sad, lonely and confused; it all depends on the perspective of the individual.

If one chooses the first option one can live a comparatively normal life despite one's age. As a doctor once said to an elderly gentleman who complained of aches and pains, "You can live a relatively normal life as long as you don't enjoy it."

Loneliness over a long period of time can develop into a mental and physical disease, which can lead to complete despondency, unless one is fortunate to have a good friend who will listen and understand one's plight. When you have occasion to listen to an unhappy person and admonish him for his behavior, do not be surprised to hear him defend his action by blaming it on loneliness. Some turn to gambling and alcoholism; some learn to accept it, and strangely enough thrive on it. They withdraw from friends and society, or take refuge in various imaginary illnesses, which become a way of life. Its progress will continue unless one is determined to use inner strength to extricate himself from such an existence, or get help from someone who cares. A family can be a big factor when one gets older; favorable family conditions and close bonds can be of great comfort.

Don't confuse solitude with loneliness. Solitude is a repose from mental strain and daily struggles; it gives one a feeling of serenity, as opposed to a feeling of being lost and forgotten when one has reached a stage of enjoying being alone. Thoreau believed that the true nature of man could not be revealed through group activities. He claimed that for each man there was a unique lifestyle, which he could discover for himself only through meaningful solitude.

Writing my autobiography and having it published was the highlight of my solitude. I found great satisfaction in the solitary process. I have learned to thrive on such tranquility, like a budding thirsty rose in a refreshing rain of spring.

It was very difficult for me to adjust to a lonely existence, but my mind was trained, disciplined over the years not to expect miracles. I have never expected to get rich quick. I have learned that wealth, quickly attained, dwindles away, but if it comes slowly over a long period of time, it multiplies; you then acquire many friends, but beware of glittering hypocrisy.

I surmise that if loneliness could be readily recognizable, one would most likely see many who feel lonely. But a person seldom wears his feelings on his lapel for everyone to know what is hidden under his crusty exterior. We yearn for sympathy in a disguised manner, but are not willing to give some in return. "If you have a little love to spare, give it to one who needs it most—the lonely" (Drs. Jean and Veryl Rosenbaum).

When you are rejected during your childhood years, you grow up with an insecure feeling of inferiority; you reject friendship because you construe it as sympathy, which you abhor. It is your basic fear of being rejected again; you live with a feeling of inadequacy, waiting for someone to reassure you, and give you a feeling of some importance. Unfortunately, friends are like leaf-covered tree branches, green and vibrant in the summertime, but come autumn the leaves begin to wilt, and finally fall to the ground, only to be blown away by blustering winds, leaving the tree bare. Friends you acquire during your prime years gradually disappear, and you are left alone, abandoned.

Self-recrimination will drain your self-esteem, making emotional adjustment difficult, unless you find a new purpose in life, and a meaning to your existense. It is that time of year when one has to find complete independence; even though the leaves have fallen off and blown away, you don't surrender—you find new interests and perhaps also new friends.

The most wretched and difficult journey through loneliness is when a loved one is lost. "Don't cry," some try to console you. This is ridiculous; you should cry as long as you have tears to shed. *Grief is the highest tribute to love. They help heal the wounds of sadness.*

—Drs. Jean and Veryl Rosenbaum

As Khalil Gibran wrote:
Yet now it cries aloud unto you, and would stand revealed before you. And ever has it been that love knows not its own depth until the hour of separation.

We have a tendency to look back at the past, rather than look ahead. The past is very precious to us; it gives some meaning to the present. We attached a price tag to the glittering promise of achievement. But it eluded us and vanished unnoticed into the void. Perhaps we failed to fulfill our role in life, which set the stage for traumatic experiences and lack of emotional needs and understanding.

If you were to ask me how I feel working alone, I would say that I am experiencing great satisfaction in the solitary process. It is rewarding; it soothes my mind and soul beyond all expectations. I am also experiencing a feeling of creativity. Feelings are emotions of unreasoned convictions. Feelings are like conscious longing for the impossible and yet possible. Feelings are synonymous with past experiences, like memories, hidden in deep crevices of the subconscious until reactivated and brought to the surface. Feelings are a by-product of impressions. I think that the following stanza from a work by Goethe describes feelings eloquently:

> *How yearns the solitary soul,*
> *To melt into boundless whole,*
> *And find itself again in peace.*
> *The blind desire, the impatient will,*
> *The restless thoughts and plans are still,*
> *We yield ourselves—and wake in bliss!*

Living alone and retired can be quite pleasant. One can put one's free time to a variety of creative and enjoyable efforts in which one can find solace and gratification in daily activities. Remember the old cliché—every dark cloud has a silver lining.

Contemplation of things spiritual can enable us to rise to unbelievable heights of contentment and tranquility, so that we can enjoy life to its fullest in spite of conditions or circumstances. Age is not a time of life—it is a state of mind. You grow old only when you desert your ideals and lose your enthusiasm; your face will get wrinkled and you'll begin to feel self-distrust; you will lose sight of the glitter of the stars and fail to see a frog on a log making love to the harvest moon. "You are as young as your love and as old as your despair" (*War Cry*—Salvation Army).

This brings to mind a story about three retired friends, two of whom played cards every Wednesday evening, while the third stayed behind. Each time he was asked why he refused to join them, he replied: "Shapiro is playing tonight. You know I am a lover of Jewish theater!" Several weeks passed and the excuse for staying behind was always the same: "Shapiro is playing tonight!" One of his two friends finally asked him, "Who is Shapiro and where is he playing every Wednesday night?"

"Don't be silly," he replied. "There is no Shapiro, there has never been a Shapiro, but when our friend Max goes out Wednesday evening to play cards, I sleep with his wife."

The crux of the joke is not as overwhelming as it may seem. The quality of life may change; it always does as we pass each year. We move constantly from one era to another. What we do with our time depends on the individual. You can waste it on your insignificant existence, or you can become involved in worthwhile activities, which can be gratifying and give you a special purpose in life, as it did to our lover of Jewish theater.

I heard a story about a man who was obsessed most of his life with a burning ambition to accumulate wealth, and was unexpectedly told by his doctor one day that he had an incurable disease. Upon hearing the bad news, he decided to turn to prayer and repentance. Not knowing how to go about practicing religion, he decided to see a Rabbi. After all, a Rabbi is in constant communication with God; perhaps he could help him get well. Failing this, he might be in a position to have his life prolonged or help him in some way to enter the Pearly Gates that lead to heaven. "I am sure he can do something for me; according to the stories I have heard about Rabbis, they can make impossible things possible, especially when God Himself is involved."

He hastily went to see the Rabbi with a proposition: "Rabbi," he said, "according to my doctor I have very little time left and would therefore appreciate that you hear me out."

"All right, I am listening," said the Rabbi.

"I hesitate to believe that you can make me well even though many things are possible for a price. I am, however, prepared to give you one hundred thousand dollars if you can be instrumental in prolonging my life for as long as possible. Should you not be successful in your attempt, you must promise me that you will intervene on my behalf and gain my admission to Heaven."

The Rabbi thought about it for a while and replied, "I cannot give you an answer now; come back in five days, at which time I will most likely have some news."

The atheist came back with great anticipation a few days later, hoping to get a favorable reply. After all, he thought, a hundred thousand dollars isn't peanuts! "Well, Rabbi, what news do you have for me?"

The Rabbi leaned back in his chair and said, "I have good news and bad news."

"Let me hear the good news first," demanded the man.

"The good news is that I have received permission to have you admitted to Heaven; that's the best I can do. The bad news is that you must leave tomorrow."

The man turned pale and mumbled, "One doesn't get much for a hundred thousand dollars these days." He slumped to the floor and passed out.

I think that was an ingenious way of dealing with an atheist.

This story leads me into another anecdote I had heard years ago about a Rabbi and a Priest. Each rode a bicycle every morning to his respective Synagogue and Church for morning services. They met at the precise corner at a precise time each morning, stopped, exchanged a few words and were on their way. A few mornings passed and the Rabbi failed to show. The Priest began to worry; perhaps the Rabbi was sick. He could think of nothing else that would detain him. He finally went to the Rabbi's house, only to be informed that the Rabbi's bicycle had been stolen and he had to walk to Synagogue each morning.

"Tell me my friend," asked the Rabbi, "how can I find out who stole my bicycle? I have a feeling that one of my congregants is guilty, but how can I be sure?"

"I'll tell you what you should do," the Priest said. "During the sermon this coming Saturday, speak about the Ten Commandments and when you come to the one, 'Thou Shalt Not Steal,' watch the faces of your congregants very closely. One of them will either blush or look embarrassed, and when that happens you'll know the guilty party."

About a week later the two met on the same corner as usual and the Rabbi was riding his bicycle. "You see my advice worked," said the Priest. "Did you do what I had suggested?"

"Yes, I did," replied the Rabbi sheepishly, "but when I got to the Seventh Commandment, "Thou Shalt Not Commit Adultery," I suddenly remembered where I had left my bicycle."

29

Retirement

"Life begins at sixty-five is a maxim that only a minority find to have some basic reality. Retirement is a time when we begin to worry how and where we will spend our free time. We have heard many times through the years how to prepare for retirement, but very few do. We can prepare to go on vacation or do something similar, but I have yet to see anyone who actually prepared himself emotionally to cope with permanent freedom. I do not think that retirement has anything to do with our position in life; whether we are rich or poor, the feeling is the same. We cannot call ourselves "unemployed," which would be an easier way of dealing with this unavoidable situation. It wouldn't carry the distasteful meaning of permanency. We are, however, compelled to face retirement despite its traumatic connotation.

What does retirement mean to me? It means imposed inactivity; it means that I have become useless and rejected by society; it gives me a sickening sensation; it is repugnant; it is gloom, and an end to dreams and aspirations. Even though I am fully aware that most of my dreams would have never materialized, I nevertheless hung on to an invisible piece of rainbow most of my life, which gave me a purpose, a goal—attempting to reach the unreachable—knowing full well that you never reach the pinnacle of material fulfillment, because greed is a by-product of success.

I am also of the opinion that retirement should not be mandatory, regardless of whether one is fifty or sixty-five years of age. Each individual should be given the opportunity to decide for himself whether to retire or not. If you feel well mentally and physically and are willing to continue working, it should be up to you to make that decision. Should one wish to retire at sixty years of age because one is anxious to get involved in something other than his lifelong occupation, one should then be entitled to the same privileges as if he were sixty-five, but no one should be ordered to retire simply because he is of pension age.

Retirement should be a personal choice and not a rule of law or social regulation. We have lived our lives and made all our decisions; surely we should be entitled to make that decision on our own.

We actually retire twice in our lifetime: once we retire from parenthood, and later from our profession and activities, which were the lifeline of our existence. To retire from parenthood is, of course, less traumatic. The quality and style of life change, however, because of the absence of unbearable noise, frustrations, and children who have grown up, gotten married, and moved out into a world of their own. We are left alone, abandoned; we miss the very same disturbing, annoying noises that were so aggravating at one time. The house becomes empty and silent. Even though we may feel retired from parenthood, concern for our children never ceases. We know that they can take care of themselves, but to us they are still children, and always will be; we feel that they need our help and guidance, and yet everything is so temporary. Before we realize it, the last stage of retirement is upon us.

I think of a man at this time who worked in a garment factory. His silent, passive behavior was unlike that of other workers, who were constantly humming melancholy melodies of their respective countries. This man was a presser; each time he pushed down on a small lever of the iron he was swallowed up in a gray cloud of steam, but he continued working like a robot without uttering a word or showing a sign of emotion. He had apparently resigned himself to his occupation many years ago.

He had occasion to speak to me one day and confided that he was due to retire within a few months. I went to the factory later in the year and noticed that there was another man at the pressing machine.

Months later I met my friend in the factory again one afternoon. "I thought you had retired months ago!" "I did retire," he replied apologetically, "but I can't stay at home—the days are endless and I have nothing to do!"

"Why don't you go fishing, play golf, get involved in community activities, or just relax and bask in the sun? This is what a person hopes for during his working years. It is a hobby, you know a ho . . ."

He did not let me finish the word, and interjected in a sad, monotonous voice, "You call that a hobby? That is something one should do for diversion while working, but if one is compelled to do some of the things you mentioned because one has no other interests in life, they are not hobbies any more; you know that you are just pushing time, which becomes monotonous and downright repulsive. I come down here twice a week to eat my sandwich at lunchtime and chat with the fellow workers. I hang around until closing time and leave when everybody leaves. I go home with a feeling of accomplishment as if I had done a day's work."

I think that retirement is one of the central factors contributing to despair. We know it is inevitable, but we find it difficult to accept. We begin to feel sorry for ourselves because we are not able to adjust to a new and unfamiliar way of life.

When we retire after all those gray years we had worked, we deserve the freedom; we have been waiting for it. Now that it is upon us, we do not know what to do with it and are overtaken by boredom. I often thought that my work was the most important part of my life. I was the central figure in the arena. Now that I have reached the so-called "Golden Years," they are far from idyllic. They do not carry the magic I had expected when I was young. They do, however, offer a lot of freedom and promise, which come with retirement. I feel liberated. The new skills and new interests I acquired are many. We have to know how to put our free time to good, creative use. In spite of various comments and statistics on the subject, if we think positively, life can be rewarding. We may not be physically as fit as we have been, but we can be just as alert and can put our time to serve or assist some who are in need of help, and thus acquire a feeling of importance, having found a new and gratifying purpose in life.

Your life will take on a new meaning, a new dimension, and you will be happy to put all your free time to good and rewarding accomplishments. You will think, today was quite rewarding and "tomorrow is another day." Think of spring, spring flowers (you could never spare the time to look at them lovingly, tenderly before); they will awaken your senses to beauty and miracles, which are so obvious after a cold winter. Spring flowers carry beauty and hope, which remind us of our potential and the contributions to happiness of which we are a part. The important thing, however, is to think positively and all things will fall into place.

Retirement is not as traumatic for a woman as it is for a man, except to some who are involved in the world of business. A woman is basically a mother and a housewife—roles she treasures dearly all her life; cooking, cleaning, taking care of her family are her main concerns. Very little changes when she retires from parenthood, except that the work load becomes easier, but this is overshadowed by worrying about her little darlings who are now married. They have their own homes and families, which demand care; only mother still clings to the past. When the husband retires, however, she begins to complain: He is constantly under my feet; I wish he would go out for a few hours, so that I can sit in the park for a while and watch my pantyhose shrivel, to match the wrinkles on my face.

A hairdo and a bit of makeup do wonders for a woman's ego. If that's not enough to make you feel better, pray a little—silently. I associate prayer with humility: one must be humble and grateful for the blessings he enjoys. To pray silently is a gratifying experience; it is an antidote to a shattered spirit that will rise and overshadow your wrinkles and your concern. As I said before, age is a state of mind; if you think young, you will feel younger.

According to Raymond Woodbury Pence, an autobiography can be compared to a "personal essay": "Thus the virtue of a personal essay or autobiography comes not from its subject but from the writer. An essayist is indeed a kind of autobiographer, one who begins anywhere and is always beginning over again. Our indifference to his subject is the mark of a real essayist. We do not care what he writes about, just as we do not care what an old friend talks about, so long as he writes, and the old friend talks; that is good enough for us. It is the writer's personality which attracts us, revealing itself in unexpected turns of thought, in new and original ways of looking at things, in flashes of fun and sadness."

I heartily agree with his observation. One person may travel to Ceylon or the Middle East, only to bore us with stories on his return. Another can go downtown or to a food market, but we are not sorry when he stops talking; whereas an imaginative person visiting the same places will keep us fascinated with his observations. In my case it is my autobiography, *Orphan of the Storm*, and its sequel. I do not write in chronological order, because an autobiography is highly personal and varied. I write as I think on any given day. I may or may not be satisfied with the material I had written a week or a month ago; as a result certain changes have to be made, because my thinking or my views have changed.

I must confess that the most boring books I have read were

those written in chronological order, which follow a pattern of daily events. I like flashbacks; they create new interests in new beginnings. Individuality and simplicity are the ingredients of a good book; one's autobiography should be indefinite in its continuity, not sound like a weather forecast. Because its sole purpose is to reflect its author's thoughts, mood, or feelings, the virtue of a book does not come from its subject as much as it does from its author.

These are some of the credentials of an interesting book, depending of course on who the reader may be, and his likes and dislikes. Nothing in this world appeals to all people all the time. Each individual thinks differently; most of us are tuned in to different wavelengths. A certain humorous anecdote may be enjoyed by many, but be completely out of tune to others. But if one were to analyze a joke or an anecdote, one would be surprised to learn that its origin basically is some pleasant or sad experience. How many of us are interested in its origin or the message it contains? We either like it or we don't, without taking time to think what motivated the author to write about something pleasant, repugnant, or depressing. If you would allow yourself time to analyze the contents of a book, you would probably gain a new fresh understanding about the individual behind the book.

Objectionable reading material spreads quickly, like a contagious disease, and invades many countries. I know a man who boasts about his trips, which take him to many parts of the world. He told me, boisterously, of course, that he had been to Mexico, Cuba, Barbados, Germany, and finally Italy. He and his wife walked into a restaurant one day and looked over the menu. He then told his wife that he would order for both of them.

"Since when do you speak Italian?" she asked.

"I speak Italian. Didn't I ever tell you?"

"No, I think you are joking."

"Just wait and see when the waiter comes to take our orders."

"Okay, I am waiting," she said in a tone of disbelief.

Our big spender began to think how to prove to his wife that he could in fact speak Italian. He was familiar with the language enough to know that many words end with *"ini"*, like *cappocini*. The waiter approached them with a friendly smile and asked in Italian what he would like to order.

"We want soupini," he replied.

The waiter brought soup. Amazing, he thought, it really works.

Next he ordered "meatini", and they were served beautiful, delicious meat. When it came to dessert he ordered "cakeini". When the meal was finally over the waiter handed him the check, saying, "Here is my checkini." The man turned to his wife and said, "You didn't believe me when I told you that I can speak Italian. Do you believe me now?" The waiter interjected before the wife had a chance to reply, "If I weren't Moishe Kaplan you would have eaten *drekini.*"

30

The Land of Infinity

According to the Jerusalem Guide Book, Jerusalem in its four thousand years of recorded history has been destroyed and invaded more often than any city in existence, but has tenaciously been restored each time. It was David's purchase of the threshing floor on Mount Moriah that set the pattern of Jerusalem's destiny, for on this place his son Solomon raised the Great Temple about 960 B.C.

In Canaanite times, Jerusalem was a stronghold and shrine for barbaric gods. It is mentioned again in 1400 B.C. in a dispatch to Egypt, warning of the approach of tribes from the East—the children of Israel; four centuries later they entered the city in triumph under King David.

This appears to have been a crucial period for Jerusalem's development. Between the seventh and eighth centuries B.C. Jerusalem acquired the South West Hill, later known as the Upper City, and today it is occupied by the Jewish quarters and Mount Zion.

Jerusalem has a history of thousands of years, being rebuilt many times, only to be desroyed again by various conquerors, until it finally fell to the Romans. Herod was appointed king by the Roman Senate in 40 B.C. He adorned Jerusalem and constructed the Second Temple. Upon his death, however, Titus captured Jerusalem and the Temple was burned to the ground.

Many wars had been fought during scores of centuries. Many generations had come and gone until in 1855 the Porte, the Sultan of Turkey, granted to non-Moslems for the first time admission to Temple Mount, and in 1856 he issued the Edict of Toleration for all religions in the Empire.

Jews began arriving from Europe. Thus, synagogues—centers of worship and learning—rose in the Jewish quarters of the city. We are familiar, of course, with the history of recent years, until

June 28, 1967, at which time Israel conquered the Old City and the partition came to an end. It is important to note that for the first time in centuries Israelis can come whenever they wish and pray at the Wailing Wall, which was forbidden territory to them for many generations. In fact, religions of all nations of the world have found a common ground to come and pray whenever they wish.

The Dome of the Rock, which was built in 1688 A.D., is situated over the site of the last Jewish Temple.

Churches, mosques, meccas, shrines and many a holy place built on and around Mount Moriah are revered and claimed by many faiths. I am not an historian to delve into history that is thousands of years old; I merely feel that a brief résumé of Jerusalem's history serves as a background to my observations and the experiences I gathered during my extended visit to Israel.

We were taken to see David's Tomb on Mount Zion and continued on to the Western Wall and the Golden Gate, blocked since 1530. It is believed that it stands on the site of the First Temple. It leads to the belief that there are more holy places and history in Israel than in the remainder of the world. Each rock, each mountain is a reminder that you are indeed in the Land of the Bible; you are face to face with sages and prophets of the Biblical times. It is an effort to control your emotions when you actually realize that you are a member of an eternal people, who made history over thousands of centuries: history that had been written because of or despite the Jewish wanderers, who finally came home—a home that has rightly belonged to them since Biblical times. Israel is a reality born of an elusive dream, even though some cynics do not share the same views.

In order to establish some chronology to my impressions, we will begin with the day of departure from Toronto. More than half a century had passed since I was taught Hebrew and farm work in a small Kibbutz in Poland in preparation to emigrate to Palestine as a Chalutz (a vanguard or pioneer), to be integrated into Kibbutz life upon arrival. However, things did not materialize for me as planned at the time, and I landed in Canada in 1927.

Today, March 7, 1976, I am on the first lap of a three-week tour to Israel, led by our capable spiritual leader, Rabbi Dr. David Monson, who is President of the Zionist Organization of Canada, and by our friend, Dr. George Liban, who is the Executive Vice-President of the Zionist Organization of Canada.

It was a hypnotic experience as the El Al airplane continued to slice into the dark of night toward the Holy Land. The fulfillment of a dream that had tormented me all my life was on the verge of becoming a reality. Emotions stirred within me, as I realized that within a few hours the plane would tip its wings over the shores of the beautiful blue Mediterranean and I would be in the lap of the land of my dreams, a land I knew only from history! The time is nearing now. I will actually walk on it, feel its mysticism and focus my eyes on infinity. I will be overwhelmed seeing the Western Wall, which holds, tucked away in its crevices, thousands of prayers and messages written in all languages of the world. I will see Mount Scopus and the Tomb of Rachel on the way to Bethlehem with an inscription of thousands of centuries ago: "If love could have saved, you would have lived."

But let us resume our flight. We are in Frankfurt, Germany, for refueling. I look out the window into the dark of night and see shadows marching up and down the tarmac—they are German security guards. A flood of memories stabs my mind. "Their kind killed six million innocent people, my family included. Even though the ocean divided us, I was nevertheless there in spirit throughout the holocaust."

Victims were thrown into infernos or gas chambers like firewood by such murderers up to the last minute before liberation. The Germans really believed that the superior Aryan race would conquer the world. It seems incredible that crimes of such magnitude and human bestiality were committed only a generation ago, which is but a pulsebeat in history, and yet everything becomes so vividly fresh in one's memory by association. How can one ever forget what is the darkest part of history since the beginning of time! It is even more astounding that the civilized world did nothing to prevent the slaughter, or in some way help the victims from being destroyed. I claim, as many others have through the years, that the democratic world was an accomplice to the acts of bestiality, but to quote the old clichés: "What the ground has covered must be forgotten," or "The passage of time heals old wounds."

It is true for the ones who died at the hands of the barbarians; they do not know nor remember the pain, the fear, and the anguish. They were stripped of human dignity prior to and at the time of slaughter. That part of history is indelible. It was written with blood that generations will read about for centuries.

Israel's legitimacy is questioned now by the very same prostituted nations who recognized her officially as a state when the British finally gave up their mandate and thus Israel was freed. A home was born for the homeless who had been in exile for thousands of years.

I know that those guards out there in the dark of night are really not to be blamed. I do, however, question my judgment, even though we know it was mass hysteria fermented by one or more psychopaths who brought the world to the brink of destruction. Nevertheless, they represent evil to this day. I feel that every human being has a duty to be just; we have a duty to condemn inhuman acts, no matter what political purpose is behind them, and we should never forget it.

When we reached the height of 35,000 feet, daylight was beginning to break above pieces of drifting clouds, although everything was enveloped in deep darkness down below. A sliver of invisible sunshine must have penetrated the dawn, and a fiery glow was riding on one of the huge wings, reflecting against the windows while the plane proceeded to cut the darkness. It was the most unforgettable phenomenon of the entire flight.

From outer space, prior to landing in Tel Aviv, the Holy Land appeared to be empty barren desert, mountains, and valleys. In the midst of this apparent desolation I could see the dark turquoise waters of the Mediterranean and small white dotted spots, which I later discovered were Jerusalem and other nearby settlements. Upon touring the country, however, I was amazed to see stretches of cultivated land, orange groves, olive trees, and many other fruits and vegetables growing all the way from the Mediterranean Sea to the cloud-covered hills and the granite mountains that form the spine of Israel. There, in the sunshine, lay the Holy Land, an oasis in the midst of barren desolation.

When we finally landed in Tel Aviv, the Hebrew National Anthem was pouring through an intercom. I saw non-Jewish French Canadians and people of many other nationalities cry openly. There is something very tangible that brings one to tears upon landing in the Holy Land; a feeling of reverence penetrates all hearts.

I can readily understand the reason why we cry. We shed tears of joy and happiness. We have a state, a country of our own, after being driven around for thousands of years like sheep without a shepherd. We have a home to which we can go if we so desire. What impressed me most was that people of all faiths from all over the world wept openly, probably because they were in the Land of the

Bible. Mysticism penetrates their hearts and souls; a divine spirit envelops them. Perhaps they weep because of the guilt they feel. The saintly atmosphere makes them aware of their unwarranted intolerance toward man. They become obsessed with a feeling that every human being—regardless of nationality or religion—has been created equal, and they realize how insignificant we all are in the face of the vast, unknown, mystic universe.

For me, expectation and realization had finally fused, culminating in the mission I had not completed—I was so close, and yet, so far, at one time, almost half a century ago.

Israel is a land that elevates one's spirit from dark depression into light. "Arise, shine, for thy Light is come" (Isaiah chapter 9). You are a brilliant reality. You are projecting dynamism that lingers in the holy air. You affect everybody with your charm. You are unique. You are a combination that invites reverence. You revolve around deserts, mountains, and seashores. You are fascinating and enchanting. You attract nations from all over the world with your sublime tranquility, for you are eternity! Jerusalem remains the Eternal City, and Mount Zion is also revered equally by all religions.

Mount Zion is synonymous with Jerusalem. It is a matter of human freedom and divine control, with the vibrant present together with glory of the past, and hope for the future. The city has, of course, been built up—expanded through the centuries—but basically remains unchanged. The sun shines brightly but sadly on the diamond-glistening dew early in the morning, and on the mountains, desert, and canyons, which conceal secrets of the past, waiting patiently for the voice of God.

The Old City of Jerusalem, known as the world of peace, is bustling with thousands of pilgrims, who are praying in and around holy places. On Friday evening hundreds of Chassidic Jews come out into the courtyard of the Western Wall, dancing and singing, welcoming the Holy Sabbath. The Wall has always been cherished by Jews as the relic of the lost Temple, where they would bribe the Romans to allow them to weep over the ruins, the reason it was formerly called the Wailing Wall. The Chassidic Jews who constantly pray there believe that redemption can be hastened only by prayer and fasting.

I believe that all faiths unite in Israel by seeking one objective— solace for the soul, and a meaning to life and its complexities. They are seeking God together, without animosity or political malice.

Jerusalem is the center for people of all faiths. They wish to die here so that they can live forever in the wind that blows over the desert, the sand dunes, and the Hills of Judea, and be reborn again spiritually.

Close, jovial participation is difficult, however, because of past memories and present conditions. The historic contrast is too extreme. Nevertheless, pilgrims with different customs and backgrounds are tolerant and unquestionably sympathetic toward each other, for this is the Holy Land, where light is sown into the righteous and goodwill shall prevail over evil. Peace and tranquility will reign over the land some day.

Israel in general, and Jerusalem in particular, is the center of the world where medieval customs and a unique philosophy still prevail, where all people share in the oldest history in the world. They deserve admiration; they are genuinely happy and content. They inspire one another with strength, which comes from hope and history thousands of years old.

There is an extraordinary degree of uniformity and invisible splendor in the dimensions and shapes of the mountains. They stand like domes, as if they had been placed there carefully by tender hands. They are terraced with rocks from top to bottom to hold rainwater from running down freely and also to prevent erosion. They project wisdom and serenity while a divine halo hovers over them. If you haven't been to Israel you cannot possibly comprehend what I am trying to say: seeing is knowing for certain that you know.

I found Israel transformed from the ancient Palestine I had been taught about, to a sophisticated country, and yet its Biblical image has remained. Hospitals, schools, and other institutions have expanded tremendously over the years. Kibbutzim are flourishing across the land. Youth centers and boys' towns are nestled in the hills and forests around Bayit V'gan, a suburb of Jerusalem; they house and educate thousands of war orphans and underprivileged children, who are drafted into the army when they reach the required military age. It is beyond understanding how these institutions can operate successfully, even though financial assistance is very limited. It is a legacy of self-sufficiency left by their ancestors, which is continuing to shape the minds of the present generation and their future perpetuation.

I believe that Israel is the only country in the world where public institutions are built three to four floors below ground level as preventive measures against attacks. From the Mellahs of Algeria,

Tunisia, and Morocco immigrants have come, and from the homes of those who survived the devastation and terror of war-torn Europe they have come; from Syria and Iran, from the wasteland of Yemen and the hovels of Egypt and Afghanistan they have come, and from the barren life of the Soviet Union. Each with his own particular background, culture, and language; they have all come together to boys' town and youth centers in Jerusalem, and to Kibbutzim across the land.

A sharp contrast can be seen between Israeli-occupied territory, which blossoms like an oasis, and the barren Arab desert. The Arab leaders are apparently not concerned about their own people, who face starvation in the desert; they are not about to give them assistance. If they were, Israel could not be blamed for their plight. Politicians need a scapegoat, and who is the most likely one? Israel of course.

Isaiah, the prophet, said thousands of years ago that the desert would flourish like a flower some day. His prophecy has partially become a reality. I can visualize that possibility, even though it may take decades of hard work and a lot of understanding. This of course will be possible only when the people are given the opportunity to think for themselves and extricate themselves from under the heels of the political forces who constantly flex their muscles with threats of war.

When we reached the top of a high mountain, an unforgettable scene revealed itself in a distant haze. The Judean Hills were standing proudly united with the sky. Although the sun was shining brilliantly, the mountains were shrouded in a thin, gray, transparent haze; infinity rested on the wings of a holy breeze. It was intangible, and yet it seemed as if creation were taking a respite. The desert was also resting lavishly, peacefully, as if it had not been touched since creation, even though it is saturated with blood from the continuous wars since and prior to the beginning of recorded history. In complete contrast, golden-colored oranges were smiling from behind the leaves of orange groves, and hundreds of beautiful bright red roses were growing out of cracks of granite rocks.

You will be mesmerized by an exhilarating experience. Just beneath you there is a garden that skirts the wall and the fascinating National Park and the Mount of Olives, which seem to be within reach of the palm of your hand. Legend has it that beacons were burned on the peaks of such mountains thousands of years ago to signal each new month, and the lights could be seen all the way to Babylon.

Do not forget to visit Mount Herzl and the family tomb. Herzl was the founder of Zionism, born in Budapest in 1860, and his remains were buried in Israel, in 1949, in accordance with his will.

Mount Herzl, Yad V'Shem, and the Mount of Remembrance left an unforgettable impression in my heart. There is a complex of monuments perpetuating the memory of the six million. I saw a dark gray-stone deteriorated building where Eichmann, one of the Nazi murderers, had been held during his trial before his execution for crimes against humanity.

An eternal light burns on the Avenue of Jews and Righteous Gentiles, and each morning a memorial service is held to honor those who helped to save some Jewish lives during the Nazi holocaust.

One is fascinated by the beautiful view of the wastelands and the Judean desert down to Masada, the Valley and the Dead Sea, which is 1,290 feet below sea level, the lowest point on the earth's surface.

We visited Jericho, which is located near the northern tip of the Dead Sea. According to history, Jericho is the oldest city in the world. There a lost city about 10,000 years old was found by archeologists. According to their reports, a clearly legible Hebrew inscription was found carved into the lower level of a wall, taken from Isaiah 6:14. It reads, "Your heart shall rejoice and your bones shall flourish like a herb."

When you are confronted with nature in its hypnotic innocence and a lifestyle of the Bible, when you see flocks of sheep grazing in the back yard of a city under the watchful eyes of a shepherd dressed in a long white robe and carrying a long staff, when you see camels silhouetted against the horizon on top of a desert mountain, you realize that nothing has really changed in the Middle East, except that the people have become more sophisticated. They live today, for there may not be tomorrow. Israelis say, "Live in Haifa, which is built on Mount Carmel overlooking the Bay of the Mediterranean—a breathtaking beautiful view where one can see forever on a sunny day; have a good time in Tel Aviv, and be buried in Jerusalem."

The Scrolls of Fire, also called The Martyrs' Shrine, is an ingenious masterpiece of art created by Nathan Rappaport. It is made of bronze or metal, I think; carved in it are many historical events depicting the annihilation of the Jews during the holocaust and the liberation of those who survived. It also portrays the history of Joseph, who was sold to a passing caravan by his brothers, and later became Minister in the Pharaoh's court.

Then you come to Mount Moriah, where Abraham was to sacrifice his son Isaac, because God had ordered him to do so.

You begin to doubt history or perhaps legend. Abraham may have had hallucinations because of his lonely existence in the vast barren desert, or did he really hear God's voice in the painful silence of the night? We can only speculate; you cannot separate the rational from the irrational. When you look at Israel in general and Jerusalem in particular, you get the feeling that this land is unique in appearance and character; perhaps it was meant for righteous nations at the time of creation! Who is to know? I know one thing for certain: when you come to Israel, regardless of nationality or religion, you begin to feel a hypnotic power embracing you. It penetrates your senses until you begin to doubt your own insignificant existence. Holiness and nobility invite reverence, pride and humility, all at the same time, for this is the Land of the Bible and history since Abraham's times.

Nations are struggling to gain freedom and peace, but the world has abolished peace and is constantly preparing or inciting wars.

The Knesset (Parliament) is a most impressive building, where the following is inscribed: "From Exile to Redemption." There is also a monument inscribed, "In their blood the world will rise."

I could probably write several books about Israel and the Middle East if that were my subject, and if I were more informed about the politics, history, and mysticism that surround it. Moreover, I would elaborate on Zionism more fully. Unfortunately, I am not prepared to do that. I do, however, wish to quote Elridge Cleaver, author of *Soul on Ice*, who recently wrote:

> *To condemn the Jewish survival and the doctrine of Zionism as racism, is a travesty upon the truth. I am surprised that the Arabs would choose to establish a precedent condemning racism because it can so easily and righteously be turned against them. Having lived intimately for several years amongst the Arabs, I know them to be amongst the most racist people on earth. I believe that the time has come to re-examine the credentials*

of all the members of the General Assembly; when votes are
cast in the reckless manner of the anti-Zionist resolution, it is
time to sit up and take notice.

This brings to mind a conversation I had with an Arab in Tel
Aviv. I wandered away from my hotel one day and couldn't find
my way back. Seeing a man leaning against a doorway, I asked
him for directions to the Dan Hotel. I felt that he was eager to
talk. He knew that I was a tourist, and that I was Jewish; his name
was Saleim. He began to talk about war and peace and the Arabs
versus the Jews. "There have been so many wars here," he said,
"that I take it all in my stride. The Arabs do not want wars, in
spite of what is being said about us. It is the leaders of the Arab
countries who incite terrorism and wars. I have lived in Israel
since the 1967 war. I like Israel; I like the people. I have a good
position and a fine life, unlike those who are wasting their lives
in camps because they are told by their politicians to stay there."

"What do you think about the future of Israel and the Middle
East in general?" I asked.

He thought for a minute and replied, "Israel is not just a
country, or a state that has Jews living here. It belongs to the Jews,
like Syria belongs to the Syrians, Egypt to the Egyptians, and so
on. Just because the Jews have been in exile for thousands of years
does not deprive them of their rights since Biblical times. Many
countries have sprung up in the last two or three decades after
they have been crushed under the heels of oppressors. I accept
Israel as I accept Allah; it is a reality beyond question or doubt."

I bade him Salaam and was on my way, thinking: If only all
the Arabs would share his philosophy, peace and tranquility would
reign in many lands.

What is incomprehensible to me is the constant manipulation
of decent people by insincere politicians who create misunderstand-
ings among nations, not to win or lose a war but to fight, regardless
of the consequences. As long as nations fight and people are killed,
that is good enough for the instigators. Territory that was gained
in a war is forced to be returned to the vanquished later, thus
leaving an opening for a new beginning of a new war. It is not
easy to resist the temptations of terror and war when duped by
expert warmongers. A country goes to war only to find out later
that nothing has been gained except loss of life, suffering, blood-
shed, and grief.

In order to understand the chaos in the world today, the public must become aware of the insincere claims and accusations directed toward one country or another by conspirators who thrive on wars. Only then will nations respect the rights of each other and realize the stupidity of it all; harmony and tranquility will then prevail. As is written in the supplementary readings in the Hebrew Prayer Book, "Righteousness maketh a nation great. But sin is a reproach to any people."

I am optimistic that the righteous will prevail some day, even though there was a deep sense of hopelessness among Jews after the Nazi holocaust. The feeling of despair was so profound that it should have marked the end of a people; instead, out of the ashes of six million innocent victims who perished in gas chambers and by other acts of inhuman destruction, the State of Israel was born, when Partition was approved by the United Nations in 1947 and the Jewish homeland was reestablished. The remnants of the holocaust and Jews from all over the world decided to become masters of their own fate, and began to emigrate to Israel, and thus the wandering homeless came home. Although we paid very dearly and the sacrifice was overwhelmingly painful, the Jewish State was established.

Being saturated with Jewish traditions, pride, and principles, which are of utmost importance to me—perhaps they are partially responsible for my convictions—it is my belief that a slave people will be redeemed from their oppression some day. You have living proof when you see the oasis they have carved out in the barren desert sands.

To quote some excerpts from an article in the *Foundation Magazine* (Vol. 3, Spring 1976), written by Father Ira under the heading "The Jews, Chosen For What?":

If you believe in history which tells us what the Jews have endured over thousands of years, if you take seriously this Covenant idea, if you know something about Exodus and Sinai, then you feel there are some kinds of obligations to act out in your life; that being "chosen" is not any special privilege, but more a sense of responsibility. Remember, the Redemption never spoke of the Jews alone—God's blessing to Abraham is to all righteous families of the earth.

The pattern is consistent throughout history, and you don't have to be Jewish to be involved in compassion and brotherly love. Jew and Gentile are finally being fused by the threat of atomic warfare, which is powerful enough to destroy the world. We should strive for equality, rather than superiority, which would lead us toward a new concept, and bring about everlasting peace to all nations of the world.

The wolf shall dwell with the lamb, and the leopard shall lie down with the kid . . . and a little child shall lead them. (Isaiah 11:61).

Epilogue

The futile battle has continued through the years, and I suddenly realize that old age is upon me. I am surprised and bewildered by this traumatic experience, but have gradually adjusted to the natural process of life. Matters that seemed of utmost importance to me at one time have vanished. Nothing matters too much any more; there are no business battles left to be won. A sort of tranquil contentment, which envelops my soul with serenity, has overtaken the once highly important aspirations and made it possible to express on paper my experiences and my present perspective on things in general.

I have come to feel that I would be losing my repose and self-respect, which I had built up so painfully over the years, if I were to be critical of my lifelong behavior and endeavors, which I have not had the opportunity to complete. I would have no alternative but to consider that all my efforts have been in vain had I not succeeded in putting down on paper a small part of my experiences: the longing of my soul, my restless life full of disappointments and frustrations, my aspirations, and finally my feelings of gratitude for the small portions of joy from the past, which make the present a bit more meaningful and acceptable. Although I have failed in many areas of my life, I have nevertheless had the satisfaction which few are able to achieve, of expressing some of my feelings in my two books. One must have affirmation in his life in order to appreciate its values.